Encountering
the Book of Romans

Encountering the Book of Romans

A Theological Survey

Douglas J. Moo

Baker Academic

Grand Rapids, Michigan

Published by Baker Academic
a division of Baker Publishing Group
P.O. Box 6287, Grand Rapids, MI 49516-6287
www.bakeracademic.com

Seventh printing, August 2008

Printed in the United States of America

Library of Congress Cataloging-in-Publication Data
Moo, Douglas J.
    Encountering the book of Romans : a theological survey / Douglas J. Moo.
       p. cm. — (Encountering biblical studies)
    Includes bibliographical references (p.) and index.
    ISBN 10: 0-8010-2546-X (pbk.)
    ISBN 978-0-8010-2546-4 (pbk.)
    1. Bible. N.T. Romans—Theology. I. Title. II. Series.
  BS2665.2 .M665   2002
  227'.107—dc21   2002018587

For the many students
all over the world
who have helped me understand
what Romans is all about

Contents in Brief

Contents

Editor's Preface

The strength of the church and the vitality of the individual Christian's life are directly related to the role Scripture plays in them. Early believers knew the importance of this and spent their time in fellowship, prayer, and the study of God's Word. The passing of two thousand years has not changed the need, but it has changed the accessibility of many of the Bible's ideas. Time has distanced us from those days, and we often need guidance back into the world of the Old and New Testaments.

To that end Baker Book House is producing an innovative series of biblical textbooks. The design of this series is to put us back into the world of the biblical text, so that we may understand it as those early believers did and at the same time see it from and for our own day, thus facilitating the application of its truths to our contemporary situation.

Encountering Biblical Studies consists of undergraduate-level texts, and two surveys treating the Old and New Testaments provide the foundation for this series. Accompanying these survey texts are two collateral volumes of readings, which illuminate the world surrounding the biblical text. Built on these basic survey texts are upper-level college texts covering the books of the Bible that are most frequently offered in the curriculum of Christian colleges.

Complementing the series is a set of standard reference books that may be consulted for answers to specific questions or more in-depth study of biblical ideas. These reference books include *Baker Commentary on the Bible*, *Baker Topical Guide to the Bible*, *Baker Encyclopedia of the Bible*, *Baker Theological Dictionary of the Bible*, and *Evangelical Dictionary of Theology*.

The Encountering Biblical Studies series is written from an evangelical point of view, in the firm conviction that the Scripture is absolutely true and never misleads us. It is the sure foundation on which our faith and life may be built because it unerringly leads willing readers to Jesus Christ.

Walter A. Elwell
General Editor

Publisher's Preface

Bible courses must be considered the heart of the curriculum for Christian colleges and evangelical seminaries. For Christians the Bible constitutes the basis for both our spiritual and our intellectual lives—indeed for *all* of life. If these courses are fundamental to Christian education, then the textbooks used for these courses could not be more crucial.

Baker Book House is launching a series of volumes for college-level Bible courses. In this series, Baker will publish texts that are clearly college-level. The textbooks for the basic college survey courses and for the more advanced college courses on individual Bible books will not be written for laypeople or pastors and seminarians, nor will they be primarily reference books. Rather, they will be pedagogically oriented textbooks written with collegians in mind.

Encountering the Book of Romans attempts to build on the basic survey text, *Encountering the New Testament: A Historical and Theological Survey* (Walter A. Elwell and Robert W. Yarbrough). While the survey text is written for college freshmen, this Romans volume is intended for upper-level collegians.

Rather than providing a sustained exegetical analysis of each verse in the Book of Romans, this volume surveys the entire book with an emphasis on drawing out its theological message and its practical significance for collegians. It consists of appropriate introduction and survey material with the necessary critical, historical, literary, hermeneutical, and background concerns woven within the exposition of the biblical text.

Guiding Principles

As part of the developing of this volume, the series editors, author, and publisher established the following principles:

1. It must reflect the finest in evangelical scholarship of our day.
2. It must be written at a level that most of today's upper-level collegians can understand.
3. It must be pedagogically sound. This extends not only to traditional concerns like study and review questions, chapter objectives and summaries for each chapter, but also the manner in which the material is presented.
4. It must include appropriate illustrative material such as photographs, maps, charts, graphs, figures, and sidebars.
5. It must seek to winsomely draw in the student by focusing on biblical teaching concerning crucial doctrinal and ethical matters.

Goals

The goals for *Encountering the Book of Romans* fall into two categories: intellectual and attitudinal. The intellectual goals are to (1) present the factual content of the Book of Romans, (2) introduce historical, geographical, and cultural background, (3) outline primary hermeneutical principles, (4) touch on critical issues (e.g., why some people read the Bible differently), and (5) substantiate the Christian faith.

The attitudinal goals are also fivefold: (1) to make the Bible a part of students' lives, (2) to instill in students a love for the Scriptures, (3) to make them better people, (4) to enhance their piety, and (5) to stimulate their love for God. In short, if this text builds a foundation for a lifetime of Bible study, the authors and publisher will be amply rewarded.

Overarching Themes

Controlling the writing of *Encountering the Book of Romans* have been three essential theological themes: God, people, and the gospel as it relates to individuals. The notion that God is a person—one and three—and a transcendent and immanent Being has been woven throughout the text. Moreover, this God has created people in his image who are fallen but still the objects of his redemptive love. The gospel is the means, the active personal power that God uses to rescue people from darkness and death. But the gospel does more than rescue—it restores. It confers on otherwise hopeless sinners the resolve and strength to live lives that please God, because they walk in the love that comes from God.

Features

The publisher's aim has been to provide an exceptionally unique resource on the one hand but not to be merely trendy on the other. Some of the distinguishing features we hope will prove helpful to the professor and inspiring to the student include the following:

- liberal use of illustrations—photographs, figures, tables, charts
- sidebars and excursuses exploring exegetical, ethical, and theological issues of interest and concern to modern-day collegians
- chapter outline and objectives presented at the opening of each chapter
- study questions at the end of each chapter
- a helpful glossary
- a bibliography to guide further study

To the Student

Encountering the Book of Romans in a systematic way for the first time is an exciting experience. It can also be overwhelming because there is so much to learn. You need to learn not only the content of the letter that constitutes this book but also important background information about the world in which the writer of the letter lived.

The purpose of this textbook is to make that encounter a little less daunting. To accomplish this a number of learning aids have been incorporated into the text. We suggest you familiarize yourself with this textbook by reading the following introductory material, which explains what learning aids have been provided.

Sidebars

Sidebars isolate contemporary issues of concern and show how the Book of Romans speaks to these pressing ethical and theological issues.

Chapter Outlines

At the beginning of each chapter is a brief outline of the chapter's contents. *Study Suggestion:* Before reading the chapter, take a few minutes to read the outline. Think of it as a road map, and remember that it is easier to reach your destination if you know where you are going.

Chapter Objectives

A brief list of objectives is placed at the outset of each chapter. These present the tasks you should be able to perform after reading the chapter. *Study Suggestions:*

Read the objectives carefully before beginning to read the text. As you read the text, keep these objectives in mind and take notes to help you remember what you have read. After reading the chapter, return to the objectives and see if you can perform the tasks.

Key Terms and Glossary

Key terms have been identified throughout the text by the use of **boldface** type. This will alert you to important words or phrases you may not be familiar with. A definition of these words will be found at the end of the book in an alphabetical glossary. *Study Suggestion:* When you encounter a key term in the text, stop and read the definition before continuing through the chapter.

Study Questions

A few discussion questions have been provided at the end of each chapter, and these can be used to review for examinations. *Study Suggestion:* Write suitable answers to the study questions in preparation for tests.

Further Reading

A helpful bibliography for supplementary reading is presented at the end of the book. *Study Suggestion:* Use this list to explore areas of special interest.

Visual Aids

A host of illustrations has been included in this textbook. Each illustration has been carefully selected, and each is intended not only to make the text more aesthetically pleasing but also more easily mastered.

May your encounter of the Book of Romans be an exciting adventure!

Author's Preface

"Of making many books there is no end," warns Solomon (Eccl 12:12). And, also, it would seem, "Of making of many books on Romans by Moo there is no end." Some readers of this book will know that I have already written two commentaries on Romans: the New International Commentary volume (published by Eerdmans) and the NIV Application Commentary (published by Zondervan). Why another book on Romans from Moo? I hope and believe that it is not just a matter of inordinate pride. To the degree that any of us can truly know our hearts, I honestly believe that I am writing not just to get my name on another book. I wrote this book because I think that my views on Romans are worth hearing. Or, more accurately, I think that the many Christian scholars and preachers who have gone before me, and whose views I build upon and adapt, are worth hearing. The contemporary scholarly world swirls with new ideas about Paul and Romans. Some of these ideas certainly are good ones. And God knows we always need to take a fresh look at old theological views, testing them against the best interpretation of Scripture we can develop. But not all the new ideas are, in my view, good ones. Some of them are bad ones, and some of them are at least questionable. So I see this book as an opportunity to revise and restate some old ideas against the backdrop of some of these new ideas. The nature of the "Encountering" series gives me the opportunity to communicate these ideas in a different way and to a different audience than I had been able to do in my earlier commentaries.

Far too many people have helped shape my thinking on Romans to mention here. But the many opportunities I have had to teach Romans—in academic contexts at Trinity Evangelical Divinity School and Wheaton Graduate School, in Sunday school classes, in extension classes, at pastors' seminars, even in a Bible study for high school students—have been deeply influential in helping me think through the letter. This volume is dedicated to those many students whose questions, papers, and class comments have forged my own thinking on Romans.

Abbreviations

Old Testament

Genesis	Gn
Exodus	Ex
Leviticus	Lv
Numbers	Nm
Deuteronomy	Dt
Joshua	Jos
Judges	Jgs
Ruth	Ru
1 Samuel	1 Sm
2 Samuel	2 Sm
1 Kings	1 Kgs
2 Kings	2 Kgs
1 Chronicles	1 Chr
2 Chronicles	2 Chr
Ezra	Ezr
Nehemiah	Neh
Esther	Est
Job	Jb
Psalms	Ps(s)
Proverbs	Prv
Ecclesiastes	Eccl
Song of Songs	Sg (Song)
Isaiah	Is
Jeremiah	Jer
Lamentations	Lam
Ezekiel	Ez
Daniel	Dn
Hosea	Hos
Joel	Jl
Amos	Am
Obadiah	Ob
Jonah	Jon
Micah	Mi
Nahum	Na
Habakkuk	Hb
Zephaniah	Zep
Haggai	Hg
Zechariah	Zec
Malachi	Mal

New Testament

Matthew	Mt
Mark	Mk
Luke	Lk
John	Jn
Acts of the Apostles	Acts
Romans	Rom
1 Corinthians	1 Cor
2 Corinthians	2 Cor
Galatians	Gal
Ephesians	Eph
Philippians	Phil
Colossians	Col
1 Thessalonians	1 Thes
2 Thessalonians	2 Thes
1 Timothy	1 Tm
2 Timothy	2 Tm
Titus	Ti
Philemon	Phlm
Hebrews	Heb
James	Jas
1 Peter	1 Pt
2 Peter	2 Pt
1 John	1 Jn
2 John	2 Jn
3 John	3 Jn
Jude	Jude
Revelation	Rv

Part

1

Encountering an Ancient Letter

Romans 1:1–17; 15:14–16:27

---

1 Getting Oriented

What Is Romans Really About?

Objectives

After reading this chapter, you should be able to

1. Appreciate why we have to get our bearings before we plunge into an ancient letter like Romans.
2. Understand the most important alternatives for reading and understanding Romans today.
3. Decide how you are going to read Romans.

Christians have always believed that God speaks to his people in the pages of the Bible. And that belief is quite justified. The Bible is a collection of books that God inspired to inform, challenge, and edify us. But how do we understand what it is that God is trying to communicate to us through the pages of the Bible? For God himself did not directly write the words of Scripture. The Bible is no book dropped from heaven. Rather, it is a collection of many different books, written by human beings over the course of two millennia. And to understand the Bible rightly, we must learn something about this human dimension of Scripture. We especially need to remind ourselves of what we might call the "contextualized nature" of the Bible when we turn to Romans. Many Christians think of Romans as a kind of theological summary and tend to pay little attention to its actual origins. But Romans, though thoroughly theological, is no textbook on doctrine. It is a *letter*—written by a particular person to particular people in a particular time and place. We will be able to understand better what God wants to teach us in Romans if we keep these circumstances in mind. In chapters 2 and 3 we will explore some of the specifics, looking in turn at the author, the readers, and the theme of the letter. But we need to begin, in this chapter, by laying a broader foundation. Specifically, we want to ask, and suggest an answer, to this question: What is Romans *really* about?

Ancient Letters and Modern Readers

The question we have just posed might seem to be the product of overheated academic imaginations. Doesn't the book tell us clearly enough what it is about? Why create needless controversy over what is so obvious? But wait. Is it obvious? That's the question. The problem is that we bring our own agendas to the reading of a letter like Romans. We come to it—inevitably—from our own culture. We in-terpret its words and sentences as if they were written by a twenty-first-century Christian. But, of course, they were not. Romans was written by a first-century Jew, Saul of Tarsus. The words of Romans have to be understood in his context before we can translate them accurately into ours. The famous philosopher of language Ludwig Wittgenstein introduced the notion of "language games" to explain this problem with understanding words. Basically, he argued, we have to know what "game" we are playing if we are going to understand language accurately. Take a simple example. The phrase "Hail Mary" uttered in the context of the "game" of a Roman Catholic religious service means something quite different from the very same phrase spoken in the "game" of a football broadcast.

And so we might rephrase our central question: What "game" was Paul playing when he wrote his letter to the Romans? The Reformer Martin Luther gave voice to a classic answer to this question in the sixteenth century. Paul was writing about the way a sinful human being can get into right relationship with a perfect and just God. Why did Luther think that this was what Romans was about? "Because it is the plain meaning of the text!" Luther undoubtedly would have responded. And he may well be right. But we also must acknowledge that Luther's reading was influenced by his circumstances. He was reading Romans from a very specific and personal vantage point. As a dedicated Roman Catholic monk, Luther used every available religious discipline to try to make himself presentable to God, but he simply could not convince himself that he was succeeding. As he looked deeply into his own heart, he saw so much selfishness and pride and rebellion there that he could not imagine what he could ever do to bridge the gap between himself and God. Then came the great realization. What Luther could never do, God had already done. God, by allowing his Son to be executed on a Roman cross, had provided a way for the sins of all human beings to be forgiven. And it was in Romans, especially, that

Luther discovered this liberating message of grace. As a result of his previous training, Luther had taken the expression "the righteousness of God" (Rom 1:17) to refer to God's own righteousness—God's impartial justice. But how, then, could the revelation of that righteousness be "good news" (see Rom 1:16)? Surely it was *bad* news, not good news, to learn that God was just and impartial, that he would punish every sin and judge every sinner. But then Luther came to understand that the "righteousness of God" that Paul was talking about was not God's justice, but God's gift. The good news that Paul preached was that God had brought into the world the possibility of a righteousness *from* God—the gift of acceptance and "right standing" offered to every sinner—and that the gift was given simply in response to faith. "Works" of religious devotion or good deeds were not needed to earn acceptance with God. All God asked was that people turn away from their sins and turn to him in heartfelt faith.

Reformer Martin Luther, 1483–1546. (Courtesy of Billy Graham Center Museum, Wheaton, Ill.)

What a sense of liberation and joy Luther felt when he first came to understand "the righteousness of God" in these terms! Indeed, so overwhelming was the experience that Luther read the entire Bible in light of this truth for the rest of his life. "Justification by faith" was the heart of the gospel, the heart of Romans, the heart of the Bible. It was precisely for this reason that Luther had his famous problem with the Epistle of James, for he did not think that this letter adequately taught the truth of justification by faith. The Protestant Reformers who followed Luther did not make "justification by faith" quite as central as Luther did, but they all followed him in reading Romans as a book about the individual human being and how that individual could be turned from a rebellious sinner into an obedient saint. Attention was focused above all on the early chapters of Romans 1–4, where the great issues of sin and God's remedy in Christ are spelled out. Eventually, as the heat of the Reformation battles died down, many Roman Catholic scholars came to interpret Romans in a very similar way. By the middle of the twentieth century, therefore, one could almost speak of a consensus about the basic message of Romans. We can summarize this consensus in two basic points:

1. Romans focuses on the individual human being.
2. Romans emphasizes justification by faith because Jews were teaching justification by works.

Preachers, Sunday school teachers, and evangelists have taught most of us to read Romans from this perspective. We might call this the "language game" of individual salvation.

The Current Debate about Romans

Scholars view a consensus as a challenge. It is the very nature of the academic approach to question what most assume to be true—to take a hard, critical look at the ruling paradigms. And that is no bad thing. We too easily can get locked into certain ways of looking at the Bible and never stop to ask whether our approach is the right one or not. If the Bible is truly to be our authority for all of life, then we must constantly be reassessing our reading of its message. Very often, in fact, our failure to appreciate the real message of Scripture lies in certain assumptions about how we read the text—assumptions that we might not even be aware that we hold.

And so it was that in the last half of the twentieth century scholars began asking some serious questions about the ruling consensus among interpreters of Romans. Two questions in particular came to the forefront and set the agenda for the current debate about the nature of Romans. These questions match the two key points in the "individual salvation" reading of Romans mentioned above.

Thus, the first question was whether Romans indeed focuses on the individual. Scholars such as Krister Stendahl argue that our individualistic reading of Romans (and of Paul generally) arose in the modern era, especially under the influence of Luther. Luther's problem was how he, as an individual human being, could find rest for his troubled conscience. But that was *not* the issue that Paul was grappling with. Indeed, Stendahl suggests, concern about what he called the "introspective conscience" arose in the modern Western world. People in ancient times simply didn't think that way. We have made the mistake of reading into Romans our own concerns.

What, then, was Paul's real concern in Romans? The "people" question: What does God's gracious work in Christ mean for the two great "people groups" of Paul's world, Jews and Gentiles? Romans is not basically about how an individual human being can get right with God; it is about how Gentiles can be added into God's people without disenfranchising God's "original" people, the Jews.[1] This was the great question that confronted

the Jewish apostle Paul in the first century as he sought to explain and defend the gospel. Generations of Jews, reading the Old Testament promises of God about the Messiah and the salvation he would bring, naturally thought that those promises would bring great blessing for the Jewish people. But by the time Paul writes Romans, something strange and unexpected has happened. Comparatively few Jews have responded to the gospel, while Gentiles have turned to Christ in significant numbers. The church is taking on an overwhelmingly Gentile profile. But if the preaching of the gospel is bringing salvation to the Gentiles while leaving most Jews hardened in their sins, how can the gospel truly be "the gospel of God" (Rom 1:1)? Did not the same God who sent his Son to the cross and raised him from the dead to usher in the age of fulfillment promise that he would bless Israel? We find Paul tackling this thorny question in chapters 9–11 of Romans. And for Stendahl and many others, those chapters, not Romans 1–4, are the heart of Romans. The "people question" is what Romans is really about. Romans is not so much about the history of the individual as about the history of salvation.

A second question attacked the second plank in the Reformation platform. Luther's conviction that God offers the grace of salvation unconditionally to anyone who believes was forged in the fires of controversy. As a monk, he struggled to understand how his acts of religious devotion, however many, could ever enable him to appear before a perfect and holy God. And as a reformer, he fought for his vision of the gospel with a Roman Catholic church that insisted on works as a necessary condition for true righteousness before God. We should not be surprised, then, that Luther tended to read Romans as an ancient parallel to his own experience. Paul was cast in the role of the reforming Luther, and the Jews took the place of a legalistic Roman Catholicism. For Luther, then, and for those who have followed in his interpretive footsteps, Paul emphasizes justification by faith in order to counter the Jewish view

covenant

new perspective

of justification by works. Jews, in the traditional consensus, tended to base a right standing with God on the quantity of good works that a person was able to accomplish. Paul, in contrast, proclaims that a person can gain right standing with God only by an act of humble faith. Again, I suspect that many of us would readily identify this understanding of matters as the one we have been taught. Indeed, many of us have probably considered this way of looking at Paul and the Jews as obvious and unquestioned.

But suppose the Jewish people in Paul's day were not teaching justification by works? This is precisely the question that a significant number of scholars have begun asking in the last thirty years. The seminal figure is E. P. Sanders, who wrote a book in 1977 that systematically argued for a very different view of the ancient Jewish faith than had been customary among both scholars and laypeople.[2] Essentially, Sanders claims that Jews in Paul's day did not believe that they would be saved by obeying the law, or by "good works." They believed that God had established a **covenant** with the Jewish people and that they would be saved because, as Jews, they belonged to that covenant. Salvation was based, then, on God's covenant election. To be sure, Jews made a great deal of obeying the law. They obeyed God's law, however, not to "get saved" but to "stay saved," not to enter into the covenant but to stay in the covenant. Sanders dubbed this way of understanding first-century Judaism "covenantal nomism." ("Nomism" comes from the Greek word for "law," *nomos*, and is a deliberate contrast to "legalism.") Although Sanders was not the first to argue this understanding of Judaism, his book came at the right time to create a significant shift in the scholarly consensus.

Many scholars now agree that Sanders's covenantal nomism describes first-century Judaism accurately. But how, then, should we read Romans? What is Paul's point when he claims, "No one will be declared righteous in his [God's] sight by observing the law" (literally, "by works of the law") (Rom 3:20)? If Jews did not

claim that a person had to do the law to be justified before God, why would Paul say this? Scholars have come up with quite a variety of answers to these questions. The most persuasive answers have come from James D. G. Dunn.[3] Picking up from the first point above—about how Paul was most concerned with the "people" issue—Dunn argues that Paul's problem with "works of the law" was that they excluded Gentiles from God's salvation in Christ. Jewish devotion to the law was wrapped up in the covenant that God made with Israel. But that covenant was made with *Israel* and not with the other peoples of the world. So when Christ came to offer salvation to all, obedience to the law could no longer be the focal point of the people of God. This is where the Jews were making their mistake, Dunn thinks. Their problem, in Paul's view, was not that they were insisting that people had to obey the law to be saved. (Sanders had already shown that this was not the case.) Rather, their problem was that they were trying to keep God's salvation to themselves by clinging to the law as their badge of national privilege. The problem Paul had with "works of the law," then, was not so much the "works" part as the "law" part. With the coming of Christ, Paul was arguing in verses like Romans 3:20, being justified by God was no longer tied to the Jewish covenant but was freely available to everyone.

The kind of interpretation that Dunn argues has become widely accepted among scholars. Indeed, people talk about a "paradigm shift" in Pauline studies and speak of the **new perspective** on Paul and on Romans. Why is it important to learn about it? Because it suggests a different way of approaching and reading Romans. Our understanding of many individual verses and paragraphs in the letter will be changed if we adopt the new perspective as the lens through which we read the book.

So we now have two different approaches to Romans on the table before us: (1) the "Reformation approach," with its focus on individual salvation and assumption of Jewish legalism; and (2) the "new perspective," with its focus on people groups and a covenantal nomistic view of Judaism. Which should we adopt? How should we read Romans?

Getting Situated: How, Then, Should We Read?

Answering this question requires us to make two important preliminary points. First, the survey of interpretation might give the impression that the Reformation approach to Romans has been replaced by the new perspective. In fact, a considerable number of contemporary scholars continue to be persuaded that the Reformation reading is more accurate than the new perspective. Second, the brief survey of the two main approaches to Romans is, of course, quite simplified. I selected two views from a broad spectrum of alternatives. These views represent fairly the two dominant directions in interpretation. But other views, and various combinations of these two views, are quite common.

Every reader of Romans must eventually make up his or her own mind about which overall approach to Romans produces the best "fit" with the actual teaching of the letter. And I encourage readers of the present volume to do just that as they work their way through the argument of the letter. As a help in this process, I often will indicate briefly how the two opposing views would interpret key texts. But I will also advocate a certain approach to the letter that I think makes best sense of Paul's teaching in its first-century context.

How, then, should we read Romans? I suggest a modified Reformation approach. Critics of the Reformers' general line of interpretation, remember, offer two basic criticisms of their focus on individual salvation: (1) they ignore the centrality of "people" concerns for Paul; and (2) they wrongly assume that first-century Judaism was a legalistic religion. Both criticisms are somewhat justified.

Most contemporary readers of Romans do not share and perhaps have difficulty imagining the situation that Paul and the early Christians faced. The Messiah promised in the Old Testament and longed for by Jews finally had come. But he had come in a way entirely unexpected. Rather than leading a revitalized Israel to new national prominence, Jesus had died ignominiously on a Roman cross. And the movement that he inaugurated quickly spread from its Jewish roots to embrace Samaritans (Acts 8) and then Gentiles (Acts 10). Paul, commissioned to bring the gospel to both Jews and Greeks (Acts 9:15), embarked on extensive missionary travels, the result being the founding of many churches filled mainly with Gentiles. It is well known that the idea of a crucified Messiah was a troublesome "stumbling block" to the Jews (e.g., 1 Cor 1:23). But the idea of a messianic community made up mainly of Gentiles was equally troublesome. Hadn't God promised salvation to Israel—to Jews? How could a church composed mainly of Gentiles truly fulfill those promises? And how should Gentiles be admitted to this new people of God? Should they be required to obey the law that God gave to Israel? Should Jews who became Christians continue to obey the law? These kinds of questions were being asked urgently in Paul's day and have left their mark all over the New Testament (see, e.g., the apostolic council of Acts 15; Galatians; 2 Cor 3; Eph 2:11–3:13; Phil 3:7–11; Col 2:16–23; Hebrews). And they have left their mark in Romans as well. Romans 9–11 is a long and involved argument about how a largely Gentile church could be the true fulfillment of God's promises in the Old Testament. The relationship of Jew and Gentile is a motif that runs throughout Romans, from the announcement of its theme, the gospel as "the power of God for the salvation of everyone who believes: first for the Jew, then for the Gentile" (1:16), to its climactic exhortation, "Accept one another, then, just as Christ accepted you" (15:7).

torah

If the question of Jew and Gentile in the messianic people of God was being asked broadly in the early church, there were special reasons why Roman Christians might have been particularly interested in the matter. The best evidence we have suggests that the church in Rome was founded by Jews and was dominated by Jews for its first two decades. But that situation would have suddenly and dramatically changed in A.D. 49. In that year the Roman emperor Claudius expelled all Jews from Rome (see Acts 18:2). A Roman historian tells us he did so because the Jews were fighting over "Chrestos"[4]—almost certainly a corruption of the name *Christos*, "Christ." At one fell swoop, therefore, all the Jews in the Roman Christian community were forced to leave the city. All that was left were Gentiles, who naturally took over positions of leadership in the community. By the time Paul wrote Romans, probably in A.D. 57, the Roman authorities had tacitly allowed Jews back into the city. But the Jewish Christians returned to a church that, in their absence, has become a largely Gentile institution. The situation was ripe for social tension. We can imagine the now dominant Gentiles moving further and further away from what they might perceive to be foolish remnants of Judaism, such as rules about food and holy days, while the returning Jewish Christians, keenly sensitive of their minority status, insist even more strongly on adherence to their ancestral customs. This is exactly the situation that Paul's warnings to the weak and the strong in Romans 14–15 presuppose. The point, then, is that the situation of the Roman church was a microcosm of the social and theological tensions that existed throughout the early church.

Faced with such a dispute in the Roman church, we should not be surprised if Paul

Law and Torah in Romans

Understanding Romans requires us to read it in its own context and to interpret its words as Paul's first readers would have done. Only after we have done that to the best of our ability can we apply the letter accurately to our own circumstances. Take a case in point: the word "law." We apply that word to a lot of different things: state law, federal law, the law of nature, biblical law. And even when we use it in this last sense—surely what Paul has in mind in Romans—we can miss the right nuance, for often we use the word "law" to refer to any commandment found anywhere in the Bible. This usage goes back especially to Luther, who made a fundamental distinction between "law" (what God requires of us) and "gospel" (what God gives to us). And both are found throughout the Bible. But we would misunderstand Romans badly if we took this meaning of the word "law" to the text. Paul's use of "law" *(nomos)* arises from his own Jewish background and context. In this context, "law" meant the law of Moses: the body of commandments that God had given the people of Israel at Sinai through Moses. Note, for instance, that Paul can speak of Jews simply as people who "have the law" and Gentiles as those who do not (Rom 2:12–16). He speaks about the period between Adam and Moses as the time when the law had not been given (Rom 5:13–14). Galatians 3:17 is especially clear: the law was introduced "430 years" after God's promise to Abraham.

One way to remind ourselves about which law we are discussing in Romans is to use the transliterated Hebrew word **torah** instead of our very ambiguous word "law." I will often do so throughout the commentary, particularly in places where the meaning of *nomos* might be especially unclear.

spent a lot of time in a letter to this church dealing with the conflict between Jew and Gentile. And so he does. But can we conclude that the "people" issue was central to the letter, as many advocates of the new perspective claim? I don't think so. Paul's focus in Romans is on the gospel. This word "gospel," as we have seen, occupies pride of place in his announcement of the theme of the letter (1:16) and appears again at critical points in both the introduction and the conclusion (1:1, 2, 9, 15; 15:16, 19 [NIV]). But the gospel, as Romans 1:16–17 makes clear, is basically about the restoration of the individual sinner's relationship to God. It brings salvation to "everyone who believes." True, Paul immediately introduces the "people" issue: the "everyone" includes Jews first and then Gentiles. But the point here is simple: the horizontal dimension, Jew versus Gentile, is subordinate to the vertical dimension, human beings versus God. The latter is primary, the former secondary. And the letter as a whole bears this out. Paul focuses on the way the good news of Jesus Christ can transform individual human beings, turning them from sinners into saints. Yet because Paul is explaining this gospel in a particular context, he constantly draws out the significance of the gospel's transforming power for the division between Jew and Gentile. Romans, then, is about individual salvation *and* the new people of God. These are not mutually exclusive options. The Reformers tended to ignore the latter, and contemporary scholars have been quite right to point this out. Yet these same scholars often have gone too far, focusing so much on the "people" issue that the vertical dimension of the gospel becomes unfairly muted.

But we still have to address the second major criticism of the Reformers' approach to Romans, that they unfairly had assumed first-century Judaism to be a legalistic religion. Here, again, balance is needed. Modern scholars are justified in claiming that interpreters of Paul often have caricatured the Jewish faith. Jews in the first century believed in God's grace (as they do today). They celebrated God's covenant with Israel as the basis for their hope of salvation. They obeyed the law out of thankfulness to God for his gift of election. But at the same time, Jews tended to put so much stress on the law that God's grace and election could recede into the background. And, since salvation in the Jewish viewpoint would not finally be granted until the end of life, obedience to God's law became, in fact, a requirement for salvation. Only Jews who acted on their covenant privileges by conforming their lives to the demands of the law would finally be saved. The law, then, was not a problem only because it separated Jew and Gentile—as advocates of the new perspective often suggest—but also because Jews were falsely putting too much weight on it as a basis for their salvation.

Ultimately, any interpretation of the background against which Paul was writing has to fit the actual teaching of Paul and the other New Testament authors. And the New Testament reveals plainly enough that "legalism" was a problem in first-century Judaism. To be sure, this was not the "hard" legalism that some have wrongly attributed to the Jews—the idea that Jews believed they had to do more good works than bad to get to heaven. Rather, it was what we might call a "soft" legalism—a dependence on their own obedience to the law as a way of activating God's grace in their lives. The advocates of the new perspective are right, then, to argue that the Reformers and their heirs did not always pay enough attention to the distinctively Jewish worldview that lay behind the New Testament focus on the law. But I think that the New Testament itself vindicates the Reformers' insistence that ultimately the issue of the law is not a *Jewish*, but a *human*, issue. Paul's "works of the law" refers to things done in obedience to the Jewish *torah*. But the Reformers were right when they took such language to include, ultimately, any "good works" done in obedience to any law. Debate over the exact shape of first-century Judaism continues. The view of Judaism proposed in the new perspective initially seemed to win the field. But challenges to specifics within that view as well as to it more generally have emerged. The reader should know that I have taken a mildly critical stance toward the new perspective in this volume.[5]

"Take Up and Read!"

The great church father Augustine was moved to pick up and read part of Paul's

letter to the Romans by the words of a child singing in a nearby house, "Take up and read! Take up and read!" And when he read, Augustine became convinced of the truth of the gospel.[6] The words of that child apply to each one of us. God asks us to take up this marvelous part of his word to us and read. It is by patient, careful, open-hearted reading that God can teach us what he wants us to know through the words of this letter to the Romans. Yet we do not read in a vacuum. God led Paul to write the letter in a specific set of circumstances, and we read the letter in a specific set of circumstances. What I have tried to do in this opening chapter is to orient the reader to a crucial aspect of those circumstances. We can misread Paul's letter by bringing to it our own assumptions about "what Romans is about" and failing to let Paul's own concerns set our agenda.

Study Questions

1. I have suggested that we can misunderstand words when we do not know the context in which they are spoken or written. Consider times when you have misunderstood someone because you did not recognize the context.

2. Read Romans 3:20. What would this verse mean if the "new perspective" were correct? What would it mean if the "Reformation approach" were right?

3. How might a balanced view of the Jewish faith affect the way we evangelize Jews in our own day?

2 Paul and the Romans

Objectives

After reading this chapter, you should be able to

1. Understand why we have to situate Romans in its first-century context before we can read it rightly.
2. Know the circumstances of Paul's situation as he writes Romans.
3. Know a bit about the Roman Christians as they received Romans.

Communication, by its very nature, is occasional and two-sided. When we communicate with someone, we always do it in a certain context, for a certain reason. That context might be very broad: a historian writing a description of Caesar's campaigns; or it might be very narrow: a student writing home for more money. But a context always exists. And so, of course, do the two parties. The historian does not write into thin air. He or she has a certain audience in mind: fellow professors, or college students, or the general public. And, if the historian hopes to sell many books, he or she will write with the needs, interests, and abilities of that audience in mind. Similarly, the student asking for an infusion of cash undoubtedly will put the plea in the terms best calculated to elicit a sympathetic response from the parents.

The letter to the Romans was written on a specific occasion and is an act of communication between two parties: the apostle Paul and the Roman Christians. Learning more about both parties and their circumstances will aid our reading of Romans.

Paul the Apostle

Information on these points comes especially from the beginning and the end of the letter. Paul follows the convention of ancient letter writers by opening with a description of himself (1:1–6), a reference to his audience (1:7a), and a greeting (1:7b). He adds to these standard items a thanksgiving (found in many of his letters) combined with a brief rehearsal of his circumstances (1:8–15). The other "bookend" around the body of Romans is the epistolary conclusion, 15:14–16:27. Here again Paul touches on matters that are typical at the end of his letters: his travel plans (15:14–29), a request for prayer (15:30–32), a prayerful wish for peace (15:33), recognition of his ministry associates (16:1–2, 21–23), greetings (16:3–15, 16b), the "holy kiss" (16:16a), a concluding grace (16:20), and a concluding doxology (16:25–27). What makes Romans a bit different than the other letters of Paul is the amount of space that Paul devotes to many of these matters. There is good reason for this elaboration. Paul did not found the Roman church, nor has he ever visited there. He has gotten to know some of the Roman Christians during his travels (see 16:3–15), but many of them he has never met. And so Paul needs to spend a little more time than usual introducing himself and explaining why he writes to a church that some would claim he has no authority over.

He establishes his credentials immediately. As a "servant" of Christ Jesus, Paul implies that he has a status equal to those famous Old Testament servants such as Moses (see Jos 14:7) and David. Moreover, he is an "apostle," one of those chosen by the Lord himself to be the "foundation" of the church (Eph 2:20). And his apostolic calling is particularly to the Gentiles (1:5). Since the Roman Christians, Paul implies in verse 6 (and see the next section), belong to the sphere of Gentile churches, they fall under his apostolic jurisdiction. Paul makes a similar point in verses 13–15, although he broadens the scope of his ministry in those verses to include Jews as well as Gentiles. And he returns to this same theme at the end of the letter. In 15:14–16, Paul claims that his rather bold words to the Roman Christians are quite justified because God bestowed grace on Paul to be "a minister of Christ Jesus to the Gentiles." Paul pursues his calling with fervor and hard work, seeking to offer Gentile Christians to the Lord as a sacrifice pleasing to him. As he puts it in 1:5, he wants these believers to come to "the obedience of faith" (I discuss this phrase in chapter 3).

And so Paul explains to the Romans why he can be so bold as to write a letter of exhortation to them: they fall within the sphere of his divine calling to bring Gentiles under the lordship of Jesus Christ. But why write the letter now? What led Paul to take up pen and send a letter to a church he had never even visited? Paul never tells us explicitly why he

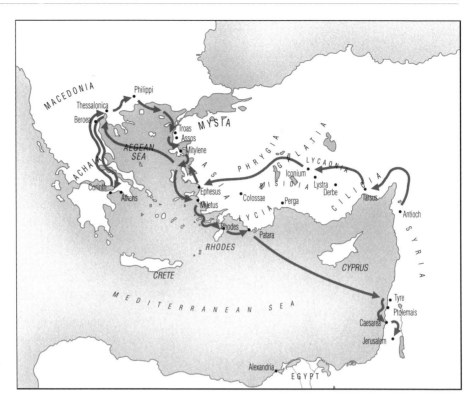

Map of Paul's
third missionary
journey, A.D.
53–57.

writes, and scholars have debated the question of the purpose of Romans for many years. But we begin to get some answers to this question when we probe the epistolary introduction and conclusion for more information about Paul's own circumstances. Beyond an expression of regret that he has been "hindered" from coming to Rome in the past (1:10, 13; cf. 15:22), Paul says nothing about this matter in the introduction. But Paul's sketch of his travel plans in 15:17–29 is much more illuminating.

First, Paul expresses a sense of closure with respect to a significant stage of his ministry. "So from Jerusalem all the way around to Illyricum, I have fully proclaimed the gospel of Christ" (15:19). Illyricum was a Roman province that occupied approximately the territory now held by Albania and remnants of the old Yugoslavia. Luke never tells us in the Book of Acts that Paul had been in this province, but the vague reference to "that area" around Macedonia in Acts 20:2 might include such a visit. At any rate, what Paul suggests in this verse is that he has completed basic missionary work in the areas roughly covered by the three great missionary journeys of Paul recorded in Acts. Thriving churches have been planted in key centers throughout

Paul's Situation in Romans (Rom 15:14–33)

The Backward Look:
"From Jerusalem all the way around to Illyricum I have completed [or, 'fulfilled'] the gospel of Christ" (v. 19b).

The Forward Look:
"But now I am going to Jerusalem to minister to the saints" (v. 25a).

"But now . . . after many years, I have the desire to come to you . . . to be sent on my way by you" (v. 23).

"As I am going on to Spain" (v. 24a).

Ruins of the ancient city of Corinth, where Paul probably wrote the Book of Romans. (Jim Yancey)

Third, however, Paul could not travel west immediately. "Now, however, I am on my way to Jerusalem in the service of the saints there" (15:25). As the following verses reveal, the service that Paul had in mind was the delivery to the Jerusalem Christians of the collection that he had been taking from his Gentile churches. This enterprise was very important for Paul. He mentions it in every letter he wrote on his third missionary journey (see also 1 Cor 16:1–4; 2 Cor 8–9). Paul viewed the collection as more than a relief effort. He also saw in it a practical way of bringing Christian Jews and Gentiles together. If he could get the Gentile Christians to give money to the Jewish Christians, and get the Jewish Christians to accept it, then a very practical step would have been taken toward the unification of the church. Hence come Paul's deep concerns for the collection and his request for prayer about it (15:30–32).

Fourth, and finally, Paul plans to stop in Rome on his way from Jerusalem to Spain (15:28). So the complete itinerary is now before us: Jerusalem, to deliver the collection; Rome, as a stopover; Spain, for extended ministry.

These details enable us to pinpoint with some precision where Paul was when he wrote Romans and, therefore, when he wrote it. All the circumstances point to Paul's stay in Corinth toward the end of his third missionary journey (see Acts 20:2–3), probably in A.D. 57. Paul's commendation of Phoebe, who was from Cenchrea, right next door to Corinth, points in the same direction (Rom 16:1–2). But if we know when and where, we still don't know much about the *why:* Why was Paul going to stop in Rome, and why did he write a letter to them? The answer to the first question is hinted at in 15:24. Paul expresses his hope that the Roman Christians will "assist" him on his journey to Spain. The Greek word behind "assist" (*propempō*) is consistently used in the New Testament to refer to missionary support.[2] So Paul apparently wants the Roman Christians to support him in his missionary efforts in Spain. His home church, Antioch, is far away from Spain,

this area. Paul, the church planter, is now free to look for other new fields "white for the harvest." And his gaze has traveled all the way to the other end of the Mediterranean.

Second, then, Paul's eventual plans are to engage in church planting work in Spain (15:24). Why Paul chose Spain we do not know, nor can we be sure whether or not he ever got there. One church father claims that Paul preached in the "limits of the West," which could refer to Spain.[1] But the reference might be to Rome, and Paul's ministry in the eastern Mediterranean, attested by the Pastoral Epistles, makes it unlikely that Paul ever reached Spain. But for our purposes the important point is that Paul was intending to evangelize in Spain as he wrote Romans.

and Paul knows that he will need help from some Christians closer to the new mission field. So Paul is, in effect, asking if he can come to Rome, show his slides, and pass the offering plate for the new missionary endeavor.

But why, then, the letter? Why go into so much detail just to introduce himself to the Romans? We need to wait to look at some possible answers to this question until after we have glanced briefly at several other issues. In the rest of this chapter we will learn about the other party in the communication that we call Romans: the Roman Christians themselves.

The Roman Christians

If Paul tells us quite a lot about his own situation in the opening and closing parts of Romans, we learn a lot less about the Romans themselves. And that is not surprising. After all, the Romans know who

The Origins of the Church at Rome

We have no direct evidence about the way the gospel was first planted in the capital of the Roman Empire. The Roman Catholic church has traditionally claimed that Peter was the founder of the church. As the first "bishop" of the Roman church, Peter established the office given to him by Christ himself: the "rock" on which the church of Christ would be built (see Mt 16:18). It is in this way that Roman Catholics validate the papacy as a divinely appointed office. But the earliest claim that Peter founded the Roman church comes fairly late, in A.D. 354 (in the *Catalogus Liberianus*). Earlier tradition associates both Peter and Paul with the founding of the Roman church (Irenaeus, *Against Heresies* 3.1.2; 3.3.1). Neither tradition has much basis in fact.[1] Paul makes clear in Romans that he had never been to the city before (1:10). And if Peter had founded the church in Rome, it is unlikely that Paul would have written

to the Roman Christians without making any reference to him (see Rom 15:20).

The New Testament portrays Peter engaging in significant missionary work in Palestine until persecution forced him to flee, perhaps in about A.D. 44 (see Acts 12:1–19). Peter at that time, according to Luke, left for "another place" (Acts 12:17), but the identity of that place is entirely speculative. We do know that he was back in Jerusalem for the council in A.D. 48–49 (Acts 15), that he wrote in Corinth at some point (1 Cor 1:12; 9:5), and that he ministered to churches in northern Asia Minor toward the end of his life (cf. 1 Peter). At this time, according to the most likely interpretation of "Babylon" in 1 Peter 5:13, Peter was in Rome with Mark, who used Peter's preaching as the basis for his gospel. All this makes it likely that Peter did not even get to Rome until after Paul had written Romans.

How, then, did the church

in Rome get its start? A tradition more likely to be right comes from the fourth-century father Ambrosiaster: the Romans "have embraced the faith of Christ, albeit according to the Jewish rite, without seeing any sign of mighty works or any of the apostles."[2] While speculative, it is not at all unlikely that Jews who embraced Jesus as the Messiah at Pentecost brought their new faith back with them to Rome and so planted the church there. The apostles we read so much about in the Book of Acts played critical roles in establishing Christian churches all over the Mediterranean world, but we should not neglect those ordinary believers who also carried the message of the good news to the ends of the earth.

1. See O. Cullmann, *Peter: Disciple, Apostle, Martyr* (Philadelphia: Westminster, 1962), 72–157.
2. The text can be found in *Patrologia Latina* 17, col. 46.

they are! But three important facts about the Roman Christians do emerge from these verses.

First, Paul intends to address all the Christians in Rome: "To all in Rome who are loved by God and called to be saints" (1:7). Yet, at the same time, he does not address this letter, as he does so many of his others, to the "church" that is in Rome (compare, e.g., 1 Cor 1:2; 1 Thes 1:1). What this probably means is that there was more than one "local church" in the city of Rome. We know that the Jews who lived in Rome had established many synagogues. The Christians in Rome seem to have followed the same pattern, worshiping in many small congregations. Evidence from the greetings in Romans 16:3–16 bears out this conclusion. Paul sends greetings to the "church" that meets in the house of Priscilla and Aquila (v. 5). And references to "the brothers with them" in verse 14 and "all the saints with them" in verse 15 also probably refer to house churches. This scattering of the Christians in Rome into at least several small house churches might explain why divisions among "strong" and "weak" have grown up (see 14:1–15:13). We might infer that these separate congregations in Rome were taking quite

different approaches to the issues that Paul deals with in these verses.

Second, Paul views the Christians in Rome as being within the sphere of his special mandate: the Gentiles. Note 1:13: "I do not want you to be unaware, brothers, that I planned many times to come to you (but have been prevented from doing so until now) in order that I might have a harvest among you, just as I have had among the other Gentiles." By referring to "*other* Gentiles," Paul makes clear that he views the Roman Christians as Gentile also. The same point emerges from the most likely interpretation of 1:5–6: "Through him and for his name's sake, we received grace and apostleship to call people from among all the Gentiles to the obedience that comes from faith. And you also are among those who are called to belong to Jesus Christ." The NIV text, quoted here, suggests that Paul's point in verse 6 is to include the Roman Christians generally among those who have been "called to belong to Jesus Christ." But the NRSV probably has more accurately captured the nuance of the Greek: "through whom we have received grace and apostleship to bring about the obedience of faith among all the Gentiles for the sake of his name, including yourselves who are called to belong to Jesus Christ." On this reading, Paul's point is to remind the Roman Christians that they are included in that category of people—the Gentiles—for whom God gave Paul a special calling.

Third, Paul makes clear that he is also writing to Jewish Christians. The clearest evidence comes from the greetings, where he names several Jewish Christians: Priscilla and Aquila (16:3), Andronicus and Junias (16:7), and Herodion (16:11). The presence of Jewish Christians in Paul's audience is suggested also by 4:1, where Paul labels Abraham "our forefather," and 7:1, where he addresses those who "know the law." A similar conclusion emerges, paradoxically, from 11:13–32, where Paul addresses Gentile Christians explicitly. The fact that he has to single out Gentile Christians here suggests that his audience includes some Christians who are not Gentile.

Study Questions

1. What does Paul's expressed desire not to "build on someone else's foundation" (15:20) suggest about the origins of the Roman Christian community?

2. Consider the implications of the several different house churches in the Roman Christian community for the relationships of the Christians there by thinking about what your own church would be like if it were divided into house churches of no more than fifteen to twenty persons each.

3. Why does Paul want to make clear that the Roman Christian community is Gentile in essence?

The points cited in the last two paragraphs seem at first sight to be contradictory: Paul addresses the church in Rome as Gentile, yet he refers to Jewish Christians as well. Scholars have sometimes chosen to follow one line of this evidence and sometimes the other. It has been argued that the Roman Christian community that Paul addresses was entirely Jewish or entirely Gentile. But doing justice to all the evidence requires a more nuanced approach. Perhaps the best way to reconcile these points is to conclude that Gentiles had become a significant enough majority in the Christian community that it could be considered Gentile, yet Jews still made up a solid minority. Recall the situation that I sketched in chapter 1. Messianic Jews returning from Pentecost establish Christian congregations in Rome. As these congregations grow, some Gentiles, especially "God-fearers," who were strongly attracted to Jewish beliefs, join the community. When Jewish Christians are forced to leave Rome by the emperor Claudius, Gentiles naturally take over. By Paul's day, some Jewish Christians have filtered back into the community, but in the meantime it has taken on the complexion of a Gentile church.

3 The Gospel of God

Outline

- **The Theme of Romans: What Is Romans About?**

  The Gospel Regarding God's Son (1:1–5)

  The Gospel and the Righteousness of God (1:16–17)

  Not Ashamed of the Gospel

  The Power of God for the Salvation of Everyone Who Believes

  The Righteousness of God

- **The Purpose of Romans: Why Romans?**

  Proposals Focusing on Paul's Circumstances

  Proposals Focusing on the Roman Church

- **The Structure of Romans: How Does Romans Unfold?**

Objectives

After reading this chapter, you should be able to

1. Identify several possibilities for the theme of Romans and point to evidence in the text in support of each view.
2. Know what Paul means by "the righteousness of God" and how that phrase fits into his preaching of the gospel in Romans.
3. Understand how the whole letter fits together as one long exposition of the gospel.
4. Appreciate Paul's purposes in writing this particular letter to the first-century Roman Christians.
5. Apply insights from these first four points to your own reading of Romans so that you can understand better God's purposes for us.

In the first two chapters we have surveyed some of the detailed questions surrounding the origin of Paul's letter to the Romans. Now we are ready to put these details together into a big picture. To get all that God wants us to get out of Romans, we must read the letter as a whole. Too often we read the Bible merely in bits and pieces, and although God surely speaks to us through those bits and pieces, think how much more we could learn if we knew how they worked together as part of a larger act of communication. This is the perspective we are after in this chapter as we draw together the threads of our discussion to get a sense of what Romans as a whole is about.

The Theme of Romans: What Is Romans About?

As we saw in chapter 1, Romans has become a critical battleground in the war between a more individualist reading of Paul, inherited from the Reformation, and a more corporate reading, the dominant scholarly approach in our own day. Both perspectives, I argued, have something to teach us about Paul and about Romans. Paul is concerned to explain how God's new work in Christ can integrate both Jews and Gentiles into one new people. Critical as this theme is in Romans, however, it is not the dominant note. That note is sounded, I suggested, in the word "gospel." In Romans, Paul sets forth the good news of Jesus Christ. That good news is first of all a message directed to each one of us: God in Christ has made it possible to overcome the terrible and deadly power of sin and to enter into an intimate and eternal relationship with God. But the individuals who experience the power of the gospel belong to different ethnic groups—Jews and Gentiles— and Romans has a lot to say about how the gospel relates to both these groups. In this section I want to pursue the issue of the theme of Romans by looking carefully at two key passages relating to this matter in the letter's introduction: 1:1–5 and 1:16–17. As we look at these texts, we also will have opportunity to note quickly some of the other significant themes in the letter.

The Gospel Regarding God's Son (1:1–5)

Some of what Paul says about himself in these opening verses is typical of his letters: he calls himself a "servant of Christ Jesus, called to be an apostle" (v. 1). But, probably because he is writing to a church he had neither founded nor visited, Paul gives details about the nature of his ministry that are unusual for his letter openings. These verses are often overlooked as readers skip over the preliminaries to get into the heart of the letter. But in these verses Paul makes five points that furnish important clues about what is to come in the letter.

First, Paul is "set apart for the gospel of God" (v. 1). Paul might be claiming that God appointed him from birth—as he did Jeremiah (Jer 1)—to serve the gospel. Or he might be thinking of his being "set apart" at the time of his vision on the road to Damascus, which was a call to ministry as well as to salvation. But in either case, I want to highlight Paul's focus on the gospel. The word "gospel" has Old Testament roots, particularly in Isaiah, where "preaching good news" is associated with the day of salvation (see esp. Is 52:7, quoted in Rom 10:15). "Gospel" can have an active sense of proclaiming good news, or a more static nuance whereby it denotes the work of God accomplished in Christ as, in itself, the good news.

Second, this gospel was "promised beforehand through the prophets in the Holy Scriptures" (v. 2). As in the overture to an opera, Paul continues in these opening verses to introduce notes that will become recurring motifs in the letter. The gospel can be the gospel "of God" only if it stands in continuity with the revelation of that same God in the Old Testament. Paul therefore repeatedly stresses in Ro-

Model of first-century Rome. (Ben Witherington III)

mans (see 3:21; chs. 4, 9–11) that God's work in Christ for all people is exactly what he had promised from the beginning. The Old Testament and its law fit smoothly with the gospel in a single plan of God.

Third, this gospel is about *God's son* (vv. 3–4). Paul does not say much about the person of Christ in the body of Romans. Christology apparently was not an issue in the church at Rome, so Paul felt no need to address it. But we should not therefore conclude that Romans has nothing to say about Christology. Point after point in the letter assumes a certain view of Christ such as we find enunciated at length elsewhere in Paul's writings. But we should not neglect what Paul says about Christ in these opening verses. They are governed by the introduction of Jesus as God's Son (v. 3a). By calling Jesus God's Son, Paul connects him with Old Testament predictions about a coming king, or messiah (see esp. 2 Sm 7:14; cf. also Ps 2:7). But the title also suggests Jesus' unique and intimate relationship to the Father (see, e.g., Rom 5:10; 8:3, 32).

After introducing Jesus as God's Son, Paul describes him in two roughly parallel statements (vv. 3–4):

"as to his human nature . . . a descendant of David"

"through the Spirit of holiness . . . declared with power to be the Son of God"

The parallelism, which is much closer in the Greek than in English translation, has been explained in two basic ways. The NIV translation, quoted above, reflects the first of these possibilities: Paul is describing *two natures* within Christ. As human, Jesus the Son is the Messiah, born in the line of David, to whose descendant God promised an everlasting kingdom (2 Sm 7:14). But as divine ("Spirit" or even "spirit" of holiness [cf. NIV margin]), Jesus is Son of God—a status "declared" to the world when he was resurrected from the dead. But true as this might be, the "two natures" interpretation probably is not right. "As to his human nature" is a paraphrastic rendering of a Greek phrase that literally translated is "according to the flesh" *(kata sarka)*. The exact significance of the word "flesh" in Paul is notoriously difficult to pin down. But "flesh," especially when contrasted with the Spirit, as here ("Spirit of holiness"), connotes the weakness of human life before and outside of Christ. Sometimes, of course, this weakness takes the form of sin (where the NIV usually will translate "sinful nature"; see, e.g., Rom 7:5). But at other times the word has a more neutral meaning, indicating rather the "purely human" dimension of life (see, e.g., Rom 8:3b). But in either case, "flesh" does not denote a "part" of the human being ("human nature"). In fact, the "flesh versus Spirit" contrast in Paul usually reflects his salvation-historical perspective (for more on this concept, see the next point). "Flesh" relates to the era before the coming of Christ, when sin reigned unopposed; "Spirit" attaches to the new era, which has dawned with the work of Christ and the pouring out of the Spirit.

The point, then, is this: Paul's typical "flesh versus Spirit" contrast suggests that he is contrasting not two *natures* of Christ but two *stages* in his existence. As God's Son, Jesus came to earth as David's descendant and accomplished the work of the Messiah; but after his resurrection, and through the work of the Holy Spirit, he entered into a new stage of existence, "Son-of-God-in-power." Note, again in contrast again to the NIV, that I have attached the words "in power" to the title "Son of God" rather than to the verb. I have done this because the Greek verb translated "declared" (*horizō*) probably should be translated "appointed" (as in all seven other New Testament occurrences of the verb [Lk 22:22; Acts 2:23; 10:42; 11:29; 17:26, 31; Heb 4:7]). Jesus, who has existed from eternity as Son of God, became "Son-of-God-in-power"

Making Contact with Readers

A good writer or speaker always tries to make contact with the audience. He or she wants to create as much common ground as possible. Paul tries to do precisely that in Romans. Since this is a church that he has neither founded nor visited, he is anxious to do what he can to make contact with the Christians there. One way in which Paul accomplishes this is by quoting from traditions or hymns familiar to the Roman Christians. To be sure, Paul never explicitly introduces such quotations, and scholars are often divided on where we might find them. But it is a perfectly natural thing for Paul to do in his circumstances. One such piece of traditional material might be found in Romans 1:3–4. As we noted, the verses are somewhat parallel, such as we might find, for instance, in an early hymn about Christ. And the verses also contain one or two expressions that are unusual in Paul. So, although we cannot be certain, it might very well be that Paul seeks to establish some common ground with his Roman readers by beginning the letter with a reference to an early Christian confession or hymn well known to the church.

Some Christians might wonder how such a quotation might affect our understanding of the Bible's inspiration. If Paul did not write these words himself, are they still inspired Scripture? The answer is yes. The inspiration of Scripture does not require that the biblical authors be the first to come up with the actual words that we find in the Bible. It requires simply that they (and, of course, God) were involved in the selection of the words that now appear in the Bible. If Paul quotes from a tradition in verses 3–4, then he would have chosen (and edited) the words under inspiration so that they communicate just what God wanted us to know.

apocalyptic

new age

salvation
history

old age

when God raised him from the dead and sent the Holy Spirit to inaugurate the new era of redemption. Jesus now reigns over a kingdom in which redeemed men and women can experience the new power of the "age to come."

Fourth, in arguing for a two-stage understanding of Paul's christological statement in these verses, I have introduced the notion of salvation history. Contemporary scholars of Paul generally agree that Paul's thinking and writing about Jesus and Christian experience are dominated by a certain way of conceiving God's work in history drawn from his Jewish background. Jews in Paul's day, especially those influenced by the **apocalyptic** movement, tended to divide the history of God's work in the world into two distinct eras: the "present age," dominated by sin and Gentile oppression of Jews, and "the age to come," when sin would be taken away and the Messiah would reign over a triumphant Israel. New Testament writers, as well as Jesus himself, adopted this scheme but modified it in light of the two separate comings of the Messiah. Jesus' first coming inaugurates the **new age** of redemption without eradicating the present, evil age. At his second coming the present age will cease to be while the new age, in an enhanced form, will remain. We use the term **salvation history** to denote this general scheme, according to which God's salvation is accomplished in the world through a historical process divided into stages.

Interpreting specific expressions often requires that we set those expressions in a larger world of discourse. "Salvation history" is Paul's world of discourse, and I will refer frequently to this overall framework to interpret and apply specific language in Romans. I introduce the matter here because it furnishes the appropriate context within which to understand the "flesh versus Spirit" contrast of verses 3–4. Within Paul's salvation-historical scheme, "flesh" relates to the **old age** and "Spirit" to the new.

Fifth, Paul's apostolic commission, he tells us in verse 5, is to "call people from

among all the Gentiles to *the obedience that comes from faith*." Paul's call to minister to Gentiles is well known. While Jews never were excluded from Paul's apostolic sphere of service, God chose him to be the "point man" in bringing the good news of Christ to the Gentiles. We therefore find Paul's successful evangelistic campaign in southern Asia Minor to be the focus of controversy at the apostolic council (Acts 15); and Paul writes an impassioned letter to defend the law-free offer of the gospel to the Gentiles (Galatians). We are offered the fruit of some of those struggles and controversies in this very letter, as Paul helps the Roman Christians—and us—to understand that the gospel is offered without the law and yet in continuity with the Old Testament.

But especially interesting in this verse is the way Paul presents his purpose in ministry: "the obedience that comes from faith." The phrase is an important one in Romans because Paul, in a sense, "frames" the letter with it, coming back to it in his conclusion (16:26 [the NIV paraphrases, but the Greek is the same]). Again the NIV translation reflects a decision: the Greek is literally translated "the obedience *of* faith" (so the NRSV). The English preposition "of" (as the Greek genitive construction it translates) allows for several possible specific interpretations of the relationship between "obedience" and "faith." Two are especially important: "the obedience that comes from faith" (NIV) and "the obedience that is faith." The second interpretation takes "faith" to be an expansion of what "obedience" means. One "obeys" God by believing him and his Son. Support for this rendering comes from places in Paul's writings where he seems to equate obedience and faith (e.g., Rom 1:8; 10:16; 11:23, 30–31; 16:19). And one might argue that the Book of Acts highlights Paul's evangelistic ministry above all else. With the former, NIV rendering, the focus is more on the life of discipleship that should follow from genuine biblical faith. Paul would be suggesting that his mission is to exhort Christians to obey the Lord whom they have believed, to live out their faith in everyday life. And Paul's letters certainly manifest a concern for this life of obedience.

At the risk of trying to have my cake and eat it too, let me suggest that we avoid the extremes of each of these interpretations. Paul seems deliberately to have chosen a phrase that preserves a careful balance between his desire to awaken faith in non-Christians and to stimulate obedience in believers. His mission is to call Gentiles to a faith that carries with it the determination to obey the Lord, and to an obedience that is stimulated by fresh experiences of faith. The NIV "obedience that comes from faith" may convey this idea, but it is capable of being interpreted as a kind of two-stage experience: one first believes and then later obeys. For Paul, however, genuine Christian faith always carries with it, right from the beginning, the call for obedience. Paul calls on people to believe in the *Lord* Jesus, and calling Jesus "Lord" means that one is committed to doing what Jesus commands. Faith and obedience are two sides of the same coin. One cannot have true faith without obedience, nor can one truly obey without believing.

The Gospel and the Righteousness of God (1:16–17)

In verses 3–4, Paul connects the good news that he preaches with the person of Christ, descendant of David and risen Lord. As risen Lord, Jesus has entered into a new stage of "power" *(dynamis)*. In verses 16–17, Paul explains the nature of that power. These verses function as the hinge between the letter's introduction and its body. They introduce the theme of the argument that follows in the book and are therefore very important in understanding the letter as a whole. Paraphrased a bit, Paul's argument unfolds in three steps:

1. Paul is not ashamed of the gospel.
2. Paul is not ashamed of the gospel *because* the power of God for salvation

is revealed in it (salvation that is available to everyone who believes, both Jew and Greek).
3. The gospel has the power to save *because* the righteousness of God is revealed in it (a righteousness based on faith, in agreement with Hb 2:4).

Not Ashamed of the Gospel

Why does Paul begin this important paragraph with so defensive a statement? He might simply be using the literary device of litotes, whereby one uses an understated negative formulation to make a positive point ("I am not without some ability at basketball" = "I'm a pretty good basketball player"). But Paul might well intend to take a defensive stance here. As I noted above, Paul was God's "point man" in bringing the good news to Gentiles. As such, he was a very controversial figure. Loyal Jews and even some Jewish Christians considered him a traitor to his people because, they believed, he had abandoned the law. Some radical Gentile Christians thought he did not go far enough in shedding the trappings of his Jewish upbringing. And so Paul might suspect that rumors about his teaching—not always accurate or positive ones—were circulating in Rome. One of Paul's purposes in Romans is to defend himself and, more importantly, the gospel he preaches from false accusations and malicious interpretations (see, e.g., 3:8).

The Power of God for the Salvation of Everyone Who Believes

When the good news about Jesus is preached, God's own power is unleashed. That power is capable of "saving" anyone who believes. Two points about this salvation are especially important in assessing the argument of Romans that follows. First, this salvation is not only negative: saved *from* sin and death; but also positive: saved *to* restored fellowship with God. Second, this salvation is accomplished only when God has finished his work for us at the end of history. Paul usually does not use "save" and "salvation" in the sense of initial conversion (although

righteousness see Rom 8:24); rather, he applies these terms to the ultimate rescue from God's wrath and deliverance into the eternal kingdom at the end of history (Rom 5:9, 10; 13:11). The gospel and the power that it releases are not intended only to convert the sinner but also to transform that sinner and rescue him or her from every possible worldly and satanic threat.

The "Righteousness of God" (*dikaiosynē theou*) in Romans

1:17 For in the gospel *a righteousness from God* is revealed, a righteousness that is by faith from first to last, just as it is written: "The righteous will live by faith."

3:5 But if our unrighteousness brings out *God's righteousness* more clearly, what shall we say? That God is unjust in bringing his wrath on us? (I am using a human argument.)

3:21 But now *a righteousness from God,* apart from law, has been made known, to which the Law and the Prophets testify.

3:22 This *righteousness from God* comes through faith in Jesus Christ to all who believe.

3:25 God presented him as a sacrifice of atonement, through faith in his blood. He did this to demonstrate *his justice,* because in his forbearance he had left the sins committed beforehand unpunished.

3:26 He did it to demonstrate *his justice* at the present time, so as to be just and the one who justifies those who have faith in Jesus.

10:3 Since they did not know *the righteousness that comes from God* and sought to establish their own, they did not submit to *God's righteousness.*

We should not overlook the words that conclude verse 16: "everyone who believes: first for the Jew, then for the Gentile." Here Paul sounds a note that will resound throughout the letter. The "everyone" motif is a critical subtheme of Romans. As a means of restoring the sinner's relationship to God apart from the law, the gospel has a universal applicability. In a way not previously seen in salvation history, God offers salvation to the Gentile as well as to the Jew. But also we should note the "first . . . then" part of Paul's assertion. The inclusion of Gentiles has not, Paul suggests, disenfranchised the Jew, or even pushed the Jew out of first place in God's purposes and plans. The gospel is, after all, "the gospel of God . . . promised beforehand . . . in the Holy Scriptures" (1:1–2). It does not, indeed it cannot, take away the legitimate rights of the Jewish people granted to them by God himself in the Old Testament.

The Righteousness of God

The connecting word at the beginning of verse 17, "for" (*gar*), shows that the revelation of God's **righteousness** in verse 17 is the basis for the power of God for salvation released in the good news (v. 16). But what is this "righteousness of God"? Note, first, that again I am modifying the NIV, which offers the paraphrastic rendering "a righteousness from God." "Righteousness of God" preserves the ambiguity of the Greek phrase as a basis for our discussion. Second, in asking this question we get into a matter crucial to the interpretation of Romans, as the phrase occurs eight times in Romans (see also 3:5, 21, 22, 25, 26; 10:3 [twice]) and only once elsewhere in Paul's writings (2 Cor 5:21). Third, we also get into a matter that has been and continues to be a point of considerable controversy among scholars. The chart summarizes the key points.[1]

Four main interpretations of the phrase should be considered: (1) the justice of God; (2) the faithfulness of God; (3) the status of righteousness given by God; (4) the act of putting people in the right

45

performed by God. Each of these interpretations (with the possible exception of the third) has precedent in the Old Testament teaching about God's righteousness, but I think that the fourth comes closest to Paul's intention here. As Luther recognized long ago, the revelation of God's justice (the first interpretation) is hardly "good news" for sinful human beings. I think that Paul does use the phrase with this meaning in 3:25, 26, but it does not fit the present context. Contemporary scholars rightly insist that Paul's use of the phrase flows from the frequent Old Testament references to God's righteousness. And those references, it is argued, come in the context of God's covenant with Israel, meaning that "righteousness," or "being in the right," must be interpreted in light of those covenant obligations. For the Israelites, therefore, "being in the right" means obeying the covenant stipulations, the law. For God, on the other hand, "being in the right" means carrying out the commitments to Israel that he has expressed in the covenant. "Faithfulness" expresses this sense very well. This notion may be part of Paul's meaning here, but I do not think that it expresses his full meaning. Paul goes on in verse 17 to make clear that this righteousness of God is attained only through faith, and it is hard to see how God's faithfulness would be contingent on our faith.

This emphasis on faith is what has led to the popularity of the third interpretation, a popularity reflected in the NIV decision to translate "righteousness *from* God." "Righteousness," on this reading, is the status of "right standing" that God gives to sinners when they believe. Again, I think that Paul intends to include this notion in his expression, but again I question whether it is broad enough to explain Paul's language. How is it that this status of righteousness is "revealed" in the gospel? Moreover, this interpretation of God's righteousness does not have strong Old Testament precedent. Yet Paul seems to assume here that his readers will know what he means when he uses the phrase, presumably because he builds on the Old

Testament use of it. And, indeed, Paul claims in Romans 3:21 that this righteousness of God is attested by the Old Testament.

If we take this last issue as our starting point, our attention is drawn to several Old Testament passages in which it is predicted that God would manifest his "righteousness" in the last days. Note particularly Isaiah 46:13:

> I am bringing my righteousness
> near,
>   it is not far away;
>   and my salvation will not be
>   delayed.
> I will grant salvation to Zion, my
>   splendor to Israel.

See also Isaiah 51:4–8:

> Listen to me, my people;
>   hear me, my nation:
> The law will go out from me;
>   my justice will become a light
>   to the nations.
> My righteousness draws near
>   speedily,
>   my salvation is on the way,
>   and my arm will bring justice to
>   the nations.
> The islands will look to me
>   and wait in hope for my arm.
> Lift up your eyes to the heavens,
>   look at the earth beneath;
> the heavens will vanish like
>   smoke,
>   the earth will wear out like a
>   garment
>   and its inhabitants die like flies.
> But my salvation will last forever,
>   my righteousness will never
>   fail.
> Hear me, you who know what is
>   right,
>   you people who have my law in
>   your hearts:
> Do not fear the reproach of men
>   or be terrified by their insults.
> For the moth will eat them up like
>   a garment;
>   the worm will devour them like
>   wool.
> But my righteousness will last
>   forever,
>   my salvation through all
>   generations.

In these important prophetic texts God's "righteousness" is another way of speaking of the salvation he plans to bring to his people in the last days. By "putting things right" again, God will vindicate himself and save his people, in faithfulness to his promises to them. This is the notion of God's righteousness that Paul has in mind here (and in 3:21, 22; 10:3). The gospel brings salvation to people because it reveals God's promised way of putting people into right relationship with himself. "God's righteousness," as Paul uses it here, implies God's faithfulness to his promises, and it culminates in the status of "being in the right" when it is met with faith. But the idea is broader than either of these two, including the entire process by which God acts to put people into this saving relationship.

One final point about this "righteousness of God" needs to be made. As virtually all scholars acknowledge these days, this "putting in the right" that God is carrying out is a forensic act. That is, it does not mean that people are "made right" in a moral sense but that they are "declared to be in the right" in a judicial sense. In the gospel God acts first of all to rescue sinners from the condemnation they stand under because of sin and to declare them innocent before him of all those sins. This is what "God's righteousness" involves and what the related idea of justification means. "Moral" righteousness, as Paul makes clear in Romans 6, inevitably must follow upon forensic righteousness. But the two are not the same, and the legal standing precedes the transformed lifestyle.

Paul concludes these verses with an emphasis typical of him and of the argument of Romans: faith. Many Jews probably believed that God would automatically bestow his righteousness on all of Israel. But Paul makes clear that it is only those who believe—and all those who believe—who will experience God's righteousness. This probably is what he intends to say in the debated phrase "by faith from first to last" (a literal rendering of the Greek). Some think that the phrase suggests a progress in faith, while others think that Paul is referring both to Christ's faithfulness (the Greek word *pistis* can have this meaning) and to human faith. But the expression probably is emphatic, as the NIV recognizes: "faith from first to last." And Paul reiterates the importance of faith with a quotation from Habakkuk 2:4. We might translate this quotation as "The righteous will live by faith" (NIV), but the argument of Romans suggests rather that we should translate it as "The one who is righteous by faith will live." Life, eternal life, is granted to the person who has been declared righteous before God through his or her faith.

The Purpose of Romans: Why Romans?

We are now in a position to return to a question left unanswered in chapter 2: Why Romans? Why would Paul write what is arguably the most important theological document ever produced to a church that he had never visited? Since Paul says nothing definitive on this point in the letter, scholars have been free to speculate—and speculate they have![2] We can categorize the suggestions under two main headings.

Proposals Focusing on Paul's Circumstances

In chapter 2 we discovered that Paul writes Romans as he is about to embark for Jerusalem, where he plans to deliver to the Jewish Christians a collection of money from Gentile Christians. He then will proceed on to Spain via Rome. We further noted that Paul hopes to receive some support from the Roman Christians for the work in Spain (15:24). Many scholars have seized on this last point in their explanation of the purpose of Romans. Paul writes Romans to introduce himself to the Roman church. And he does this at such length because he knows that false rumors about the gospel he preaches have reached them. He must

Model of first-century Jerusalem. (Donald Hagner)

defend himself against such charges if he hopes to enlist their support. Probably most commentators on Romans allow this factor to have some role in Paul's decision to write this letter to the Roman Christians, but most are equally convinced that there is more to the purpose of Romans than this. One intriguing suggestion is that Paul is dominated as he writes by his impending visit to Jerusalem. As 15:30–33 makes clear, Paul is deeply concerned about the prospects for that visit. So, it is suggested, Paul writes Romans as a kind of rehearsal of the speech he plans to make in Jerusalem.[3] While it is unlikely that Paul would go to such effort in a practice speech, the proposal does have the merit of drawing our attention again to the issue of Jewish/Gentile relationships that so marks the argument of Romans.

Proposals Focusing on the Roman Church

The trend in recent scholarship is to insist that Romans be treated as a real letter—not a doctrinal treatise, not a personal meditation, but a letter, written to real people with real problems. And then the conclusion is drawn that the purpose of Romans must be found in the needs of the Roman community, for it is to meet the needs of churches that Paul writes his letters. What might the issue in Rome have been? Romans 14:1–15:13 seems to furnish the best answer. Paul there rebukes the Roman believers for dividing into two parties and standing in judgment over one another. The issue, as I will explain more fully when we come to that text, has to do with the place of the Mosaic law in the Christian community. The "weak," mainly Jewish Christians, insist on observing certain ritual requirements of the law; the "strong," mainly Gentile Christians, insist that all such rules are passé and mock the "weak" for insisting on them. A large number of contemporary scholars think that Paul writes Romans to confront this division within the church. The theology in chapters 1–11 is designed to provide the foundation for his general appeal in chapters 12–13 and his direct appeal for unity in 14:1–15:13.

Healing the division in the Roman community undoubtedly was one of Paul's purposes in writing Romans, but there is too much in the letter not directly (or even indirectly) related to this purpose to see that as the sole purpose. In fact, I suggest that we should abandon the quest for a single purpose for Romans.[4] Paul writes with one eye on the division of the church, but he writes also to prepare for his visit and to explain the gospel. The various purposes of Romans do share a common denominator: the missionary situation of Paul. As Romans 15:19–20 reveals, Paul has reached a significant stage in his missionary work. He is about to embark on a new work in Spain. He is on his way to Jerusalem with money that he hopes will bring some measure of reconciliation to Jew and Gentile. And he writes to a church divided between Jew and Gentile. He therefore writes about the gospel that he preaches. The Roman Christians need to understand the power of that gospel: it can both justify and transform the sinner. And they need to understand how that gospel, in bringing Jew and Gentile together into one people of God, both continues the one plan of God set out in the Old Testament and inaugurates a new stage in that plan. *The gospel in its salvation-historical context* is the theme of Romans. Paul's purpose in elaborating that theme is to help the Roman Christians understand and appreciate their situation in the flow of salvation history. And, because Paul is dealing in Romans with such basic and enduring theological issues, Romans transcends its time and place (as, of course, does all Scripture, in different ways) to speak to the church of every generation. As James Denney puts it,

> Is it not manifest that when we give [the conditions under which Paul wrote] all the historical definiteness of which they are capable, there is something in them which rises above the casualness of time and place, something which might easily give the epistle not an accidental or occasional character, but the character of an exposition of principles?[5]

The Structure of Romans: How Does Romans Unfold?

How does this timeless, yet time-rooted, exposition of the gospel unfold? We will be looking at the specific turns of that argument as the book unfolds, but it helps in reading any book to have some idea of the lay of the land before plunging into the details.

At the outset we have to be careful about imposing our own neat structure on what is a very complex book. We sometimes seem to think that biblical books have to fall into a clear "Roman numeral I, point A, subpoint 1" kind of outline. But a glance at most of the letters we write reveals that this idea might grossly oversimplify the situation.[6] Still, Romans, just because Paul is writing rather generally about the gospel without too much regard for specific issues, unfolds with a certain internal logic of its own. Here are the chief points in that logic:

I. The Letter Opening (1:1–17)
   A. Prescript (1:1–7)
   B. Thanksgiving and occasion: Paul and the Romans (1:8–15)
   C. The theme of the letter (1:16–17)

II. The Heart of the Gospel: Justification by Faith (1:18–4:25)
   A. The universal reign of sin (1:18–3:20)
      1. All persons are accountable to God for sin (1:18–32)
      2. Jews are accountable to God for sin (2:1–3:8)
         a. The Jews and the judgment of God (2:1–16)
         b. The limitations of the covenant (2:17–29)
         c. God's faithfulness and the judgment of Jews (3:1–8)
      3. The guilt of all humanity (3:9–20)

49

B. Justification by faith
(3:21–4:25)
1. Justification and the righteousness of God (3:21–26)
2. "By faith alone"
(3:27–4:25)
   a. "By faith alone": initial statement (3:27–31)
   b. "By faith alone": Abraham (4:1–25)

III. **The Assurance Provided by the Gospel: The Hope of Salvation (5:1–8:39)**
A. The hope of glory (5:1–21)
1. From justification to salvation (5:1–11)
2. The reign of grace and life (5:12–21)
B. Freedom from bondage to sin (6:1–23)
1. "Dead to sin" through union with Christ (6:1–14)
2. Freed from sin's power to serve righteousness (6:15–23)
C. Freedom from bondage to the law (7:1–25)
1. Released from the law, joined to Christ (7:1–6)

2. The history and experience of Jews under the law (7:7–25)
   a. The coming of the law (7:7–12)
   b. Life under the law (7:13–25)
D. Assurance of eternal life in the Spirit (8:1–30)
1. The Spirit of life (8:1–13)
2. The Spirit of adoption (8:14–17)
3. The Spirit of glory (8:18–30)
E. The believer's security celebrated (8:31–39)

IV. **The Defense of the Gospel: The Problem of Israel (9:1–11:36)**
A. Introduction: the tension between God's promises and Israel's plight (9:1–5)
B. Defining the promise (1): God's sovereign election (9:6–29)
1. The Israel within Israel (9:6–13)
2. Objections answered: the freedom and purpose of God (9:14–23)
3. God's calling of a new people: Israel and the Gentiles (9:24–29)
C. Understanding Israel's plight: Christ as the climax of salvation history (9:30–10:21)
1. Israel, the Gentiles, and the righteousness of God (9:30–10:13)
2. Israel's accountability (10:14–21)
D. Summary: Israel, the "elect," and the "hardened" (11:1–10)
E. Defining the promise (2): the future of Israel (11:11–32)
1. God's purpose in Israel's rejection (11:11–15)
2. The interrelationship of Jews and Gentiles: warning to Gentiles (11:16–24)
3. The salvation of "all Israel" (11:25–32)

Study Questions

1. What is the difference between Jesus as eternal "Son" (1:3) and Jesus as "Son-of-God-in-power" (1:4)?

2. What is "salvation history" and how are we Christians today placed within that history? What significance might our place in that history have?

3. How does our faith affect the revelation of God's righteousness? What happens to a person when he or she experiences that righteousness?

4. Why did Paul write Romans? How should your understanding of its purpose affect the way you read the book?

F. Conclusion: praise to God in light of his awesome plan (11:33–36)

V. **The Transforming Power of the Gospel: Christian Conduct (12:1–15:13)**
   A. The heart of the matter: total transformation (12:1–2)
   B. Humility and mutual service (12:3–8)
   C. Love and its manifestations (12:9–21)
   D. The Christian and secular rulers (13:1–7)
   E. Love and the law (13:8–10)
   F. Living in light of the day (13:11–14)
   G. A plea for unity (14:1–15:13)
      1. Do not condemn one another! (14:1–12)
      2. Do not cause your brother or sister to stumble! (14:13–23)
      3. Put other people first! (15:1–6)
      4. Receive one another! (15:7–13)

VI. **The Letter Closing (15:14–16:27)**
   A. Paul's ministry and travel plans (15:14–33)
   B. Greetings (16:1–16)
   C. Closing remarks and doxology (16:17–27)

Key Terms

apocalyptic

new age

salvation history

old age

righteousness

Part
2

Encountering the Human Dilemma

Romans 1:18–3:20

4 God's Wrath against Sinners

Romans 1:18–32

Outline
- The Revelation of God's Wrath (1:18)
- The Reason for God's Wrath (1:19–21)
- The Results of God's Wrath (1:22–32)

Objectives
After reading this chapter, you should be able to

1. Appreciate the reality and nature of God's wrath.
2. Define and give examples of God's revelation in nature.
3. Trace the manifold nature of human sin to its roots.

natural revelation

special revelation

After the wonderful announcement of God's good news of salvation through God's righteousness in 1:16–17, we would expect Paul to dwell on the nature and blessings of that salvation. What a shock, then, to read about wrath, sin, idolatry, degradation, judgment. But Paul has made no mistake. He knows that we cannot appreciate the good news until we thoroughly understand the bad news. Only when we have really come to grips with the extent of the human dilemma will we be able to respond as we should to the answer to that dilemma found in the good news about Jesus. A popular evangelistic strategy used to be called "The Romans Road" because it was based on the structure of Paul's argument in Romans. No one evangelistic approach will fit every situation, but getting people to take the gospel seriously will often require us first to get people to take their own dilemma seriously. This is Paul's strategy in Romans.

The Revelation of God's Wrath (1:18)

The notion of "the wrath of God" is not a welcome one, even among many Christians. We prefer to dwell on God's love and grace. But we will never understand God or the work he accomplished for us in his Son until we appreciate the reality of God's wrath. As presented in Scripture, God's wrath is no capricious emotion but the necessary response of a perfect and holy God to violations of his will. Paul usually associates God's wrath with a coming day of judgment (e.g., Rom 2:5). Here, however, he announces that God's wrath "is being revealed" in the present. This might mean simply that God makes clear to people that his wrath is a reality to be reckoned with. But "reveal" here probably has the active notion of "manifest" or "accomplish." God will inflict his wrath on sinners in a climactic way in the last day. But even now, in ways that verses 19–32 will make clear, God is punishing human sin with his wrath. Noting

the parallel between verses 17 and 18, some scholars suggest that the revelation of God's wrath is part of the revelation of his righteousness. But this is unlikely. God's righteousness, as I argued earlier, is a saving activity. God's wrath is the reason why God's righteousness is needed, but it is not part of that righteousness.

Verse 18 stands as the heading for the entire argument of 1:18–3:20. In the rest of this section Paul will detail the ways in which God's wrath is inflicted and, especially, the reason why he inflicts that wrath. The first part of this argument, in the rest of chapter 1, concerns people generally, as they are confronted with the truth that God reveals to all people in the world that he has created.

The Reason for God's Wrath (1:19–21)

The last words of verse 18, though easily overlooked, furnish the clue to the direction that Paul's argument now takes. God's wrath, Paul has said, is visited upon people who "suppress the truth." Think for a moment about that word "suppress" and what it implies. People cannot suppress something that they do not have. So Paul implies that people have access to the truth. In verses 19–21, Paul therefore elaborates this point and shows that people have not responded as they should have to the truth that God has revealed to them. Paul makes three basic points.

First, God has manifested his truth to all human beings. God has "made it plain to them" (v. 19). To be sure, the text does not explicitly claim that the antecedent to "them" is all human beings. But the "them" picks up the "men" of verse 18 who are ungodly and wicked and who suppress the truth. And Paul makes clear that all people are included in this category (e.g., 3:9). In theological terms, Paul here is teaching about **natural revelation.** By contrast, **special rev-**

The beauty of the created world reveals God's existence and power. (Jim Yancey)

natural revelation. It is best, then, to think that verses 19–32 speak of the condition of all human beings faced with God's natural revelation.

Second, the truth contained in natural revelation is limited. In verse 20, Paul spells out just what information God has "made plain" to human beings. In an ironic apparent contrast (called an oxymoron), Paul claims that "God's invisible qualities . . . have been clearly seen." Specifically, he lists God's "eternal power and divine nature." From what God has revealed in nature, people can know that a god exists and that that god is powerful, but of course they cannot know about the specific requirements of God's law or about the plan of God or about the culmination of that plan in the cross of Christ.

Third, precisely because natural revelation is so limited, it cannot mediate salvation to sinners. Paul hints at this conclusion at the end of verse 20. The purpose of God's revelation in nature, Paul affirms, is that people might be "without excuse." They cannot claim ignorance when God visits his wrath upon them, for (note this transitional word at the beginning of v. 21) people actually "knew God." This language in Scripture often refers to a saving relationship with God. Here, clearly, that is not the case. It is Paul's way of making the point that people do have some knowledge about God. The problem, as the rest of verse 21 makes clear, is that they do not respond appropriately to that knowledge. Rather than glorifying or giving thanks to God, their hearts are darkened and their thinking perverted.

What Paul says in these verses is critical to our assessment of the situation of people who do not have access to special revelation. The current climate of pluralism and tolerance makes it especially important to listen carefully to Paul here, for he makes it clear that natural revelation, by itself, cannot rescue people from their sinful state. People have enough information about God in the world around them to be justly condemned, but not enough to discover the

elation includes God's direct acts of speaking and acting, recorded, for instance, in Scripture. Not everyone, of course, has access to special revelation. But God also reveals truth about himself in a general, more indirect way, in the created world itself. The fascinating and intricate web of created things in the world around us speaks of the existence of a powerful and intelligent Creator. Since Paul is talking here about natural revelation, many interpreters think that he is speaking only of Gentiles, because Jews, of course, have been given special revelation, and Paul will speak to their condition in chapter 2. However, while what Paul teaches here undoubtedly is most relevant to Gentiles, he never so restricts his analysis. And we must remember that Jews also have access to

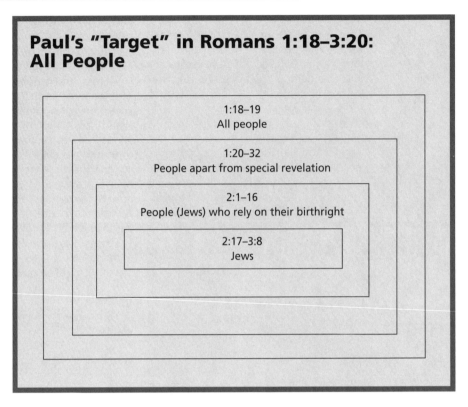

Paul's "Target" in Romans 1:18–3:20: All People

1:18–19
All people

1:20–32
People apart from special revelation

2:1–16
People (Jews) who rely on their birthright

2:17–3:8
Jews

good news that is the only path to salvation. To be sure, God can graciously use natural revelation as a means of stimulating people to look for further information about the God who created the world around them. And so, in keeping with the approach of Paul in his speech to the Athenians in Acts 17, natural revelation can become the springboard to the gospel.

The Results of God's Wrath (1:22–32)

In the remaining verses of chapter 1, Paul describes the devastating effects of the universal human decision to spurn the God who reveals himself in the natural world. Paul pictures human beings making an "exchange" to which God responds by "giving people over." Three times Paul depicts this pattern and its tragic consequences:

"[They] exchanged" . . . "Therefore God gave them over" (vv. 23–24)
"They exchanged" . . . "Because of this, God gave them over" (vv. 25–26a)
"Their women exchanged" . . . "[God] gave them over" (vv. 26b–28)

In each case human beings put aside the truth God has revealed in nature and put in its place their own perverted notions and activities. Paul focuses on two kinds of sins in this passage: idolatry (vv. 23, 25) and sexual perversion (vv. 24, 26–27). These are precisely the sins that the Jews often attributed to the Gentiles as evidence of the Gentiles' estrangement from God. But Paul also follows Jewish custom in providing a broad list of sins that result from people's refusal to worship God (vv. 28b–31). The passage ends with a final verdict on the perverse pleasure people find in encouraging rebellion against their Creator (v. 32).

God responds to people's decision to exchange the true God for idols by condemning people to the consequences of the sins they have chosen for themselves. This "giving people over" is not an entirely passive matter—as if, as one commentator puts it, God simply ceases "to hold the boat as it was dragged by the current of the river."[1] Rather, we should view this action as a positive, judicial decision on God's part, whereby he sentences people to the very sins they have chosen for themselves. Especially instructive for the sequence of Paul's teaching here is Wisdom of Solomon 11:15–16: "In return for their [the Gentiles'] foolish and wicked thoughts, which led them astray to worship irrational serpents and worthless animals, you sent upon them a multitude of irrational creatures to punish them, so that they might learn that one is punished by the very things by which one sins." And so the downward spiral of sin that we see in the world around us comes about. Although Paul does not explicitly say so, we probably are justified in thinking that this giving over of people to sin is one of the ways in which God is now revealing his wrath.

Jewish Condemnation of the Gentiles

We have noted that Paul's description of the condition of people in light of natural revelation resembles Jewish condemnation of the Gentiles. Jews in Paul's day were appropriately proud of their status as God's chosen people. The scattering of Jews all over the Mediterranean world (the Diaspora) meant that most Jews lived in minority groups within an overwhelmingly Gentile culture. As a typical, natural reaction, the Jews emphasized their privileged condition and tended to look down on the Gentiles as inferior people. Several Jewish passages reflect this teaching in various degrees, but the clearest and most detailed example comes from an intertestamental book that is part of the Apocrypha, Wisdom of Solomon. Toward the end of chapter 12 in this book, the author begins to castigate the Gentiles for their depravity and continues his tirade against them all the way to the end of chapter 14. The similarities to Romans 1:18–32 are striking. The author:

- criticizes the Gentiles for idolatry: "For they went far astray on the paths of error, accepting as gods those animals that even their enemies despised; they were deceived like foolish infants" (12:23–24);

- treats idolatry as the root of many other sins: "the beginning of fornication" (14:12);

- claims that the Gentiles are "not to be excused" (13:8), because they had ample evidence for God's existence and qualities in creation (13:1–5);

- shows that the Gentiles' rejection of knowledge of God led to all kinds of evil: "Then it was not enough for them to err about the knowledge of God, but though living in great strife due to ignorance, they call such great evils peace. For whether they kill children in their initiations, or celebrate secret mysteries, or hold frenzied revels with strange customs, they no longer keep either their lives or their marriages pure, but they either treacherously kill one another, or grieve one another by adultery, and all is a raging riot of blood and murder, theft and deceit, corruption, faithlessness, tumult, perjury, confusion over what is good, forgetfulness of favors, defiling of souls, sexual perversion, disorder in marriages, adultery, and debauchery" (14:22–26).

The similarities are close enough that Paul might have had this very passage in mind when he wrote Romans 1. On the other hand, Paul might be repeating common Jewish polemic against the Gentiles, of which this passage in Wisdom of Solomon is just one example. In either case, Paul again seems to be making contact with his readers by repeating traditional teaching.

Roman household gods were worshiped in shrines like this one. (Ben Witherington III)

ated beings. This was the form that idolatry typically took in the Old Testament period. Paul heightens the distinction between God and the created world by imitating the language of the creation story itself: "birds and animals and reptiles" (cf. Gn 1:20, 24). We should keep in mind that idolatry is not restricted to worshiping an image on an altar. Anything that we put in place of God—sex, money, power, golf, ministry—is an idol. Jewish sources often made a connection between idolatry and sexual sin. Thus it is not surprising that Paul would portray God's reaction to people's idolatry as giving them over to "sexual impurity." We should note that God does not therefore initiate a sin that was not present before. Paul makes clear that people already had "sinful desires." And the teaching of a text like this must be balanced with the human side of the matter: "Having lost all sensitivity, they have given themselves over to sensuality so as to indulge in every kind of impurity, with a continual lust for more" (Eph 4:19).

In the first "exchange . . . give over" sequence (vv. 22–24) Paul focuses on the root sin of idolatry. It is one of the marks of sinful human beings that they dress up their descent into foolishness as the very height of wisdom. People seek to justify their rejection of the only true God by speaking of advances in knowledge, the maturation of human intellect, and the like. But any truth that is put in the place of the truth of God is idolatry. Paul uses traditional language to portray this idolatry in verse 23. Note Psalm 106:20, "They exchanged their Glory for an image of a bull, which eats grass," and Jeremiah 2:11, "Has a nation ever changed its gods? (Yet they are not gods at all.) But my people have exchanged their Glory for worthless idols." Interestingly, both texts describe the idolatry of Israel, confirming the suggestion that Paul has all human beings, not just Gentiles, in view in these verses. Equally traditional is the portrayal of idolatry in terms of the worship of cre-

The second "exchange . . . give over" sequence (vv. 25–27) covers the same ground in a bit more detail. Again it is idolatry that initiates the sequence: "They exchanged the truth of God for a lie, and worshiped and served created things rather than the Creator." God again responds by "giving people over" to "shameful lusts." In this case, however, Paul elaborates on these lusts in terms of homosexuality (vv. 26b–27). Paul follows typical Jewish teaching in labeling homosexuality as being "unnatural" or "against nature" (para physin). Some contemporary apologists for homosexuality have tried to interpret this language to mean that only sex conducted against the nature of the individual person is sinful. If a person is heterosexual, sex with people of the same sex would be "against that person's nature" and therefore wrong.[2] But Paul holds no such individualized notion of "nature." He uses the word, following Jewish custom, to refer to the natural order as God has made it.[3] Following the Old Testament (e.g., Gn 19:1–28; Lv 18:22; 20:13; Dt 23:17–18), Paul sees in homosexual activity a particularly striking manifestation of the way in which human beings have twisted God's created intention into something quite different from what God ever intended.[4]

Those who engage in homosexual activity, Paul concludes, receive "in themselves the due penalty for their perversion" (end of v. 27). It has become popular in our day to think that AIDS might be a particularly clear manifestation of this penalty. This is possible, but we must quickly remind ourselves that all kinds of physical diseases are direct (e.g., cirrhosis of the liver for those who abuse alcohol) and indirect consequences of sin. And Paul himself almost certainly is not thinking only of physical consequences to sin (particularly when we remember that AIDS was, of course, nonexistent in his day). What Paul does want to emphasize is that the flouting of God's creation will in sexual matters brings God's rightful judgment.

The third "exchange . . . give over" sequence is not as clear as the first two. In fact, the "exchange" part is buried in Paul's discussion of homosexuality at the end of verse 26, while the "give over" part

Key Terms

natural revelation

special revelation

does not come until verse 28. Moreover, the "giving over" is not directly tied to the exchange, but is said to be the result of people not thinking it "worthwhile to retain the knowledge of God." The Greek here features a word play that is difficult to preserve in English translation. The best we can do is the awkward "Because people did not *approve [edokimasan]* God in their thinking, God has given them over to minds incapable of *approving [adokimon]* what is right." We should emphasize that the fall into sin affects not just our affections and our actions, but our thinking as well. Human beings now have minds that are incapable of consistently thinking about divine things in an accurate way.

In verses 29–31 Paul provides us with a list of representative sins, as he elaborates "to do what ought not to be done" at the end of verse 28. The three sentences into which the NIV divides these sins accurately convey the structure of Paul's list. He begins very generally, moves on to the cardinal sin of envy and its consequences, and concludes with a wide spectrum of sins. The focus throughout is on what we might call social sins—the evil that we do to one another. Idolatry may be the root sin, and sexual perversion one of its key consequences, but Paul does not want us to forget the many forms that our rejection of God's truth has taken. None of us reading such a list can come away without a sense of conviction.

Paul wraps up his description of the results of God's wrath in human history with a general indictment. Again he reminds us of natural revelation: people know that certain actions deserve death, that God justly punishes people who sin in these ways. Thus, not only do people

Study Questions

1. In what ways might the wrath of God be evident in the world of our day? How might we know what events or circumstances are the product of that wrath?

2. What does the limited power of natural revelation mean for the state of those people who have never heard the gospel?

3. Name some modern idols that Christians may not be recognizing as idols at all.

4. How should the Christian go about integrating the claim of some modern scientists that homosexuality is a genetic predisposition with Paul's teaching in Romans 1:18–32?

know about God's person and power from the natural world, but also they have some kind of inbuilt recognition of good and evil and sense that God is just when he punishes wrongdoing. Paul will say more on this matter in 2:14–15 as he describes the "natural law" to which all people have access. In condemning, at the end of the verse, those who commit sin as well as those who approve of those who commit sin, Paul may again be echoing Jewish teaching (e.g., *Testament of Asher* 6.2, "The two-faced are doubly pun-ished because they both practice evil and approve of others who practice it"). But Paul goes further. His "not only . . . but also" construction implies that he views those who approve of sinners as worse than the sinners themselves. Paul is not minimizing the seriousness of sin. He is implying that people who label sin as good or natural or noble are doing great damage to the morals of a society, for eventually it becomes an acceptable behavior and people are no longer conscious of their sin.

5 Jews Are "without Excuse"

Romans 2:1–29

Outline

- **Jewish Sin and God's Impartial Judgment (2:1–11)**

  Jews Are as Guilty as Gentiles (2:1–5)

  God's Impartial Judgment (2:6–11)
- **Jews, Gentiles, and the Law (2:12–16)**
- **Jewish Sin and the Covenant (2:17–29)**

Objectives

After reading this chapter, you should be able to

1. Understand how Jews are doing "the same things" Gentiles do.
2. Identify the way in which God confronts all people with his law.
3. Appreciate the value and limitations of the covenant that God entered into with Israel.
4. Appreciate more fully the situation of human beings outside of Christ.

diatribe

The Gentile Christian in Rome listening to the end of Romans 1 being read in a church service might wonder about this Paul. The apostle had the reputation of being favorable to Gentiles, but in these verses Paul seemed to be repeating the same old Jewish polemic against the Gentiles. Had nothing changed with the coming of Christ? Were Gentiles still going to be treated as a race inferior to the Jews?

As the reader moved into chapter 2, these questions would quickly have been answered. Paul has announced in 1:18 that God's wrath is revealed against all human sin. He has shown in 1:19–20 that all people deserve God's wrath because they have access to God's truth but have turned away from it. In the rest of the chapter he concentrates on the way people have spurned God's natural revelation. But now, in chapter 2, he turns to special revelation. God has made his will known to the Jewish people in very particular ways, especially through his law. But, as all people fail to live up to the expectations of God revealed in nature, so also Jews have failed to live up to the demands God has made of them in his law. To be sure, the Jews are not quite in the same position as the Gentiles, for God did single them out from all the peoples of the world and entered into a covenant relationship with them. But Paul will show that this covenant, apart from the grace available in the gospel, cannot shield Jews from God's judgment.

Jewish Sin and God's Impartial Judgment (2:1–11)

This passage falls into two distinct units. In 2:1–5, Paul places Jews in the same category into which he has placed the Gentiles (1:21–32): guilty of sinful acts and "without excuse." He then shows how this equal treatment of Jews and Gentiles fits with an important attribute of God: impartiality (2:6–11).

Jews Are as Guilty as Gentiles (2:1–5)

By the time Paul writes Romans, he has been preaching the gospel for over twenty years. He knows how people will react to his teaching and what questions they are likely to raise. As he writes about the gospel to the Roman Christians, Paul uses this experience to structure his presentation. He therefore frequently pauses to ask questions about and raise objections to what he has just taught. The transition from chapter 1 to chapter 2 reveals just this kind of circumstance. Paul was well accustomed to preaching about the sinfulness of all human beings based on natural revelation. As he did so, he was familiar with people in the crowd who would be quite eager to join in his condemnation and pride themselves as superior to the idolators and fornicators whom he was raking over the coals. We can imagine Paul suddenly turning on such people and shocking them with a direct accusation: "You, therefore, have no excuse, you who pass judgment on someone else, for at whatever point you judge the other, you are condemning yourself, because you who pass judgment do the same things" (v. 1).

Like any good writer, Paul uses the literary devices of his own day to communicate effectively with his readers. One of the devices that Paul uses quite often in Romans is **diatribe**. More a style than a genre, a diatribe usually took the form of a dialogue using questions and answers to make its points. The writer entered into a discussion with a fictional opponent as a way of advancing his or her own argument. Perhaps the best example comes in the *Discourses* of Epictetus. Paul uses this style in the beginning of Romans 2. As the English word "yourself" toward the end of verse 1 reveals, Paul is using the second person *singular* in these verses. This does not indicate that he is singling out one person in the Roman congregation; rather, he is using the diatribe style, letting the Roman Christians overhear his fictional discussion with a typical Jew. To be sure,

Paul does not come out and explicitly label his discussion partner as a Jew at this point. This is for rhetorical effect, as he allows the Jew gradually to self-identify in the accusation that now unfolds. But how can Paul say that Jews are doing "the same things" as the people he has condemned in chapter 1? Jews were not known for idolatry at this period of time, and generally they avoided serious sexual sins. But they were guilty of many of the sins Paul has listed in 1:29–31. And perhaps Paul thinks of the Jews' preoccupation with the law as a kind of idolatry.

In verses 2–5 Paul elaborates the judgment to which Jews, like Gentiles, will be subjected. He makes two basic points.

First, God's judgment is based on "the truth" (v. 2). What Paul means by this is that God will judge every human being in accordance with the actual facts of the case. Paul returns to this point in verse 5, emphasizing that it is because of "stubbornness" and an "unrepentant heart"

Salvation through Works?

Most interpreters in the past have taken Paul to teach quite forthrightly that only faith in Christ can put a person in right relationship with God. Yet three times in Romans 2, Paul appears to suggest that people might be saved by works:

2:7: "To those who by persistence in doing good seek glory, honor and immortality, he will give eternal life" (cf. 2:10).

2:13: "For it is not those who hear the law who are righteous in God's sight, but it is those who obey the law who will be declared righteous."

2:26–27 "If those who are not circumcised keep the law's requirements, will they not be regarded as though they were circumcised? The one who is not circumcised physically and yet obeys the law will condemn you who, even though you have the written code and circumcision, are a lawbreaker."

These texts have received renewed attention in light of current debates about the exclusivity of faith in Christ for salvation. Of course, each of these texts has its own point to make and cannot simply be equated with the others, but scholars tend to take one of three tacks in dealing with these passages. Quite a few, as I have noted in the commentary, think that Paul might be referring to Christians. Their "works," as James stresses (Jas 2:14–26), will stand as evidence in the judgment of their faith in Christ. Although this is not, I think, the most likely interpretation, it poses no threat to the notion of salvation through Christ by faith alone. But a second interpretation does pose such a threat. It suggests that Paul here recognizes the possibility of salvation for people who do not know Christ but who, through God's grace, are enabled to respond positively to the light they have been granted. However, such an interpretation is not required by the evidence and stands in considerable tension with Paul's claim in texts such as Romans 3:20. A better way to view these texts is to see them as making one point in an argument that Paul advances in these chapters. This argument can be summarized by citing three texts:

A person can be justified by doing the law (2:13), [but]

All human beings are under sin's control (3:9), [therefore]

No human being can be justified by doing the law (3:20).

What Paul claims is theoretically possible in 2:13, he denies as a possibility in practice in 3:20. And the reason why it is impossible in practice is clear from 3:9: sin's hold over all people makes it impossible for anyone to do the law sufficiently well to be saved through it.

that God will judge these people. The facts that God takes into consideration have to do above all with the inner condition of a person. Not just outward actions, but the attitude of the heart will be decisive when God judges people on the day of his wrath.

Second, God's judgment cannot be avoided through outward identity. We saw that Paul was indebted to Jewish polemic against the Gentiles in 1:18–32, and we identified a particularly clear example of this polemic in Wisdom of Solomon 12–15. But in that book, after condemning the Gentiles for their sin over the course of three chapters, the author suddenly turns to the situation of the Jews, saying this about them: "But you, our God, are kind and true, patient, and ruling all things in mercy. For even if we sin we are yours, knowing your power; but we will not sin, because we know that you acknowledge us as yours. For to know you is complete righteousness, and to know your power is the root of immortality" (Wis 15:1–3). Paul's language in verses 3–4 seems to be a deliberate echo of this text, or one very much like it. What the passage reflects is the Jewish assumption that their privileged covenant status put them in such a different category from other people that they did not need to worry about their sin. But, like Jeremiah before him, when confronted with a similar attitude (Jer 7), Paul insists that mere covenant status will not be enough to shield God's people from judgment. Always, God insists on a heart response to him and a life of obedience reflecting that heart response.

God's Impartial Judgment (2:6–11)

These verses are carefully organized, falling into a pattern called **chiasm.** The word comes from the letter of the Greek alphabet that resembles our letter X. At the points of the X are the elements of the argument, structured in an A-B-B'-A' sequence (often extending beyond four points). One can readily identify verses 6–11 as falling into this kind of structure:

A God will judge people according to their works (v. 6)
  B People who do good will attain eternal life (v. 7)
    C People who do evil will suffer wrath (v. 8)
    C' Wrath for those who do evil (v. 9)
  B' Glory for those who do good (v. 10)
A' God judges impartially (v. 11)

The main point of a chiasm often comes in the middle, but in this case the main point is found at the outside: God's impartiality, revealed in his assessing every human being according to the same standard, works. The application of this standard means that people who do evil things will suffer God's wrath (vv. 8, 9). On the other side of the coin, those who do good things will experience eternal life and glory (vv. 7, 10). The argument is designed to puncture the Jewish assumption of superiority. God treats every person the same, but the Jews have a greater accountability because they have been the recipients of the clearest revelation of God. Therefore they will be "first" in receiving judgment for sin (v. 9) and "first" in being granted eternal life for doing good (v. 10).

But how can Paul promise that people who do good will be given eternal life (vv. 7, 10)? Doesn't this claim contradict his insistence later on that no person can be put right with God by works (3:20; 4:2–3)? Several solutions to this problem have been offered, but two are the most likely. First, Paul might be referring to Christians, who, because of God's grace in Christ and the indwelling Spirit, are enabled to produce works that will count favorably in the judgment of God (see, e.g., 2 Cor 5:10; Jas 2:14–26).[1] Second, Paul here simply might be stating the condition that a person must meet, apart from Christ, to go free in the judgment of God. Whether any person meets that standard is quite another question, and Paul will answer it decisively in the negative as his argument moves forward (see 3:9).[2] On the whole, I think that the second interpretation fits best in the context.

Torah scroll, consisting of the first five books of the Old Testament, from which the law is read. (Jim Yancey)

Jews, Gentiles, and the Law (2:12–16)

Paul's claim that God would impartially judge Jews on the same basis as Gentiles seems to ignore a crucial point: the Jews, because of God's covenant with them, are not in the same situation as the Gentiles. How can God treat the two groups the same? Paul responds to this kind of objection in the rest of the chapter. He begins in this paragraph with a focus on the law. As we saw in chapter 1, "law" in Romans refers first of all to the law God gave Israel through Moses, the *torah*. In verse 12, therefore, "all who sin apart from the law" are Gentiles and "all who sin under the law" are Jews, for only

Jews stand "under the law" (the Greek is literally, "in [the sphere of] the law"). Nevertheless, Paul alleges, the result for both groups is the same. Gentiles will "perish" as they sin without direct awareness of the *torah*, while Jews will "be judged" through that *torah*. And the parallelism requires that this judgment have a negative verdict: condemnation. So Paul begins by reasserting the equality of Jew and Gentile before God in the judgment.

Verse 13 substantiates the last point of verse 12. Jews will be condemned even though they have the *torah* because ("for" at the beginning of v. 13) God justifies doers of the law, not those who only hear it. All Jews "hear" the law. They read it, hear it read in the synagogue, and study it. But the standard by which God judges, as Paul has made clear in verses 6–11, is "works"—what is actually done. Paul here infers that Jews have not adequately "done" the law. Their doing has not matched their hearing. Paul's claim that "those who obey the law will be declared righteous" again raises the issue of salvation through works. And again, I suggest, Paul is setting out the standard by which God judges and is not claiming that anyone actually meets that standard.

The place of verses 14–16 in Paul's argument is debated. Some interpreters attach these verses directly to the end of verse 13. They think that the Gentiles who "do by nature things required by the law" (v. 14) are the same as those in verse 13 "who obey the law" and are justified. Paul therefore would be referring in verses 14–15 to Gentile Christians who, though not having the law by birth, now fulfill the law's demand because of the indwelling Spirit (see 8:4). (The phrase "by birth" in the preceding sentence represents Paul's "by nature," which can be attached to the phrase "who do not have the law" as well as to the verb "do" [as in the NIV].) Advocates of this interpretation often point to the language about "the requirements of the law" being "written on their hearts" in verse 15. This sounds a lot like the famous "new covenant" prophecy of Jeremiah 31:33, where God promises, "I will put my law in their minds and write it on their hearts." And, of course, the New Testament proclaims that this prophecy is fulfilled in Christians, who possess the Spirit of God (e.g., Heb 8:8–12).[3] But it might be significant that Paul says not that "the law" is written on the heart, but that "the requirements of the law" are written on the heart. And, for other reasons, I think it unlikely that Paul is referring here to Gentile Christians. For one thing, Paul would be unlikely to say that Gentile Christians "are a law for themselves" (v. 14). For another, Paul's language resembles ancient discussions about the "natural law." Originating with the Greeks, who speculated about "natural law" as a way of making certain moral norms universal, discussion of the natural law was taken up by Jews such as Philo of Alexandria. Paul seems to be alluding to these discussions, and his purpose would then be to show that, though Gentiles have not been given God's law in the specific form of *torah*, they nevertheless have knowledge of God's moral requirements. They may not have the Mosaic law (*torah*), but they do have law—moral demands that God puts in the conscience of every human being. Once again Paul levels the playing field between Jew and Greek. Even *torah*, in which Jews took so much pride, does not distinguish them as much as they might think from the Gentiles, for Gentiles also have law.

On this reading, verses 14–15 are a kind of parenthetical addendum to verse 12, with its simple contrast between those who have the law and those who do not (note the parentheses around these verses in the NIV). By keeping verse 16 outside the parenthesis, the NIV translators imply that this verse goes with verse 13: God will declare righteous those who obey the law "on the day when God will judge men's secrets." But it is better to attach verse 16 to the end of verse 15. Because Gentiles have some knowledge of God's moral demands, their consciences are in a conflicting state. They sense approval for doing what that law requires, but they also feel condemned because of the sins they commit. This "bearing witness" of the conscience takes place throughout life but will find its ultimate importance on the day of judgment.

Jewish Sin and the Covenant (2:17–29)

Paul now returns to the diatribe style of 2:1–5, for the first time addressing his discussion partner as a "Jew." The basic point of verses 17–29 is to show that the legitimate Jewish boast in possessing the law and circumcision (the mark of the covenant) falls short of bringing salvation to the Jewish people. For Paul again insists that it is not the possession (or the "hearing") of God's law and covenant that matters—it is the doing. We must underline the importance of this argument for Paul's ultimate purposes. In 1:18–3:20 he sets the stage for the revelation of

Granite mountains of the Sinai near modern Eliat are a reminder of Mount Sinai, where God's law was revealed to Moses. (Chris Miller)

God's righteousness in Christ by delineating the human dilemma. All people need God's righteousness because all people sin. Few people in Paul's day would quarrel with the claim that all people sin. But Jews still would see no need for the righteousness of God in Christ, for their sin, they would argue, is taken care of through God's covenant arrangement with them. Paul therefore must show that they have misunderstood that covenant if they think that it, in itself, suffices to take care of their sin problem. Thus he focuses in these verses on the two key components of that covenant: the *torah*, which spelled out Israel's covenant obligations, and circumcision, the mark of covenant entrance.

In the first paragraph, verses 17–24, Paul contrasts the Jews' possession of the law with their failure to perform it. Verses 17–20 consist of a series of "if" clauses spelling out the benefits and privileges that the Jews possess through the covenant. Some interpreters think that Paul engages in sarcasm here, mocking the Jews for their inordinate pride. But that misses Paul's point. Each of the items listed here is a legitimate cause of pride on the part of the Jewish people. God has entered into a special relationship with the Jews (v. 17), has revealed his will to them in the law (v. 18), and has appointed Israel to be a guide to the other nations, who do not have that law (vv. 19–20; cf. Is 42:6–7). The problem, however, is that the Jews have not lived up to their privileges. Paul summarizes his point in verse 23: "You who brag about the law, do you dishonor God by breaking the law?" Verses 21–22 lead up to this summary with three examples of the contrast between Jewish teaching and Jewish behavior. The first two—stealing and adultery—are clear enough. But what Paul might intend with the third is more difficult to say: "You who abhor idols, do you rob temples?" The most obvious possibility is that Paul is accusing the Jews of stealing from pagan temples. We know that Jews at this time were relaxing the Old Testament strictures about using the metal melted down from pagan idols.

Paul might be reminding the Jews how this practice tacitly involves the Jews in idolatry. Another possibility is that Paul refers to Jews who robbed the Jerusalem temple by not paying the money required of every Jew for its upkeep.[4] Still another option is to interpret the verb that Paul uses here *(hierosylein)* to mean "commit sacrilege." He might then be referring to the tendency of Jews to make the law so important as to infringe on God's own prerogatives.[5] The first of these options, the majority view among commentators, is best because it provides the most natural contrast with the Jews' abhorrence of idolatry.

Paul's argument in the second paragraph (vv. 25–29) is roughly equivalent to what he has argued in verses 17–24. Paul has made clear that the *torah* will be of ultimate benefit to the Jews only if they obey it. Similarly, he now alleges, circumcision will rescue Jews from judgment only if the law is obeyed. Circumcision was a very important mark of Jewish identity in Paul's world. Its great symbolic value was why it was such a contentious matter in the early church (see Acts 15; Galatians). It marked God's covenant with Abraham, and God himself insisted that Abraham's male descendants be circumcised as a mark of covenant status. The attempt of Antiochus Epiphanes IV to stamp out the Jewish religion at the time of the Maccabean Revolt focused on circumcision. Loyal Jews naturally responded by making the rite even more important than before. And the danger of accommodation to Gentile culture in the Diaspora also elevated the importance of a distinguishing rite such as circumcision.

In verses 25–27, Paul does not deny the value of circumcision. His point, rather, is that circumcision by itself cannot assure the Jew of membership in the covenant people of God. Only fidelity to the law can accomplish this. For Jews, therefore, circumcision is useful if they "observe the law" (vv. 25, 26). But if they break the law, their circumcision is, in effect, canceled. At the same time, in what would have been quite a radical turn in the argument for first-century Jews, Paul claims that uncircumcised Gentiles who "keep the law's requirements" will be treated as though they were circumcised (v. 26). Such a law-obedient though uncircumcised Gentile even will stand in judgment over the Jew (v. 27). We face here again the question of the identity of these Gentiles. Certainly the realistic-sounding language of verse 27 gives greater credence than ever to the view that identifies these law-observing people as Gentile Christians. But, with considerably less certainty, I think again that Paul is arguing hypothetically.

The radical nature of Paul's argument becomes even more pronounced in verses 28–29. Here Paul relativizes the whole concept of "Jew." Paul is using the language of "Jew" here to mean "a member of God's true people." And he argues that membership in that people has nothing to do with outward or physical matters

such as circumcision. Belonging to God's people is, rather, an inward matter. It is not physical circumcision that counts, but the circumcision of the heart. Of course, the demand for the circumcision of the heart is standard Old Testament teaching (e.g., Dt 10:16; Jer 4:4). But nowhere in the Old Testament was it suggested that physical circumcision could be dispensed with. Moreover, Paul adds that this circumcision of the heart must be carried out by the Spirit and not in terms of the "written code." The latter phrase is the NIV rendering of an important Greek word, *gramma*, "letter." Three times in his letters Paul contrasts "Spirit" (*pneuma*) and *gramma* (see also Rom 7:6; 2 Cor 3:6–7). While its meaning is debated, *gramma* seems to be Paul's way of referring to the Old Testament law as a "written" instrument. It therefore comes to represent the old salvation-historical era. "Spirit," on the other hand, stands for the new era of redemption that has dawned with the coming of Christ (see 1:4). Here, therefore, Paul clearly looks ahead to his claim that it is only Christians, filled with God's Spirit, who truly can experience the radical internal transformation indicated by the language of the "circumcision of the heart." Jews need to understand that their covenant status cannot, by itself, protect them from the judgment of God. And they need ultimately also to understand that only a relationship with Christ through the Spirit of the new age will bring them into the true people of God.

Study Questions

1. Why did Jews in Paul's day think that their sin would not count against them in the judgment?

2. How can we understand Paul's claim that a person might inherit eternal life by doing good (2:7)?

3. What does Paul refer to when he uses the word "law"?

4. What is the point of Paul's contrast between *gramma*, "letter," and *pneuma*, "Spirit"?

5. Are there contemporary parallels to the tendency of the Jews in Paul's day to think of their inherited birthright as a basis for salvation?

6 The Universal Power of Sin

Romans 3:1–20

Outline
- Jewish Privileges and Their Limitations (3:1–8)
- Concluding Indictment: All Are "under Sin" (3:9–20)

Objectives
After reading this chapter, you should be able to
1. Understand both the genuine benefits that Jews possess as well as the limitations of those benefits.
2. Appreciate the depth of the problem that sin creates for human beings.
3. Identify at least two key interpretations of the phrase "works of the law" and understand how these interpretations affect our broader interpretation of Paul's theology.

Romans is full of traps for the unwary reader. Just when we think we have understood what the letter is teaching, the argument takes an unexpected turn and once again we are left puzzled and uncertain. Of course, this is one of the glories of Romans. No book capable of being understood on a first reading is likely to hold our attention or to stimulate our thinking for very long. Romans requires many readings; even then, we feel that there are points in the letter that still escape our gaze.

The beginning of Romans 3 is one of those surprising turns in the argument. By the end of Romans 2 we think we have understood Paul's basic point: Gentile and Jew stand on the same footing before God. Both were given revelation about God; both have failed to live up to that revelation; both stand under God's wrath. And so, when Paul asks in 3:1, "What advantage, then, is there in being a Jew?" we are ready to answer, "None." But what does Paul answer? "Much in every way!" (v. 2). Paul's unexpected response forces us to look more deeply at the nature of Paul's argument in Romans 2. And when we do so, we realize that God has relativized the Jews' position vis-à-vis Gentiles at only one point: both stand in need of additional help if they are to escape God's judgment. Yet Paul knows that we might draw the wrong conclusion from what he has taught in chapter 2, and so he warns against false conclusions. And, as we will see, he continues also to emphasize that the Jews' real privileges are also limited.

But 3:1–8, where this argument unfolds, is something of a detour in Paul's argument. The main point of this section comes in 3:9–20, and the backbone of this section is found in two verses: verse 9, where Paul places all human beings under the power of sin, and verse 20, where he draws the conclusion from this sad state of affairs: no one can be justified by obeying the law. With this claim Paul concludes the bad news; he is ready now to come back and elaborate the good news.

Jewish Privileges and Their Limitations (3:1–8)

Paul continues to unfold his argument by raising the questions that he knows by experience people will ask. Here he heads off any idea that his argument in chapter 2 undercuts his claim from the theme of the letter (1:16) that the gospel is "for the Jew first." In this new stage of salvation history God has provided for equal access to his salvation for both the Jew and the Gentile, but he does so without destroying the genuine privileges enjoyed by Israel. Paul strikes a careful balance on these matters throughout the letter and gives extended attention to the issue in Romans 9–11. In verses 1–8 he briefly anticipates some of this more extended discussion. These verses again feature the vigorous question-and-answer diatribe style. And because Paul writes so compactly here, it is not always easy to know who is asking the questions and what position the imaginary dialogue partner is taking. Interpreters therefore disagree quite strongly about the specifics of the issues in these verses. A key turning point comes in verse 5 with the reference to "our unrighteousness." This might refer to human evil generally, but the Jewish flavor of the whole paragraph suggests rather that "our" refers to Paul's fellow Jews and that "unrighteousness" means something like "unfaithfulness to the covenant"—failing to live up to the "right behavior" demanded in God's covenant with Israel. Paul again is concentrating, then, on issues of salvation history and of God's integrity in carrying out that plan.

Paul begins by asking whether the status of Jews and the circumcision that marks them as God's covenant people gives them any advantage. "Much in every way!" he emphatically responds. Paul mentions "first of all" the fact that they have been entrusted with "the very words of God" (v. 2). No "second" or

Traditional site of King David's tomb on Mt. Zion. (Jim Yancey)

"third" follows this "first of all." Paul probably intended to list other privileges but got deflected as he elaborated on this first blessing. He gives a fuller list in 9:4–5. "The very words of God" is a good rendering of the Greek *logia*, "oracles." The reference clearly is to the Old Testament, but this Greek word draws attention to the fact that God himself has spoken to his people (see *logia* in Dt 33:9 and in Ps 119 [twenty-four times] in the Greek translation of the Old Testament). To be sure, Paul acknowledges, the Jews have not always lived up to the requirements that God imposed on them (v. 3), but God remains faithful to his own pledged word. Nothing will deflect him from accomplishing what he has promised to do. No, Paul exclaims, "let every man be a liar" (v. 4); God will still be found "true," or faithful. Paul confirms this idea with a very suggestive quotation from Psalm 51:4. The words he quotes state David's purpose in confessing his horrible double sin of adultery (with Bathsheba) and murder (of Uriah): that God might be "proved right" in his judgment on David. By acknowledging his sin, David vindicates God's sentence of judgment. What makes this quotation suggestive is the negative effect of the word to which God here is faithful. What Paul is suggesting is that God's faithfulness to his word (vv. 3–4a) includes his commitment not only to bless his people but also to punish them for their sin.

If this is the logic implied in verse 4, then we can better understand the next question Paul raises (v. 5). What he is asking is how it can be "fair" for God to punish the Jews when their very unfaithfulness to God has manifested his righteousness. After all, Jewish disobedience led to the need for Christ and for the new revelation of his righteousness. Why, then, does God judge them for what has contributed to his own glory and plan? Paul's response to this question is not easy to sort out from the series of questions and answers in verses 6–8, but it seems that basically he is reminding us of a simple truth: the ends do not justify the means. Even if human sin and unfaithfulness have been used by God to bring good and enhance his own glory, the sin and unfaithfulness are no less evil and deserving of punishment. God, as the Old Testament makes clear, will judge the world, and he will "do right" in judging it (see Gn 18:25). He cannot overlook sin, even when it becomes the occasion for a greater display of God's mercy and glory. Paul knows that some of his detractors accuse him of emphasizing the power of God's grace to the extent that human sin becomes actually a good thing (v. 8). But he implies that the Jews would be no better off if they claimed that their own sin could be excused or overlooked because it had contributed ultimately to God's purpose.

Concluding Indictment: All Are "under Sin" (3:9–20)

Paul accomplishes three purposes in this final paragraph in the first major section of the letter (1:18–3:20): (1) he concludes his indictment of humanity with the chilling verdict that "Jews and Gentiles alike are all under sin" (v. 9); (2) he illustrates his indictment from the Old Testament (vv. 10–18); and (3) he draws a conclusion from his indictment: the law cannot save (vv. 19–20).

The translation of the second question in verse 9 is difficult. But the NIV—"Are

Modern Answers to the Human Dilemma

The last two decades have brought a rude awakening to those who thought that the human race was finally making significant progress on the road to maturity. Genocides in Rwanda and Kosovo, to name just two incidents, have made it clear that human beings are as selfish, violent, and intolerant as ever. While not as many people died in these massacres as in Stalin's Russia or Hitler's Germany or Pol Pot's Cambodia, the parallels are clear. We must come to grips with the sad truth that the human problem is not going away. What, then, is the answer to that problem? Modern thinkers advance all kinds of answers. Some track the problem to the inequalities of material possessions and propose that we do away with private ownership of wealth (the Marxist solution). Some advance universal education as the answer. Some think that various Eastern religions, with their emphasis on communion with nature and with one

another, might provide the solution. And probably most people, without thinking the matter through very clearly, feel that technological advances will inevitably spill over into an improvement in human relationships.

History shows that people come up with many of the same basic answers to the human dilemma in every age. The specifics change, but the basic impulse remains the same. Surely we might have learned by now that none of these solutions is capable of solving the problem. To be sure, Christians should be in the vanguard of those who seek to improve society by all appropriate means. But Christians also take seriously Paul's reminder that we are all "under sin." And as long as this remains the case, the human predicament will not go away. Only as individuals embrace Jesus in faith and find liberation from the terrible power of sin does real change take place.

Michelangelo's depiction of Moses, who received God's law on Mt. Sinai. (John McRay)

"alike are under sin." This concluding indictment is a natural consequence of Paul's argument in 1:18–3:8. He has shown that Gentiles and Jews have both been given revelation from God, but they have equally failed to respond appropriately to that revelation. And that universal failure points to one inescapable conclusion: all human beings are locked up under sin's power. It is important to notice how Paul puts the problem. He does not simply claim that people are sinners (though that, of course, is true). What he says is that people are "under sin." People are imprisoned under the power of sin. The point is vital if we are to appreciate the need and power of the gospel. If people simply were sinners, then perhaps all they would need would be a teacher to inform them about what is right. But people are under sin. They need a liberator. And Paul will present Christ, through the power of God's righteousness unleashed in the gospel, as just such a liberator (3:21–26, esp. v. 24).

Following a practice that the rabbis called "pearl-stringing," Paul now adduces a series of Old Testament passages to buttress the conclusion he has drawn in verse 9. Some interpreters think that Paul might be quoting a preexisting document that had already gathered these passages together.[1] At first sight, these passages seem to be thrown together haphazardly, but a closer look uncovers some logical arrangement. The opening line (v. 10b) introduces the key idea: "there is no one righteous, not even one." The final line, verse 18, then comes back to restate this theme in different language (the two also are connected by a verbal similarity, "there is no" [ouk estin]). Verses 11–12 develop the theme of the opening line. They echo the "there is no one" language of verse 10b, restating the truth of universal human sinfulness. The entire series in verses 10b–12 is drawn from Psalm 14:1–3. Paul then uses language from Psalm 5:9 (v. 13a–b), Psalm 140:3b (v. 13c), and Psalm 10:7 (v. 14) to illustrate the universal sway of sin with respect to human speech. Verses 15–17 turn to sins of violence against other people. Here Paul uses

we any better?"—has it right (note, however, the NIV margin: "Are we any worse?"). The "we" is probably again the Jews (see my comments on v. 5), and Paul strenuously denies that the Jews are any better off. But how does this response square with his equally emphatic assertion in verses 1–2 that Jews indeed do have an advantage? The answer lies in distinguishing the two different issues that Paul is dealing with. In verses 1–2, Paul affirms that the Jews have undeniable and continuing salvation-historical advantages. They were the recipients of God's covenant and the law that was the heart of that covenant. In verse 9, however (as in ch. 2), the issue is not salvation history but salvation. And when it comes to being saved, Jews are no better off than Gentiles. Both Jews and Gentiles

Study Questions

1. How is it consistent for Paul to say both that Jews have an "advantage" (3:1–2) and that they are "no better off" (3:9)?

2. What does Paul's teaching about God's faithfulness to all his words say to Christians today?

3. What are the implications of 3:20? What does it say to those of us who are not Jews and who have never been "under" the law?

language from Isaiah 59:7–8a to illumine the propensity of people to harm one another. A look back at the context from which these quotations are drawn reveals that many of them refer to wicked people within Israel. This may be a subtle attempt on Paul's part to remind the Jews once again that they cannot claim any special exemption from sin and judgment. They are in the same situation as the "wicked sinners" who opposed Israel.

In verses 19–20, Paul states the result of the human dilemma as a transition to his positive presentation of the gospel in verses 3:21–4:25. He begins by drawing a conclusion from his Old Testament quotations in verses 10–18. I have noted that Paul usually uses the word "law" to refer to the Mosaic legislation. However, since the Mosaic law was so basic to the Old Testament in the Jewish perspective, the whole Old Testament could also be called simply "the law." Paul clearly uses the word in this sense at the beginning of verse 19. "Whatever the law says" refers back to the Old Testament quotations in verses 10–18 (drawn from the psalms and the prophets). This law is directed, Paul reminds us, to "those who are under the law"—a reference to the Jews (see 2:12). But, since the Jews, God's own people, are indicted by their own law, it becomes clear that "the whole world is accountable to God." The language is legal: all people are guilty before the bar of God's

justice. Verse 20 draws the conclusion: "no one will be declared righteous in his sight by observing the law."

The NIV conceals an issue of great debate among modern scholars. "Observing the law" translates a Greek phrase that is rendered literally as "works of the law" (*erga nomou*). Paul uses the expression eight times in his letters (Rom 3:20, 28; Gal 2:16 [three times]; 3:2, 5, 10). In the past, interpreters usually took it to refer to anything done in obedience to the law of Moses. And, since Paul excludes these works from any part in justifying the sinner, it was thought legitimate to conclude that all works were implicitly condemned as well. The Reformers therefore taught that nothing a person did could ever suffice to put that person in relationship with God. The way of "works" was a dead end; only the way of faith was left. But many modern scholars think that Paul might use the phrase to refer to Jewish works in a particular sense. They argue that the emphasis is not so much on the "works" as on the "law." What Paul is talking about is not so much the *performance* of the law but the *possession* of the law. He is saying, basically, that Jews cannot be justified before God through the Mosaic covenant.[2] Implications about "works" in general therefore are excluded. Making a decision between these two interpretations turns on the evidence from the use of the phrase in Jewish sources and on the context in which Paul uses the phrase. On both scores, I think that the traditional interpretation should be preferred.[3] We have no good reason to remove the emphasis on "doing" in the occurrences of the phrase in Jewish literature. And the sequence of Paul's argument in Romans 3–4 suggests that he views the phrase "works of the law" as a subset of the larger category "works." For in chapter 4 he says much the same thing about the "works" of Abraham as he does in chapter 3 about the "works of the law" of the Jews after Moses. Thus, even though the Reformers did not always pay sufficient attention to the Jewish context of Paul's argument, I think that their ultimate application of verse 20 is legitimate: no "work" that a human being does can ever put him or her in relationship with God.

Broaching a theme that will become a key motif in the letter (see 4:15; 5:20; 6:14, 15; 7:1–6), Paul concludes by reminding us of what the law *does* accomplish. It cannot overcome the problem of human sin (v. 20a); rather, the law makes us "conscious of sin." A more literal rendering would be "knowledge of sin." What Paul means by this is not simply that the law defines sin by telling us what we should not do, for often in Scripture, "knowledge" carries the deeper nuance of "familiarity," "intimate understanding." By revealing God's will so clearly, the law fully reveals the power of sin. It makes us realize just how far short of the ideal we fall and how powerful an enemy sin really is.

Part

3

Encountering God's Provision in Christ

Romans 3:21–4:25

7 God's Righteousness in Christ

Romans 3:21–31

Outline

- The New Era of Righteousness (3:21–26)
- Justification and the Law (3:27–31)

Objectives

After reading this chapter, you should be able to

1. Identify the different meanings that Paul gives to the phrase "God's righteousness."
2. Understand the way in which God has overcome the problem of sin through his Son.
3. Appreciate both the continuity and discontinuity in salvation history.

justification

Martin Luther called Romans 3:21–26 "the chief point, and the very central place of the Epistle, and of the whole Bible."[1] High praise indeed! I suspect that most of us would like to advance some other candidates for the honor of being the central place of the Bible, and I know that I would have a very hard time choosing even among the top twenty-five contestants. But no one can doubt that Romans 3:21–26 is one of the most theologically important passages in Scripture. Here Paul weaves together many of the key threads in the biblical view of salvation. The result is a tapestry of awe-inspiring intricacy and beauty. The passage should inspire us to think deeply about the way God has arranged the salvation of his rebellious creatures. But, more than that, it should inspire a new depth of worship and devotion. All true theology should lead to doxology.

Paul's presentation of God's righteousness in Christ in 3:21–26 is the introduction and heart of the next section of the letter. This section runs from 3:21 to the end of chapter 4. It focuses on the way in which God has revealed his righteousness, making it possible for sinners to be "justified" before him through faith. Before and outside of Christ, people are helpless captives of sin and are unable to do anything to escape sin's tyranny (1:18–3:20). But God has acted to rescue sinners from their plight. In revealing his righteousness, he makes it possible for every person who responds in faith to be "justified." Righteousness and **justification** are, indeed, two sides of the same coin. The two translate words from the same root in Greek (*dik-*). In 3:27–4:25, Paul explores the implications of his central teaching about justification by grace through faith. The short paragraph at the end of chapter 3 (vv. 27–31) briefly sets out those implications. Then, in chapter 4, Paul expands on those implications with reference to a key biblical test case, Abraham.

The New Era of Righteousness (3:21–26)

"But now" signals the transition from the sobering and depressing portrait of sinful humanity (1:18–3:20) to the celebration of the salvation available through God's righteousness in Christ. As in 1:17 (see the notes there), the NIV translates the critical phrase as "a righteousness from God," but again, a better rendering would be "the righteousness of God." As in 1:17, which this passage harks back to, Paul is talking about God's activity of putting people in the right with himself. The "now," then, refers to the new era of salvation that has dawned with the coming of Christ. Paul's presentation is ruled by his basic conception of salvation history, according to which the old era of sin and condemnation gives way to the new era of righteousness and life. Partly because of the disputes between Jewish and Gentile Christians within the Roman community, Paul is especially concerned throughout Romans to show how God's revelation in the Old Testament fits into this salvation-historical scheme. The end of verse 21 neatly summarizes his balanced approach. On the one hand, the righteousness of God has been made known "apart from law." A definite article would make Paul's point clearer: "apart from the law." As is usually the case, "law" (*nomos*) refers to *torah*, the law of Moses. Paul thinks of this law as a central ruling agent in the old era, and God's righteousness in Christ cannot be fit within that old era, for it breaks new ground. On the other hand, what God has done in Christ stands in continuity with the Old Testament witness as a whole. The "Law and the Prophets testify" to it. This phrase is a Jewish way of referring to the Old Testament. So Paul makes clear that although God's activity of making people right before him takes place outside the parameters of the law of Moses, it is an activity that the Old Testament looks forward to and predicts. While falling into two distinct stages, God's plan for salvation history nevertheless is single and continuous.

In verse 22 Paul qualifies God's righteousness in a typical fashion: it "comes through faith in Jesus Christ to all who believe." God acts in Christ to put people in right relationship with himself. But that act cannot finally be accomplished without human response. People must believe in Christ to experience for themselves God's righteousness. Before elaborating this point any further, we should be sure of our ground in the Greek text. Almost all English versions translate along the same lines as the NIV: "through faith in Jesus Christ." But the Greek is ambiguous. "Faith" and "Jesus Christ" are connected with a construction (in the genitive case) that can indicate several different kinds of relationship. The English versions, along with most commentators, take "Jesus Christ" to be the *object* of "faith"; hence, "faith *in* Jesus Christ." But a growing number of scholars think that Jesus Christ is the *subject* of faith: "the faith *of*, or *exercised by*, Jesus Christ." They point to a similar construction in 4:16, where "the faith of Abraham" clearly means "the faith that Abraham exercised." Also, the word for "faith" in Greek, *pistis*, can also mean "faithfulness" (see 3:3). So what Paul might be saying is that God's righteousness comes "through the faithfulness of Jesus Christ to all who believe." We are put right with God through Christ's faithful giving of himself to death for us and by our grateful acceptance of that gift in faith.[2] No objection to this interpretation can be made on doctrinal grounds. God's righteousness comes to us only because Jesus was faithful in carrying out the commission that God the Father had given him. Nevertheless, I think that the usual rendering is to be preferred. Nowhere does Paul clearly speak of Christ "believing" or "being faithful," whereas he regularly (and in this very context [see 4:3]) speaks of human beings believing in God or in Christ. So Paul's own habits of speech suggest that "through faith in Jesus Christ" is the best translation.[3] He adds "to all who believe"

to underline the critical point that both Jew and Gentile are now invited, on the same grounds, to experience the righteousness of God in Christ.

Paul reminds us that the universal invitation to believe is the flip side of the universal need for salvation. "There is no difference," he affirms at the end of verse 22, continuing in verse 23 with the well-known summary of 1:18–3:20: "all have sinned and fall short of the glory of God." In the situation Paul addresses, this universalism especially had in mind Jew and Gentile, but of course it applies to any distinction among human beings that we might imagine: race, ethnicity, nationality, and so on. Because all human beings have sinned, all are offered the opportunity to believe in Christ and so experience God's righteousness.

In the NIV, verse 24 is presented as the continuation of verse 23: "all have sinned . . . and are justified. . . ." A better option is to view verse 24 as the continuation of verses 21–22a, with verses 22b–23 as a parenthesis in the argument. As we saw, the verb "justify" (v. 24) and the noun "righteousness" (vv. 21 and 22) come from the same Greek root. So it would be natural for Paul to continue his discussion of God's righteousness by talking about the way in which God justifies people. And how does he do so? First, as to mode, God justifies us "freely by his grace." The adverb "freely" simply emphasizes the idea inherent in God's grace. As the sovereign Creator, God is always supreme over his creation. Never can any creature force him to act in any way. All that God does, he does of his own free will. And so his act of justifying sinners is one that he does out of his own loving nature, giving us as a gift what we never could earn or merit. Second, as to means, God justifies us through an act of "redemption." The Greek word underlying redemption (*apolytrōsis*) was applied to the money that a slave would pay in order to secure his or her freedom.[4] The root idea is a "price paid for release." The Jews who translated the Old Testament into Greek used words from this same Greek root for the release that God attained for the Israelites

Linguistics and the Meaning of Romans 3:25

In my exposition of verse 25, I have argued that the Greek word *hilastērion* alludes both to the idea of propitiation and to the Old Testament "mercy seat," or "atonement cover." Some might object, claiming that I have illegitimately given the word a double meaning. Indeed, modern linguistic theory usually does look askance at double meanings, insisting that we give a word the least amount of meaning that the context requires. But modern linguistic theory also reminds us of a very important principle when we are talking about the significance of words: the distinction between "meaning" and "referent." Many words have a certain meaning but refer to something as well. An illustration will help make this distinction clear. President Nixon got into trouble by trying to cover up a politically motivated break-in at the Watergate office building in Washington, D.C. The publicity surrounding this event led to the name of this building taking on a meaning of its own. Eventually, it could even be abbreviated, with "-gate" added to the end of another word to convey the idea of a political cover-up—for example, "Travelgate," during the administration of President Clinton. The point is this: "Watergate" *refers to* a building in Washington, D.C.; but it has come to *mean* a political cover-up. The word has both a reference and a meaning.

And this is precisely the point I would make to defend my interpretation of *hilastērion*. It *means* "propitiation," but it *refers* to the cover of the ark. Paul's readers, who, though Gentile, are obviously well acquainted with the Old Testament, would recognize immediately the reference to this piece of furniture in the tabernacle. But they also would have given it the meaning that the word *hilastērion* conveys: an object that deflects God's wrath and thereby provides atonement for the people of God. What we therefore have in verse 25 is a beautiful example of typology. The Old Testament mercy seat foreshadows the cross, on which Christ poured out his blood in an atoning sacrifice, forever taking care of the sins of the world. The Old Testament Day of Atonement, repeated every year, thus also foreshadows *the* Day of Atonement, Good Friday, the day when God once-for-all provided for the forgiveness of sins.

from their slavery in Egypt (Ex 15:13; Dt 9:26). In Christ, God paid a price to secure release from the ultimate slavery: slavery to sin (see 3:9).

In verse 25 Paul elaborates further on how God in Christ redeemed sinful human beings. But exactly what it is that Paul intends to say is debated. He claims that God presented Christ as a *hilastērion*. Some English versions translate this word "propitiation" (KJV; NASB). To "propitiate" means to "placate" someone's wrath, as in the sentence "I propitiated my wife's wrath by taking her out to dinner." The Greeks used the word to refer to memorials or sacrifices that were intended to placate the wrath of the gods, and Paul's focus on God's wrath in his description of the human dilemma (see 1:18; 2:5) makes it likely that he refers to Christ as a means of propitiation here.[5] To be sure, some interpreters have objected to the whole notion of the wrath of God, suggesting that it represents the God of the Bible as a capricious tyrant in the mold of the Greek gods.[6] But the concept of wrath has to be interpreted against the backdrop of the larger religious conception. Because the Greeks portrayed their gods as all-too-human in their petty jealousies, intrigues, and self-seeking, the wrath they attributed to those gods was often selfishly motivated or senseless. But of course the biblical view of the true God

Model of the Ark of the Covenant, showing the mercy seat beneath the two cherubim. (Jim Yancey)

mercy seat

atonement

The temple platform in modern-day Jerusalem. (Jim Yancey)

of its twenty-seven occurrences there it refers to the **mercy seat,** the cover over the ark on which sacrificial blood was poured. The mercy seat, or "atonement cover" (NIV), figures prominently in one of the crowning events in the Jewish calendar: the sacrifice offered on the Day of Atonement (see Lv 16). Since the only other occurrence of *hilastērion* in the New Testament (Heb 9:5) also has this meaning, we are justified in thinking that Paul probably intends to refer to this key Old Testament institution. On the cross, Paul in effect is saying, God has presented Christ as the new covenant "mercy seat"—the place where God takes care of the problem of sin.[7] But since God can only take care of sin by satisfying his own wrath, the concept of propitiation is included in the wider idea of Christ as our "sacrifice of atonement" (NIV).

In the last part of verse 25 and verse 26, Paul turns to a final point: the purpose for which God has presented Christ as our sacrifice of **atonement.** He has done so, Paul claims, to "demonstrate his justice"—with reference both to sins in the past (v. 25) and at the "present time" (v. 26). The NIV translation reflects a key interpretive decision: to take the word

is quite different. Attributed to him, wrath is not an uncontrolled emotion but the settled and necessary reaction of a holy God to sin of any kind. We have no good grounds, then, for rejecting the notion of propitiation from the word that Paul uses here.

Still, however, I question whether the translation "propitiation" finally does justice to Paul's intention. What this translation overlooks is the significant use of the word *hilastērion* in the Greek translation of the Old Testament. In twenty-one

dikaiosynē, "righteousness," to refer here to God's attribute of righteousness. The problem with this view is that Paul has used this same word in verses 21 and 22 to refer to God's activity of putting people in the right before him: his saving righteousness. And many interpreters argue that it is illegitimate to give the same word a different meaning within the same paragraph. They think that Paul is simply asserting again that God has sent Christ as our atoning sacrifice to manifest his saving righteousness to sinners. But in fact, the context of verses 25b–26 justifies giving a different meaning to the word here. Paul claims that God had to send Christ to demonstrate his righteousness "because in his forbearance he had left the sins committed beforehand unpunished." The allusion is to sins committed before the coming of Christ. How could God simply leave them "unpunished"? Would not his holy nature demand that he judge those who sinned? Yes, indeed, it would. And Paul suggests that it was Christ, our atoning sacrifice, who bore the brunt of that judgment. Thus, God demonstrated his righteousness. But it now becomes clear that this can only mean God's attribute of righteousness, that intrinsic part of his character that requires sin to be punished.

The end of verse 26 is a fit summary of this marvelous paragraph. Paul has shown how God can both justify the one who has faith in Jesus and, at the same time, remain just. James Denney captures the point very well:

> There can be no gospel unless there is such a thing as a righteousness of God for the ungodly. But just as little can there be any gospel unless the integrity of God's character be maintained. The problem of the sinful world, the problem of all religion, the problem of God in dealing with a sinful race, is how to unite these two things. The Christian answer to the problem is given by Paul in the words: "Jesus Christ, whom God set forth a propitiation. . . ."[8]

Justification and the Law (3:27–31)

In verses 21–26 Paul has brought together in a paragraph of unparalleled theological density the several aspects of God's righteousness in Christ, but he has not taken the time to explore any of them in detail. He does this now, but very selectively. We hear no more about God's redemption, atoning sacrifice, or justice. Paul devotes all his attention to one key element in the establishment of God's righteousness: the way human beings respond to it. The classic Reformation doctrine of justification through faith by grace is the topic of 3:27–4:25. Paul introduces the key points in verses 27–31 before going on to elaborate them with reference to Abraham in chapter 4.

Paul draws three implications from the truth that people are justified by faith (see vv. 22, 24, 28): (1) human boasting is excluded (vv. 27–28); (2) Jews and Gentiles alike can experience the benefits of the one God (vv. 29–30); and (3) the requirement of the law is not put aside, but established.

Some interpreters think that in verse 27 Paul is talking narrowly about Jewish boasting in their covenant privileges.[9] The wider context certainly makes this a possibility (see 2:17), but the narrower context points instead to human boasting in general. The issue is how any person, Jew or Gentile (see vv. 22b–23 and vv. 28–29), can come into a relationship with God in Christ. Since that can happen only by faith rather than by works (vv. 27b–28), no person can brag about his or her contribution to the process. Our "works," whether done in obedience to the law (in regard to the phrase "doing the law" in v. 28, compare the comments on v. 20) or to some other moral code, never can bring us into God's favor. Only faith, the humble acceptance of God's offer of salvation, can do so. And just as a person receiving a gift has no right to boast, so the sinner accepting the gracious gift of salvation has no basis for pride in the accomplishment. Note that I am accepting the NIV decision to translate the Greek word *nomos* in verse 27 as "principle." Some contemporary scholars object, insisting that we should translate it as "law" and understand Paul to be contrasting two different approaches to the Mosaic law: one that focuses on works and one that focuses on faith.[10] But Paul is quite consistent in defining law as something that people do rather than something that people believe (see, e.g., Gal 3:12). So it is more likely that Paul is contrasting two principles of justification: one by works and one by faith.

One of the doctrines at the very heart of Judaism is the belief in one God, monotheism. In verses 29–30, Paul turns that belief against the tendency of Jews to confine justification to the law and therefore to Israel alone. If there is only one God, reasons Paul, then he must be the God of all people, and all people must have equal access to a relationship with him. But the law, having been given only to Israel, does not give Gentiles a way to be saved. So God justifies both Jews (the

---

Key Terms

justification

mercy seat

atonement

---

circumcised) and Gentiles (uncircumcised) in the same way: through faith.

In verse 31, Paul again is careful to guard what he has said against misinterpretation. "Do not think that my emphasis on being justified by faith in any way nullifies the law," Paul is saying. Quite the contrary, this insistence on the centrality of faith "upholds the law." But how does faith uphold, or establish, the law? Paul does not explain immediately, so we have to decide where else in Romans he might elaborate this point. Most interpreters think that the very next chapter supplies the answer. Paul's stress on faith upholds the law because the law itself teaches that Abraham was justified by faith (Gn 15:6, quoted in 4:3). This might be right. But note that the word "law" is not being given its usual meaning. To include Genesis 15:6, uttered centuries before the Mosaic law, "law" must refer to the Pentateuch. But, as we have repeatedly seen, Paul usually uses "law" to refer to the commands of God given to Israel through Moses. We therefore are encouraged to look for other possible interpretations of "upholding the law." In Romans 13:8–10, Paul claims that loving one's neighbor fulfills the law. So 3:31 might mean that Christians uphold the law by obeying the command of love that Christ made the heart of new covenant ethics. But a better alternative is to look to Romans 8:4 for elaboration of 3:31. In this verse, Paul claims that the righteous requirement of the law is fulfilled in believers. How is it fulfilled? Not by us, for we always fall short of the law's demands, but by Christ, who perfectly obeys the law. Those who are "in Christ" therefore

---

Study Questions

1. How does the language of "righteousness of God" in verses 21 and 22 relate to the idea of God's "justice" in verses 25 and 26?

2. What is an alternative translation of the phrase "faith in Jesus Christ" in verse 22? What would be the theological implications of adopting this alternative?

3. How is God's grace related to our faith?

4. What other passages in the New Testament teach ideas similar to what we have found Paul to be teaching in verse 25a about Christ as our "sacrifice of atonement"? What might this relationship suggest about the source of Paul's language?

5. How can we avoid inappropriate boasting?

fulfill the demand of the law. I suggest that Paul is alluding to this idea when he claims that his teaching of justification by faith "upholds the law." It does so by bringing people into relationship with Christ so that Christ's own perfect fulfillment of the law might be applied to them.

8 The Faith of Abraham

Romans 4:1–25

Outline

- Faith versus Works in Abraham's Justification (4:1–8)
- Faith versus Circumcision in Abraham's Justification (4:9–12)
- Faith versus the Law in Abraham's Justification (4:13–17)
- Faith versus Sight in the Experience of Abraham (4:18–25)

Objectives

After reading this chapter, you should be able to

1. Understand the relationship between Abraham's faith and his circumcision and its theological consequences.
2. Compare and contrast the way Abraham was viewed by Jews and how he was viewed by Paul.
3. Understand how Abraham can stand as the head and representative for all believing Christians.
4. Enunciate and be motivated to imitate the nature of Abraham's faith in God.

As knowledge of the Bible declines—even among Christians—fewer and fewer people have any handle on the story line of the Bible as a whole. We hear or read bits and pieces of the Bible but rarely take the time to stand back and see the whole picture. As a result, many believers have little idea about how their faith in Christ fits into the wider plan of God in history. Indeed, in what C. S. Lewis would call "chronological snobbery," we can make the mistake of thinking our own time is the only important one and ignore all that we can learn from the past.

Paul was determined not to make this kind of mistake. He well knew that his vision of the gospel, if it was to make sense to the Roman Christians, had to fit into the plan of God as revealed in the Old Testament. From the beginning of the book, therefore, Paul has been concerned to show that the gospel he preaches was "promised beforehand . . . in the Holy Scriptures" (1:2). Chapter 4 marks a significant contribution to this purpose. Abraham is, of course, a key figure in Old Testament history. God's promise to him in Genesis 12:1–3 marks the beginning of the formation of a people of God. The writers of the Old Testament and Jews after them regularly traced their national and spiritual standing back to him. Therefore, if Paul's gospel is to make sense of the Bible as a whole, he has to show how it stands in continuity with God's promise to Abraham. This he seeks to show in Romans 4, appealing especially to the key text of Genesis 15:6: "Abraham believed God, and it was reckoned to him as righteousness." Paul quotes this text at the beginning (v. 3) and at the end (v. 22) of his exposition and alludes to it throughout (see vv. 9, 10, 11, 13, 18).

Abraham and the Promise

Following Paul's argument about Abraham in Romans 4 is easier if we have in front of us a brief chronology of Abraham's experience with the promise of God.

Genesis 12:1–3: God calls Abram to leave his home and take up residence in the Promised Land. God promises to:

1. make of Abram a great nation;

2. bless those who bless Abram;

3. bless all peoples of the earth through Abram.

Genesis 15: God confirms his promise by entering into a covenant with Abram. He promises that Abram will have a child from his own body to inherit God's promise. Abram "believed the Lord, and he credited it to him as righteousness." God goes on to promise that Abram would take possession of the Promised Land and confirms his promise in a sacrificial ceremony.

Genesis 17: When Abram is ninety-nine years old, God again appears to him and renews his promise to give him innumerable descendants. As a sign that Abram would be the father of many nations, God changes Abram's name to Abraham ("father of many"). He also reaffirms the promise of the land.

In recognition of God's promise, God requires Abraham to circumcise his male descendants.

God also tells Abraham that the many nations that Abraham is to foster will come through his wife, Sarah. She will bear a son, Isaac, who will carry on the line of promise.

Genesis 21:1–7: God fulfills his promise by blessing Abraham and Sarah with a son.

Genesis 22:1–18: God tests Abraham's faith by requiring him to sacrifice his son Isaac. Abraham obeys the Lord, but his hand is stayed at the last minute.

Parallels between Romans 3:27–31 and 4:1–25

The same things that Paul says briefly and generally in 3:27–31, he says again in more detail with reference to Abraham in chapter 4. Note the parallels:

Romans 3:27–31	Romans 4
Boasting is excluded (v. 27)	Abraham had no right to boast (vv. 1–2)
. . . because one is justified by faith, not works of the law (v. 28).	. . . because Abraham was justified by faith, not works (vv. 3–8).
Circumcised and uncircumcised are united under the one God through faith (vv. 29–30).	Circumcised and uncircumcised are united as children of Abraham through faith (vv. 9–17).

Faith versus Works in Abraham's Justification (4:1–8)

As he reveals in Galatians (see 3:6–18), Paul views Abraham as a central figure in his understanding of salvation history. And so it is natural for Paul to spend a chapter on Abraham here in Romans. But there is another reason why Paul does so. Jews in Paul's day also venerated Abraham, but often they attributed to him a significance that runs counter to Paul's view. Jews revered Abraham as their "father" (see Is 51:1–2; *Mishnah Qiddushin* 4.14; Rom 4:1), the ancestor to whom they could trace their own unique status as God's covenant people. They pictured his life as a model of pious devotion: "Abraham was perfect in all his deeds with the Lord, and well-pleasing in righteousness all the days of his life" (*Jubilees* 23.10); "Abraham . . . did not sin against you" (Prayer of Manasseh 8). Especially interesting for our purposes is the tradition preserved in 1 Maccabees 2:52 (and alluded to by James in ch. 2 of his letter): "Was not Abraham found faithful when tested, and it was reckoned to him as righteousness?" Here we find Genesis 15:6 quoted, but it is attached to Abraham's offering of his son Isaac (Gn 22). Paul uses Genesis 15:6 to make a very different point. What strikes Paul is that God credits righteousness to Abraham immediately after Abraham believes God with reference to the promise that he would have a multitude of descendants (see Gn 15:5). Abraham's faith leads directly to his "justification" (another word for "righteousness"). Paul draws two important conclusions from this interpretation in the opening paragraph of the chapter.

First, Abraham has no basis for boasting before God (vv. 1–2). Paul has already claimed that the principle of justification by faith excludes all boasting (3:27). But some Jews might wonder whether that applies to Abraham, whose life was held up as such a model of piety. Paul insists that it does. Paul does not deny the reality of Abraham's piety (though the Genesis story, of course, also makes clear that Abraham was less than perfect in his piety), but he quotes Genesis 15:6 in verse 3 to show that Abraham's relationship to God, his righteous standing, was based on faith. Only if Abraham's works were the basis for that righteousness would he have anything in which to boast.

And this leads us directly into the second point: the fundamental distinction between faith and works (vv. 4–8). Paul may again be motivated in what he says by Jewish tradition, which tended to view Abraham's faith as a work. He draws a heavy line between faith and works by setting them in the context of God's grace. Paul never argues the case that God is gracious. God's grace is for him a theological axiom, an assumed truth that he never dreamed of trying to prove. So, in verses 4–5, Paul uses God's grace to spotlight the contrast between faith and works. Works, by their nature, create a relationship of obligation. A person who works puts an employer under a certain obligation to reward that work. So if people were accepted by God because of their works, he would be under an obligation to accept them. But this would violate the bedrock

Abraham's faith is demonstrated by his willingness to sacrifice Isaac. (Phoenix Data Systems)

truth of God's grace. God cannot be under obligation to any human creature. If he is to act graciously toward us, it cannot be on the basis of works. Faith, on the other hand, because it involves the humble acceptance of what God offers to give, does not create any such obligation. Thus, Paul concludes, it is the "wicked" whom God justifies by faith (v. 5). This statement is a justly famous expression of a fundamental biblical truth: God does not justify people who are already in any way worthy of being justified; he justifies people who are still lost in their sin, the "wicked."

Paul follows Jewish procedure by confirming the truth of a verse from the Pentateuch (Gn 15:6, quoted in v. 3) with a verse from the Writings (Ps 32:1–2, quoted in vv. 7–8). Another similarity to typical Jewish interpretive procedure is the verbal link between the Psalms text and Genesis 15:6. Both passages use the language of the Lord "crediting" or "counting" with reference to a person's spiritual status. (Though the NIV uses "credit" in Gn 15:6 and "count" in Ps 32:2, the underlying word in the Greek Old Testament is the same *[logizomai]*.) David's words from the psalm confirm Paul's basic point in this section: a person's relationship with God comes not by works but by God's gracious act. The person who

is blessed, David claims, is the one whose sins are covered by God, the one whose sins are not counted against him or her. Forgiveness, David implies, is not a state that a person can earn by works. It can be obtained only as a gift from God.

Faith versus Circumcision in Abraham's Justification (4:9–12)

Abraham, Paul has shown, was justified by faith. And God's very nature, his graciousness, means that Abraham's faith was not a work and that works, in fact, could have no part in his justification. In this new paragraph, Paul makes a similar point with respect to circumcision. The rite of circumcision was tied closely to Abraham from the beginning. It was after God confirmed his promise to Abraham that God required that every male descendant of Abraham be circumcised (Gn 17:1–14). The rite would be a constant reminder of God's covenant with Abraham's descendants. In obedience to God's command, the Jews circumcised their male babies on the eighth day after birth throughout the Old Testament period. But the rite became in some ways even more important during the intertestamental period. In response to persecution and to the dispersal of Jews throughout the Mediterranean world, tangible symbols of the Jewish faith became ever more important. By insisting on the careful observance of circumcision, food laws, and the Sabbath, Jews could maintain their identity as a "people apart." This context explains why circumcision became such a burning issue in the early church (see, e.g., Acts 15; Galatians).

Paul therefore had very good reasons to tackle the matter of circumcision in defending his understanding of justification. Paul argues historically. The faith that was credited to Abraham as righteousness (v. 9, alluding again to Gn 15:6) could have had nothing to do with circumcision, for God pronounced Abraham righteous (Gn 15) before he introduced circumcision (Gn 17). The biblical text does not tell us how much time elapsed between the two events, although some of the rabbis claimed that it was twenty-nine years. But the point is clear enough: Abraham's justification could not have been based on his circumcision, since he was uncircumcised when God accounted him righteous. What, then, was circumcision? It was, Paul claims, a "seal of the righteousness that he had by faith while he was still uncircumcised" (v. 11). Circumcision did not establish Abraham's righteousness; it put the capstone on that experience. But, of course, Paul has more than historical interest in what happened to Abraham. Abraham's experience of being justified first and circumcised afterward qualifies him to have a unique position in salvation history. Abraham unites all believers. He is the father of believing Gentiles (v. 11b) and of believing Jews (v. 12). From a strictly human standpoint, Abraham is the father of the Jewish people (cf. v. 1), but from the spiritual standpoint, Abraham is the father of all believers. So, again, it is Abraham's faith, not his works of obedience or his circumcision, that Paul thinks is vital in understanding Abraham's salvation-historical significance.

Faith versus the Law in Abraham's Justification (4:13–17)

The faith that gained Abraham his status of righteousness excludes works (vv. 3–8) and circumcision (vv. 9–12). Now, Paul explains, it also excludes the law. In Galatians, where Paul also discusses the significance of Abraham's role in justification, the argument about the law is strongly historical. The law could have played no role in the promise that God gave to Abraham, because it came "430 years after" the promise (Gal 3:17). In Romans, Paul argues more from principle. He states his key point at the beginning and the end of this brief paragraph: Abraham and his descendants received God's promise of blessing through faith and not through the law (vv. 13 and 16a). Paul explains in verses 14–15 why the law could not have been the basis for this promise. If the inheritance of blessing that God promised to Abraham's descendants had come via the law, Paul explains, then "faith has no value and the promise is worthless." Exactly what Paul means by this is not clear. He might mean that any mixture between the works that the law calls for and faith would evacuate the word "faith" of its basic meaning. No longer would it be a humble reception of God's gracious gift; it would involve the sinner in a relationship in which God is under obligation (see vv. 4–5). On the other hand, Paul might mean that the addition of law would make it impossible for faith to reach its goal. The last part of verse 14 suggests that this might be what Paul has in view. If faith is to secure God's promised blessing, it cannot have anything to do with the law, for the law demands works, and human beings are forever unable to produce sufficient works to gain God's favor.

So, if law is involved, the promise becomes worthless; it will never be fulfilled. In verse 14, then, Paul tells us what the law cannot do: secure the promise. In verse 15, he tells us what the law does do: it stirs up wrath. The key to the meaning of this verse lies in the word Paul uses at the end: "transgression." The Greek word here, *parabasis,* is always used in Paul's writings with a very specific meaning. It refers to the violation of a known law or commandment (see Rom 2:23; 5:14; Gal 3:19; 1 Tm 2:14). When Paul says, then, "where there is no law there is no transgression," he is reminding us of the very nature of law. It sets out in considerable detail the demands of God for his people. No one can claim ignorance or uncertainty about God's requirements once the law is promulgated. Failure to obey those commands is therefore a more serious matter even than our failure to follow the will of God expressed in the conscience of people and in the "natural law" (see Rom 1:32; 2:14–15). If my sixteen-year-old daughter comes home later than our generally agreed upon deadline, she will be in trouble. But she will be in even greater trouble if she comes home after the time I had specifically set for her that very night. So it is with God's law. He reveals his general moral will for all people through the natural law. To Israel, however, he spells out his demands in great detail. So when Israel fails to obey those demands, its punishment is more severe. It is in this sense, then, that Paul can claim that the law brings wrath. It does not solve the problem of human sin. Indeed, by turning "sin" into "transgression," it makes the problem even worse.

In the middle of verse 16, Paul makes a transition back to an earlier point. In verses 11–12, he has shown how Abraham's faith enables him to become the father of all believers, Jewish and Gentile alike. He now repeats that idea. Since the promise comes by faith, it can be "guaranteed to all Abraham's offspring." In breaking down the category "offspring," Paul mentions two groups: "those who are of the law" and "those who are of the faith of Abraham." A few commentators

think that Paul might be anticipating his argument in Romans 11 by claiming that Abraham's offspring includes the nation of Israel as well as believers.[1] But the parallel with verses 11–12 suggests instead that "those who are of the law" is shorthand for "those believers who are of the law," meaning Jewish Christians. Paul quotes Genesis 17:5 to support the notion that Abraham is the father of "us all." It is not clear whether the "many nations" in Genesis refers to Abraham's physical descendants or to his spiritual descendants. Paul, of course, applies the text to believers, Abraham's spiritual progeny.

Faith versus Sight in the Experience of Abraham (4:18–25)

The end of verse 17 marks the transition into the last part of Paul's exposition about Abraham and his significance for the Christian church. The focus now turns from the results of Abraham's faith to the nature of that faith itself. First, Paul focuses, appropriately, on the object of that faith (v. 17b). The God in whom Abraham believed is "the God who gives life to the dead and calls things that are not as though they were." In light of verse 19, which reminds us that God created life in the "dead" womb of Sarah, Paul must be thinking of that miraculous event in the life of Abraham and his wife. God's calling "things that are not as though they were" might refer to a popular ancient teaching about God's creation of all things "out of nothing" *(ex nihilo).*[2] The context, however, suggests that the referent is the "many nations" that were to come from Abraham. They did not exist yet, but still God could speak as though there were already present.

Paul next goes on to remind us of the way Abraham believed the promise of God even when all the tangible evidence seemed to point in the other direction (vv. 18–21). In brief, as Paul succinctly summarizes the matter in verse 18, Abraham

Monument over the cave of Machpelah in Hebron, the traditional burial site of the patriarchs and their wives. (Donald Hagner)

believed "against all hope" yet "in hope." Specifically, he did not allow all the many reasons to distrust God's promise to

Study Questions

1. How did Jews in Paul's day understand the significance of Abraham? How does what Paul says about him change that perspective?

2. What problem might Paul create by asserting so strongly that God "justifies the wicked"?

3. How does Paul's argument about the sequence of Abraham's faith and circumcision apply to Jews who had been circumcised as children?

4. If "the law brings wrath," why did God give it to his people?

5. What does Abraham's significance as the father of "many nations" mean for the Christian church today?

6. What is the history of Abraham's experience of God's promise?

weaken his conviction that God would do just what he had promised. Abraham was about one hundred years old, well past the normal age for procreation; Sarah, his wife, was barren. What chance, then, from a physical standpoint was there that God's promise to bring him descendants through Sarah would come to pass? Yet Abraham trusted God to follow through on his promise. He "was fully persuaded that God had the power to do what he had promised" (v. 21). The attentive Bible student might wonder about Paul's emphasis on Abraham's unwavering faith, because, according to Genesis 17:17, Abraham "fell on his face and laughed" when God told him he would have a son through Sarah. A few Jewish and Christian interpreters have tried to avoid the problem by suggesting that Abraham's laughter was the product of intense joy in God's promise. But that certainly is not the natural sense of the Old Testament passage. A better approach is simply to recognize that Paul is generalizing. He is not claiming that Abraham's faith was perfect or that he never had any doubts whatsoever. Rather, his point is that Abraham, despite some very human doubts, always came back in the end to faith in the promise of God. He therefore is an outstanding biblical example of a person who walked by faith rather than "by sight."

At the very end of chapter 4, Paul makes clear a point that has been implicit throughout: what the Bible records about Abraham, especially in Genesis 15:6, is valuable for Christians, because as God credited Abraham's faith for righteousness, so he does for us as well. We also believe in a God who gives life to the dead. Our God has raised Jesus from the grave to become our Savior and Lord (v. 24). Our faith, like Abraham's, must be a faith that looks beyond contrary evidence to rest secure in the promise of God. In verse 25, Paul adds a brief reference to the work of Jesus on our behalf. The careful parallelism of the verse might point again to an existing confession that Paul quotes to establish common ground with his readers: Jesus was handed over to death to win atonement for our sins, and he was raised to life to secure our justification.

Part
4

Encountering Life and Hope in Christ

Romans 5:1–8:39

9 Rejoicing in Life and Hope

Romans 5:1–21

Outline

- **The Hope of Glory (5:1–11)**
- **Eternal Life in Christ, the Second Adam (5:12–21)**

Objectives

After reading this chapter, you should be able to

1. Describe the similarities and differences in the salvation-historical work of Adam and Christ.
2. Appreciate the results of our justification in Christ.
3. Identify and explain at least three different ways that we can understand the teaching of "original sin" in Romans 5:12–21.
4. Rejoice in the assurance that believers can have because of the work of Christ, our second Adam.

We sometimes summarize the message of the New Testament with the renowned triad of faith, hope, and love. Faith enables us to receive and maintain our relationship with God through Christ. Hope focuses our attention on the grand climax of our faith, when all the uncertainties and difficulties of this life give way to the glory of being with our Savior forever. Love reminds us of our obligations to live as God's people in our present redeemed but not yet glorified state.

Risking considerable oversimplification, we nevertheless might suggest that Paul's argument in Romans matches this triad. In chapters 1–4, he has emphasized faith as the means by which we experience the righteousness of God. In chapters 12–16, he will focus on our responsibility to live a life of love in the midst of a fallen world. And now, in chapters 5–8, he turns to the subject of hope. To be sure, these chapters at first sight are not so clearly about hope. Paul talks about Adam and Christ (ch. 5), victory over sin (ch. 6), the weakness of the law (ch. 7), and the Holy Spirit (ch. 8). But a closer look reveals that these various topics all revolve around one central pivot: the confidence believers can have that they will one day share in the glory of God. In what we call a "ring composition," Paul begins and ends Romans 5–8 on this note of hope. Both 5:1–11 and 8:18–39 teach us that God's work for us in Christ, his love, and the ministry of the Spirit will overcome our present difficulties and bring us safely home to glory in the end. Here, as bookends to Romans 5–8, Paul announces his overall theme. At the next step between these bookends, Paul tells us why we can have such confident hope: Christ, the second Adam, has conquered the sin and death that the first Adam unleashed in the world (5:12–21), and the Holy Spirit is also working to overcome sin and death (8:1–17). And in the middle he tackles two potential hurdles in our attaining of glory: sin (ch. 6) and the law (ch. 7).

Romans 5–8, therefore, is about assurance. Paul wants those of us who have been justified by faith to know that we will be delivered in the end from God's wrath. He wants us to rejoice in the certainty of a victory already won, though not yet consummated. He wants us to understand that nothing in all creation "will be able to separate us from the love of God that is in Christ Jesus our Lord," as he says in concluding this section.

The Ring Composition of Romans 5–8

We can appreciate what Paul is teaching us in Romans 5–8 by taking a bird's-eye view of the argument. The argument falls into what we call a "ring composition" or "chiasm." In this structure, which appears quite often in the Bible, the author develops an argument by matching the opening and concluding parts and then doing the same with the parts in between. A visual display will help us see how Paul has done this in Romans 5–8.

A We believers can be confident that we will experience **future glory** (5:1–11)

  B We can have this confidence because we have new life <u>in Christ</u> (5:12–21)

    C *Sin* cannot keep us from this glory: we are no longer in bondage to it (6:1–23)

    C′ *Law* cannot keep us from this glory: we are no longer in bondage to it (7:1–25)

  B′ Because we are <u>in Christ</u>, we are sure of life; for the Spirit conquers the power of sin, law, and death (8:1–17)

A′ We believers can be confident that we will experience **future glory** (8:18–39)

The Hope of Glory (5:1–11)

The many different issues that Paul addresses in this paragraph—peace, hope, the Spirit, the cross, salvation—make it difficult to identify the central topic. I think that the topic of hope emerges as the best choice. Rejoicing in "the hope of

Following the Argument of Romans

We have to be careful about assuming that Romans falls into clearly distinct stages of argument. After all, most of us don't write letters with so careful a structure. But there is evidence that Paul has given thought to the organization of his letter. Almost all commentators agree that chapters 1–8 are a distinct section of the letter, but they disagree about where that larger section is to be divided. Note these representative opinions:

Chapter	1	2	3	4	5	6	7	8
Calvin	Justification by Faith					Sanctification		
Leenhardt	Theological Aspect of the Gospel					Anthropological Aspect of the Gospel		
Nygren	"The one who through faith is righteous . . .				. . . will live"			

I think that this last alternative is best. Nygren's wording for the two sections comes, of course, from the statement of the letter's theme in 1:17b. And additional evidence that Romans 5–8 forms a discrete section comes from an analysis of key words and concepts in Romans 1–8:

Word or Concept	Romans 1–4	Romans 5–8
Faith	24	2 (both refer back to 1–4)
Believe	9	1
Life	1	12
Live	1	12
Justify, Righteous, Righteousness: Attribute or Activity of God	5–7	3
Justify, Righteous, Righteousness: Status with God	18	3
Justify, Righteous, Righteousness: Means to Further Blessing	1	5
Justify, Righteous, Righteousness: Ethical Focus	——	5

One can, of course, prove anything by selective statistics. But these numbers pertain to key words in each section and reveal a shift from justification as a status attained by faith (chs. 1–4) to the new life and ethical expectations of the justified believer (chs. 5–8).

the glory of God" is the climax of verses 1–2. The final stage in the series of virtues in verses 3–4 also is hope. Verses 5–8 explain why hope will not "disappoint us." Verses 9–10 reassert hope in a new way, attaching our certainty of salvation in the last day to our present status as people who are justified and reconciled. There is good reason for Paul to move to this topic after finishing his elaboration of justification by faith (3:21–4:25). Jews in Paul's day generally thought that God's justification was something that would take place only at the end of one's life. God would analyze a person's adherence to the law, as evidence of covenant faithfulness, and determine whether he or she was to be justified or condemned. Jesus reflects this view when he warns the Pharisees, "By your words you will be acquitted [= 'justified'], and by your words you will be condemned" (Mt 12:37). Paul transforms this Jewish view of justification by proclaiming that a person can experience this eschatological verdict in the here and now. The minute a person believes in Christ, he or she is justified. But we have no concrete evidence of this justification. God does not hand us a document attesting our innocence. So people in Paul's day might well wonder what the verdict of justification that Paul makes so much of will mean in the last day, because Christians, like all other people, still have to face the Judge of all history at the end of life. What will the verdict of the Judge be? Paul encourages us by making it absolutely clear that the verdict of justification that we experience in this life will be confirmed in the life to come. Those who have been justified *will be* saved (vv. 9–10).

"Since we have been justified through faith" picks up the key theme of chapters 1–4 as a basis for what Paul will next say. He announces that justified believers enjoy three wonderful blessings: "peace with God" (v. 1); "access . . . into this grace in which we now stand" (v. 2a); and "the hope of the glory of God" (v. 2b). The first blessing, we should note, is "peace *with* God," not the "peace *of* God." The latter refers to the subjective feeling of harmo-

nious well-being that we can have because we are accepted by God (see, e.g., Phil 4:7). But Paul is referring here to the objective state of peace that comes to the justified believer. The enmity between God and the sinner is removed (cf. v. 10). The Greek word for "access" (*prosagōgē*), like our English word, was used to refer to one's approach to an eminent person. We would expect, then, Paul to say that the believer has "access" to God. But he does not. Instead, he claims that we have access to grace. Again we see how important this concept is for Paul. That word, "grace," can summarize the blessed state enjoyed by the justified believer. And note also that Paul says that we "stand" in this grace. Grace is important not only at the beginning of the Christian life but also for all of Christian experience. The third blessing of the justified believer is the one that is most important to Paul in this context: rejoicing in the hope of the glory of God. What Paul means is that we have the hope of some day experiencing God's glory, of having a share in his own eternal character. What we lack as sinners, even justified sinners (3:23), we will one day have.

The transition from verse 2 to verse 3 is abrupt and unexpected. We can all understand how we can rejoice in the hope of sharing God's glory. But rejoicing in our suffering? Paul reveals here that he is no pie-in-the-sky dreamer. He well knows, from personal experience, the problems that believers still have in this life. And so he launches a preemptive attack on those who would accuse him of ignoring the harsh realities of life in this world. Various kinds of sufferings will come to us, but we can rejoice in them when we recognize that they serve a purpose: to develop our Christian character. In verses 3b–4 Paul shows how a godly response to suffering can initiate a series of virtues, culminating, strikingly, in hope. Note, however, that Paul is not saying that we should rejoice *because of* suffering. Evil things are still just that—evil— and we never should be happy about them. But by looking beyond the suffer-

reconciliation

ing to its divinely intended end, we still can rejoice in the midst of them.

In verses 5–8, Paul reassures us about the hope that joy in suffering produces. That hope will not "disappoint us." A more literal rendering would be, "will not put us to shame." "Shame" is one way that Jews sometimes speak of a negative verdict in the judgment. Paul's language here picks up Old Testament passages that remind the saints that their hope in God will not "be put to shame" (Ps 25:3; Is 28:16). And why can we believers have this assurance about the outcome of our hope? In a word, love. In sending Christ to die for people who had spurned and rejected their Creator, God demonstrated his unquenchable love for us (vv. 6–8). He therefore reveals a love that is far deeper than we find in human experience, where a person would die only for someone near and dear. God, however, reveals his love not only on the cross, but also through his Spirit, making us deeply aware of that love (v. 5b). In an effusion of grace, God "pours out" his love into our hearts.

Verses 9–10 are the heart of this paragraph; indeed, they are the heart of Romans 5–8. And just in case we miss the point, Paul says basically the same thing twice. Note the parallels between the verses:

v. 9: justified by his blood . . . how much more saved from God's wrath
v. 10: reconciled through God's Son . . . how much more saved through his life

In both verses, our present spiritual status is shown to be the guarantee of future eternal life. The verses thus powerfully underscore the theme of hope that Paul is developing in this part of the letter. God, Paul is arguing, has already done the harder thing: taken rebellious sinners and brought them back into relationship with himself. We can, for that reason, be quite confident that he will accomplish the easier thing: vindicate on the last day those whom he has justified and reconciled. As is customary in the New Testament, Paul applies the language of salvation to our ultimate deliverance from sin and the

wrath of God in the last day (see, e.g., Rom 13:11; 1 Cor 3:15; 5:5; Phil 2:12). "We must all appear before the judgment seat of Christ" (2 Cor 5:10), but believers know what the verdict at that judgment seat will be.

Paul wraps up this passage by returning to two earlier themes: joy and **reconciliation.** In verses 2b and 3, Paul reminds us that we can rejoice in hope and in suffering. Now, as a summary of what has come before, he joins us in rejoicing generally in God. It should be noted that the word translated "rejoice" in these verses represents the Greek *kauchaomai,* a verb that also has the nuance "boast" (as in the NRSV; cf. "exult" in the NASB). Paul has used the verb "reconcile" in verse 10, and the idea of "peace with God" in verse 1 refers to the same basic concept. If "justification" (vv. 1, 9) is taken from the legal realm, "reconciliation" (v. 11) comes from the realm of personal relationships. Through Christ, God both declares us innocent of the sins we have committed and also enters into a new and intimate relationship with us.

Eternal Life in Christ, the Second Adam (5:12–21)

When Christians hear "Romans 5," many of them immediately think "original sin." And, indeed, Romans 5:12–21 furnishes the most important data in the Bible for understanding the nature and effects of Adam's sin. But what we must grasp if we are to understand this paragraph is that its focus is not on sin, original or otherwise. Rather, it focuses on righteousness and life. Paul compares and contrasts the two "Adams" or "human beings" (remember that the Hebrew word *adam* means "human being"). The first Adam brought death into the world through sin. The second Adam, Jesus Christ, through his righteous act of obedience to the Father on the cross, has overcome the disastrous results of Adam's sin.

In place of death he has brought eternal life. Paul makes this argument by means of four "just as . . . so also" comparisons:

v. 12:	Just as sin and death came via Adam	———
v. 18:	Just as Adam brought condemnation	so also Christ brought life
v. 19:	Just as Adam made many sinners	so also Christ made many righteous
v. 21	Just as sin reigned in death	so also grace reigns, leading to life

Two observations about these comparisons are to be noted. First, the first comparison is incomplete. Paul gives us the "just as" side in verse 12 but never completes the sentence with the "so also" side. English versions recognize this break in

Artist's depiction of Adam and Eve, whose sin brought death into the world. (Phoenix Data Systems)

the syntax by putting a dash at the end of verse 12. Second, the main point in such a "just as . . . so also" comparison comes in the second clause. I might say, for instance, "Just as the Chicago Cubs have been a model of baseball futility for years, so also they will be again this year." Everyone knows what I have said in the first part of the sentence (unfortunately!). I am assuming that first point to make another one: the Cubs will be bad again this year. So, in Romans 5:12–21, Paul assumes certain things about Adam, sin, and death to make a point about Christ, righteousness, and life.

Once we understand that Paul is making a positive point about the overwhelming power of Christ's work, we can fit this passage into its context. In the first paragraph of Romans 5, Paul assures believers that they surely will be saved from God's wrath on the last day. Now, in the second paragraph, Paul explains why believers can be so certain of this final salvation: Christ has more than overcome all the negative effects of Adam's sin. Those who are in Christ no longer need fear the condemnation that Adam's sin has brought to all the world. They are destined, through the power of grace, for life.

Paul's initial statement of the relationship between Adam's sin and death (v. 12) is one of the most controversial verses in Romans. And yet, taken at face value, Paul actually does not assert anything new here. The verse falls into a chiastic arrangement, with "sin" and "death" as the key elements:

> A *Sin* entered the world through one man
> > B *Death* came through sin
> > B′ *Death* came to all people
> A′ Because all people *sinned*

There is some debate about whether "death" is spiritual or physical. Probably, it is both. God warned Adam that he would "die" if he ate fruit from the tree of the knowledge of good and evil (Gn 2:17; cf. 3:3). This death involved both physical mortality and the spiritual penalty of separation from God—so

But It Isn't Fair!

Our natural reaction when we come to grips with Paul's teaching about original sin is that it isn't fair. How can God hold me responsible for something that Adam did millennia ago?[1] We can offer no finally satisfying answer to the fairness question, but two points can help.

First, some such idea as original sin seems required if we are to explain the amazingly universal perverseness of human beings. Listen to the words of Blaise Pascal:

> Original sin is foolishness to men, but it is admitted to be such. You must not then reproach me for the want of reason in this doctrine, since I admit it to be without reason. But foolishness is wiser than all the wisdom of men. For without this, what can we say that man is? His whole state depends on this imperceptible point. And how should it be perceived by his reason, since it is a thing against reason, and since reason, far from finding it out by her own ways, is averse to it when it is presented to her?[2]

In the doctrine of original sin, God offers to us an explanation of why human beings so persistently and so universally turn away from God, look only to their own concerns, steal from others, abort babies, make war on one another, slaughter masses of people. They do it because all people were involved in Adam's sin and are stained by its consequences.

Second, we need to take seriously Paul's clear assertion that we all die because we all sin. Ultimately, we do not die because Adam sinned; we die because we sinned. Yes, our sin is the sin of Adam, in which we share. But the point is this: according to Paul, we really did sin when Adam did. Admittedly, we do not understand perfectly the mechanics of how that takes place. Some theologians think that Adam is our legal representative. Others suggest a more organic relationship: we are all genetically tied to Adam, the ancestor of all humans (compare to this the argument of Heb 7:10). However we might explain it, the Bible teaches that we can be responsible for that sin of Adam because we did, in fact, sin also at that same time.

1. Theologians raise the same objection. See W. Pannenberg, *Anthropology in Theological Perspective* (Philadelphia: Westminster, 1985), 124.

2. Blaise Pascal, *Pensées,* no. 445.

vividly captured in the image of Adam and Eve hiding from God after their sin.

In claiming that Adam brought death into the world and that death spread to all people because of sin, Paul is rehearsing standard biblical and Jewish teaching. But difficulties begin when he probes a bit deeper and asks why, or how, all people sinned. Clearly, at the minimum, Adam's sin must have introduced a fatal bent into human nature itself, predisposing human beings to turn from rather than toward God (see Rom 1:18–32). But is Paul teaching more than that? A comparison between verse 12 and verses 18–19 seems to suggest that he is, because in those verses Paul attributes the condemnation and sin of all people to the sin-gle sin of Adam. In other words, in verses 12–21, Paul attributes the death of all people to two different causes:

> All die because all sinned (v. 12)
> All die because Adam sinned (vv. 18, 19)

How do we bring these two together? The best solution is to think that Paul views Adam as a representative figure whose action affects all who "belong" to him.[1] As the representative of all human beings, Adam's sin is at the same time the sin of all human beings. When he sinned, we all sinned—and died. If this way of thinking seems strange to us, we must remember that the Bible teaches a closer re-

Christ's obedience was demonstrated in the Garden of Gethsemane. (Ben Witherington III)

corporate solidarity

his comparison. Thus, in verses 13–14, he touches on the way that the law of Moses has affected the nexus of sin and death introduced by Adam. And then, in verses 15–17, he notes a key contrast between the generally similar roles played by Adam and Christ in salvation history.

Paul knows well that Jews will object strenuously to any rehearsal of salvation history that ignores the law, because Jews believed that God's gift of the law, and the covenant it represents, significantly altered the dire situation that Adam's sin had brought about. So Paul takes a short detour from his main line of thought to assert that the coming of the law did not change the situation, and, in fact, it made that situation even worse. Sin existed before the law was given, Paul reminds us, and people during that time, from Adam to Moses, died for their sins. But it was only when the law came that sin was "taken into account." The only way to make sense of Paul's argument is to recognize that "taking into account" is bookkeeping language. Before the law, people died for sinning against the generally revealed will of God, but the coming of the law enabled God to record sins as infractions of specific commandments. "Sin" was turned into "transgression." This is a more literal rendering of the Greek word (*parabasis*) that is translated as "breaking a command" in the NIV of verse 14. And, as I noted in the comments on 4:15, this word in Paul's writings has the specific sense of "violating a known commandment." The bottom line, then, is this: the law of Moses did not cancel the effects of Adam's sin; it made them even worse.

Central to Paul's whole argument in verses 12–21 is his brief aside at the end of verse 14: Adam is a "pattern [*typos*, 'type'] of the one to come" (Christ). But before drawing out the exact nature and implications of this typological relationship, Paul pauses in verses 15–17 to note some of the differences between the two. The key phrase in these verses is "how much more" (vv. 15, 17). Although there is an equivalence in the work of Adam and Christ, there is also a power opera-

lationship among humans than we are accustomed to in the modern West. **Corporate solidarity** is the term that scholars use to describe this perspective. It can explain, for instance, how the sin of Achan, when he stole some of the booty from battle for himself, can be called also the sin of Israel (Jos 7:11), and how it could lead to judgment on Israel as a whole (Jos 7:12). So in Romans 5, Paul can remind us that Adam's sin brought death to all people, who belong to him through physical birth, while Christ's righteous act brought life to all who belong to him.

As we saw, verse 12 is the first part of an incomplete sentence. We have the "just as" clause but no "so also" clause. Paul apparently wants to make sure a couple of things are clarified before he finishes

tive in Christ that enables his work on our behalf to more than cancel the tragic effects of Adam's sin. That sin brought death and condemnation to the "many" (a Semitic way of saying "a great number of people"), but in Christ, God has given the gift of justification to the "many." And that gift, a product of God's grace, came after innumerable sins. Because of that, Paul concludes, the reign of life that Christ inaugurates completely overpowers and sweeps aside the reign of death that Adam's sin initiated. Paul's basic purpose shines through again: to assure those of us who belong to Christ that certainly we will enjoy eternal life.

Paul now finally states the full comparison between Adam and Christ, and he does it twice so that we do not miss the point. Verses 18 and 19 follow the "just as . . . so also" structure that is central to this passage. Adam's action is the "just as": his "one trespass," his one act of disobedience, made "the many" into sinners and brought condemnation to "all men." The "so also" clauses speak of the effects of Christ's "one act of righteousness," his obedience: "many" are made righteous, life comes to "all men." These verses bring

to a head a pressing issue in the way Paul presents the comparison between Adam and Christ: does Paul think that the scope of their work is equivalent? His language would seem to suggest so. Adam's sin affects the "many," and so does Christ's obedience (vv. 15, 19). Adam's sin affects "all men," and so does Christ's act of righteousness (v. 18). In other words, one could build a pretty convincing case for universal salvation from Romans 5. Just as all people die in Adam, so all people (in the future if not in this life) find new life in Christ.[2] The problem with this view, of course, is that it conflicts with rather clear indications elsewhere in the New Testament that not all people eventually will find life—that hell, sadly, will never be unpopulated.

And so it is preferable to read verse 18 differently. Two possibilities are to be considered. First, Paul might simply mean that Christ's work has the same *potential* universality that the death introduced by Adam has had. Christ has died to make salvation for all people a possibility, but to actualize that possibility, people must respond to the gracious offer of God in Christ. Note in this regard an important difference in the way Paul, in verse 17, portrays the work of Adam and of Christ. Through Adam's trespass, death reigns— death seems to follow as a matter of course. But it is only those who "*receive* God's abundant provision of grace*" (my emphasis) who will reign in life. A second way we can avoid the idea of universal salvation in verse 18 is to assume that the equivalence between the work of Adam and of Christ lies not in the number of people that they represent but in the certainty that those they represent will be affected by their work. All those who are "in Adam" die; similarly, all those who are "in Christ" live. But whereas we are "in Adam" simply by virtue of being born, we are "in Christ" only when we receive the gift God offers (v. 17).

Paul again reveals his concern to relativize the importance of the law when it comes to the sin problem by claiming in verse 20 that it has increased the trespass. How has it done so? Paul does not elab-

---

Study Questions

1. What is Paul's overall purpose in Romans 5–8, and how does that purpose fit into his presentation of the gospel in Romans?

2. How should we view suffering in light of Romans 5:3–4?

3. What are the implications of the argument of verses 9–10 for the doctrine of eternal security?

4. What is Paul's main point in verses 12–21, and how does that point further his argument in this part of Romans?

5. What are the differences between Adam and Christ, and why (and how) do those differences matter to the believer?

orate, but other passages (see esp. 5:13–14; 4:15; 7:7–12) suggest that the law increases the problem of sin introduced by Adam by making people directly responsible for a body of specific commandments and prohibitions. In knowing all the better what sin is, our accountability rises. Paul, however, will not let sin have the last word, because the increased seriousness of sin has been matched by an even greater increase in the extent and power of God's grace. The result, spelled out in verse 21, summarizes the main lines of Paul's teaching in verses 12–21: "just as sin reigned in death, so also grace might reign through righteousness to bring eternal life through Jesus Christ our Lord."

Key Terms

reconciliation

corporate solidarity

---

10 Freedom from the Power of Sin

Romans 6:1–23

Outline

- **Released from Sin's Power through Union with Christ (6:1–14)**
- **Freed from Sin, Enslaved to God (6:15–23)**

Objectives

After reading this chapter, you should be able to

1. Explain what the metaphor "death to sin" means for the Christian.
2. Explain the nature of the believer's union with Christ in death and resurrection.
3. State and explain at least three different ways that we can understand the relation between water baptism and our union with Christ.
4. Appreciate the balance between God's gift (the "indicative") and God's command (the "imperative") in the Christian life.

The Christian, who has been justified by faith in Christ, has assurance for the future. We do not need to fear the day of judgment, for we have the "hope of glory," confident that we will be delivered from God's wrath when we stand before him on the last day. And we can have this confidence because our faith in Christ means that we belong to him. Adam, whose sin brought death to all human beings, no longer represents us. Christ does. And his act of righteousness, his death on the cross, wins for all who belong to him eternal life. Such is the basic argument of Romans 5. The chapter should lead believers to rejoice in the security they enjoy because of their relationship to Christ, but Paul knows that we are likely to have some remaining questions about this secure future. Especially we will want to know about the rest of our time on earth. Are we merely treading water here until we can be delivered from this life and enjoy the blessings of heaven? Do we have to wait for our death or Christ's return to enjoy the benefits of new life in Christ? And if that eternal life

has already been given to us in Christ, what about sin? Does it really matter anymore what we do in this life? This last question clearly is the one uppermost in Paul's mind at this point. Remember: he has preached the gospel for many years. He knows how people will react to the good news of eternal life in Christ. He knows that some people will think that they have now had their admittance ticket to heaven punched and that they can do anything they want until then. Hence, Romans 6.

Released from Sin's Power through Union with Christ (6:1–14)

Paul reverts to the question-and-answer style that he has used so effectively in Romans. The immediate stimulus for his question in verse 1 is what he has said in 5:20b: "But where sin increased, grace

Church of the Holy Sepulchre, traditional site of Christ's burial. (Jim Yancey)

increased all the more." Paul is talking about salvation history, about how God reacted to the rebellion of Israel with renewed promises of grace and blessing. But one can understand how people might take this promise of grace as a general principle that says, basically, "The more sin, the more grace—and since we all want as much grace as possible. . . ." Paul reacts to any such suggestion with a strong negative: "By no means!" (*mē genoito;* literally, "may it never be"). And then he offers this explanation: "We died to sin; how can we live in it any longer?"

What does Paul mean when he claims that we Christians have "died to sin"? Three contextual indicators help us to unpack the meaning. First is an obvious point, but we might miss its significance. Paul speaks of dying to sin (singular) not sins (plural). And, in fact, this language mirrors the pattern of Romans 5–8, where Paul uses the word "sin" twenty-two times, all of them in the singular. Paul's focus seems to be not on the various sins that people actually commit but on the underlying fact, or principle, or power, of sin. Second, Paul reverts quickly and

The Keys to the Christian Life

What gives Christians the power to lead a new life, to respond to Paul's exhortation that we no longer allow sin to reign over us (v. 13)? Popular seminar speakers and writers often claim to have "the key" that will open the door to victorious Christian living. In fact, however, the New Testament makes clear that there is no single key. Rather, there are many keys, many theological truths and practical considerations that can assist us to live in ways pleasing to the God who has redeemed us. One such key is given to us in Romans 6: union with Christ. Paul significantly portrays that union as involving each of the three core events that made up the early Christian preaching about Jesus. Note the parallels between Romans 6 and the well-known passage 1 Corinthians 15:3–4:

1 Corinthians 15:3–4	Romans 6
For what I received I passed on to you as of first importance:	
that Christ died for our sins	we died with Christ (v. 8; cf. vv. 3, 5)
according to the Scriptures,	
that he was buried,	we were buried with him (v. 4)
that he was raised on the third day	we will live with him (v. 8; cf. vv. 4, 5)
according to the Scriptures	

We participate with Christ in these transforming moments in salvation history. What Christ experienced, we experienced. When he died on the cross "to sin" (Rom 6:10), we were with him. When he was raised, we were with him. And it is because we share in what he did that we have a whole new relationship to sin. The Christian life does not begin in something we do; it begins in something Christ did, something that really happened. Because Christ has been liberated from the dominating power of sin, so have we. Because Christ has been raised to a new life, we have the power of a new life available to us. It is for these reasons, Paul insists, that we have both the potential and the responsibility to "walk in newness of life." So when we become discouraged about ever gaining control over a nagging sin, we need to turn to the cross. There we find not only the message of forgiveness for that sin, but also the power to overcome it.

repeatedly in chapter 6 to the metaphor of freedom from slavery. Christians have been "freed from sin" (vv. 7, 18, 22) and are therefore no longer "slaves to sin" (vv. 6, 17, 20). So "death to sin" must have something to do with being set free from the mastery or lordship (see v. 14) of sin. Third, Christ also is said to have "died to sin" (v. 10), so the phrase must indicate an experience that could apply to him. Christ, of course, was never under sin's power in the sense that it dictated his behavior and led him to commit actual sins. Nevertheless, by becoming genuinely and fully human, Christ did enter into the sphere in which sin dominates. Putting these three indicators together, we arrive at the conclusion that "death to sin" refers to release from the dominance of the power of sin. Paul uses the imagery of "death" for two reasons: (1) he will show that it is our union with Christ in his death that brings freedom from sin; (2) passing from life to death is a natural metaphor for a radical change in state.

Thus, Paul's point is this: we Christians have been set free from the domination of sin, so how can we continue to live as if sin is still calling the shots? Paul, of course, is not claiming that Christians cannot sin anymore. Such a radical claim would make nonsense of his frequent appeals to Christians to avoid sin and live for the Lord. In this very passage, he tells believers that they must not let sin "reign" in their bodies. No, Christians will continue to sin as long as this present evil age endures. What Paul is saying, however, is that sin can no longer be the characteristic pattern of the believer's life. Sin is not in control anymore. And that new relationship to sin must reveal itself in the way we live. No one who has been set free from sin's dominating power can continue to live as if sin were still in control.

In the rest of Romans 6, Paul explains how this new relationship to sin came about and draws out the consequences of this new relationship to sin. Verses 3–10 focus (though not exclusively) on the first of these two purposes. Paul's argument unfolds in three stages: (1) baptism puts us in contact with the death of Christ (vv.

3–4); (2) because we share in Christ's death, we also will share in his resurrection (vv. 5, 8–10); (3) sharing in Christ's death means freedom from sin (vv. 6–7). The last of these clearly is the main point, with verses 3–5 leading up to it and verses 8–10 elaborating it further.

The main point of verses 3–4 is clear enough. Our release from the power of sin takes place through our union with Christ. We have participated in his death (v. 3) and his burial (v. 4), and this means that through Christ's resurrection power, we have the power to "lead a new life." But why does Paul make baptism the means by which we experience this union with Christ? We should first note that he is almost certainly speaking about water baptism.[1] The language that he uses (esp. the noun *baptisma* in v. 4), along with the importance of the rite in the early church, makes a reference to some kind of baptism "in the Spirit" unlikely. Interpreters give three basic answers to the question as to why Paul refers in this context to water baptism. First, some think that baptism is a sacrament that in itself has the power to transfer a person into relationship with Christ. So baptism itself (as an act of God's grace) joins us to Christ, enabling us to experience Christ's death, burial, and resurrection. Proponents of this view give insufficient attention to the overwhelming focus on faith as the critical factor in joining us to Christ. Paul highlights faith throughout Romans; he mentions baptism only in 6:3–4. Second, then, other interpreters, reacting against a sacramental viewpoint, insist that Paul uses water baptism simply as a symbol of what happens to the believer at conversion. Going under the water of baptism symbolizes our death to sin, being under the water the burial of our old life, rising out of the water the new life of resurrection power.[2] Paul, however, does not say that we experienced a death, or burial, or resurrection "like" Christ's; rather, he claims that we died "with" Christ (vv. 5, 6, 8), that we were "buried with Christ" (v. 4), and that we will be "raised with Christ" (vv. 5, 8). Baptism does not symbolize what happened at our conversion;

Jordan River, in which John the Baptist practiced water baptism. (Ben Witherington III)

it is the means by which these "with Christ" experiences take place. Note verse 4: "we were buried with him *through baptism*" (my emphasis). So the evidence of the text requires that we give baptism significance in its own right as a point at which we become joined with Christ. But how can we do so without erring in the direction of the sacramental interpretation, with its undervaluing of faith? The third view seeks to avoid this difficulty by seeing in water baptism a kind of shorthand for the conversion experience. The New Testament consistently views the believer's baptism as part of a complex of events, including especially faith, repentance, and the gift of the Holy Spirit. I suggest, therefore, that when Paul refers to water baptism here, he does not intend it to be seen in isolation but as part of this larger complex of conversion events.[3] When we come to Christ in faith, God gives us his Spirit and we submit to water baptism. And this complex of events—not water baptism by itself—brings us into union with Christ and the salvific events of his death, burial, and resurrection. In other words, in a situation roughly parallel to the sinning of all human beings "in and with" Adam, Paul views be-

lievers as having died, been buried, and been raised "in and with" Christ. Our new relationship to sin is the product of our having died with Christ to the power of sin (see v. 10).[4]

In verses 5 and 8–10 Paul explicitly states the relationship between identification with Christ in his death and identification with Christ in his resurrection that the end of verse 4 implies. Our new life finds its parallel and basis (note the "just as") in Christ's resurrection. So Paul now goes on to show that being with Christ in death also means being with him in life. Scholars debate the significance of the future tenses in verses 5 and 8: "we will certainly be united with him in his resurrection"; "we believe that we will also live with him." We might understand these as "logical futures," where the future tense is used to indicate an event that inevitably follows another event. In this case, our union with Christ in resurrection might be a present experience of believers.[5] What Paul says here would be parallel, then, to his claim in Ephesians that believers *have been* "raised up with Christ" (Eph 2:6; cf. Col 2:12). But we probably should regard the future tenses as temporal futures. Paul normally presents our resurrection as an event that will happen when Christ returns in glory (for a close parallel, see Phil 3:21). Still, the power of Christ's resurrection is already operating in us, so that Paul can say that we are people who have "been brought from death to life" (v. 13).

At the heart of Paul's presentation of the believer's union with Christ are verses 6–7. Here he asserts the transformed re-

---

Old Self/New Self in Paul's Writings

Generations of Christian teachers have used Paul's contrast between "old self" and "new self," or "old man" and "new man," to conceptualize the Christian life. Yet two quite distinct views of the Christian have been built on the contrast.

The "Two Natures" View

Very popular is the notion that Christians possess two "natures": the old nature, dominated by sin, that we are born with; and a new nature, dominated by the Spirit, that we are given at conversion. Paul's "old self" is equated with the old nature, and his "new self" with the new nature. An ongoing battle between these two natures marks the Christian life. Success comes when we, through Bible study, prayer, and devotion, enable the new nature to win out over the old.

The "New Creation" View

Advocates of this view focus on the language in 2 Cor 5:17, according to which the believer is a "new creation" in Christ. They think that the old nature, or "old self," that people are born with is replaced by a new nature, the "new self," when they are converted. Success in the Christian life therefore will come when the believer simply gets out of the way of the new nature.

Proponents of both views appeal to Paul's "old self/new self" language. Paul uses this language in two other passages besides Romans 6:6: Ephesians 4:22–24 and Colossians 3:9–11. The "new creation" view emphasizes Romans 6:6, which appears to teach that the old self is eradicated—crucified with Christ—at conversion. Those who espouse the "two natures" view, on the other hand, cite Ephesians 4:22–24, where Paul apparently commands Christians to put off the old and put on the new.

Neither view, in fact, does a very good job of explaining all the texts. Two points are especially important. First, the "old self" is in some sense both removed at conversion (Rom 6:6) and a continuing problem for the Christian (Eph 4:22). Second, the "new self" is more than a "nature" or even a single individual; in Colossians 3:11 Paul seems to think of it as the Christian community in Christ. These factors suggest that we need to avoid talk of "nature" or "parts" of the individual Christian when we interpret this language. A better starting point is to remember that, for Paul, the "old man" first of all is Adam, and the "new man" is Christ. Probably, then, he uses "old self" to denote our relationship to Adam and "new self" to denote our relationship to Christ. Conversion marks a decisive break with Adam and a new connection with Christ (Rom 6:6). But the Adamic influence is still active, holding the power to attract us despite our new and unbreakable relationship to Christ. Hence, we must continue to avoid falling into the habits of the "old man" and to seek resolutely to let our new self, our Christian identity, rule our thinking and acting (Eph 4:22–24).

Realm Transfer in Romans 5–8

Throughout this book, we have seen how Paul uses the scheme of salvation history to present the truth of the gospel. Paul portrays what God has done in Christ against the backdrop of a sequence of events. Christ is at the center of that history. He divides it into two eras, and in each era, we find certain ruling powers. As we move into Romans 5–8, Paul utilizes especially often the imagery of rulership. Thus, we might more accurately speak of two realms rather than two eras. Note how much of what Paul says in these chapters can be summarized with this overall scheme:

The Old Realm (The Non-Christian)	The New Realm (The Christian)
In Adam	In Christ
Old man (5:12–21)	New man (5:12–21)
Slaves to Sin (6:17, 20; 7:14)	Slaves to Righteousness (6:17, 20)
Doomed to Eternal Death (5:12–21; 7:5; 8:3)	Destined for Eternal Life (5:12–21; 8:1–13)
Ruled over by Law (6:14; 7:7–25)	Ruled over by Grace (6:14; 8:1–39)
Dominated by the Flesh (7:5, 7–25)	Dominated by the Spirit (7:6; 8:1–39)

When we come to Christ, we are transferred into the new realm. We must, however, introduce one important qualification into this simple contrast, for the old realm does not simply cease to exist for the Christian when he or she is transferred into the new. That realm will last until Christ's return in glory at the end of history, and it still has the ability to influence the way Christians think and act. While celebrating our new status as members of the new realm, therefore, we also must be vigilant against the insidious influence of the old realm, with its non-Christian ways of thinking and behaving.

lation to sin that believers enjoy because of their identification with Christ. "Our old self" (which can be translated "our old man" [anthrōpos]) is Paul's way of connoting our connection with Adam and the sin and death it brought (see Rom 5). "Who we were in Adam" has been done away with when we were crucified with Christ. Paul's shift to the language of crucifixion reveals again that he conceives of us as having been with Christ in his own death. And through this union with him in death "the body of sin" has been "rendered powerless" (so the NIV margin, preferable to the text's "done away with"). Paul, of course, does not think of our bodies as being innately sinful (that would be a most unbiblical conception); rather, his point is that our bodies, inasmuch as they are dominated by sin, have been dethroned. And that means—Paul's bottom line—"we should no longer be slaves to sin."

In verses 1–10, Paul teaches that the justified believer has been placed in an entirely new relationship to sin. As Adamic people, we are all helpless slaves of sin; but, as Christian people, we have been set free from sin's tyranny. The change is so radical that Paul uses the analogy of death to speak about this transfer. But, as verses 11–14 now make clear, this transfer, as radical and fundamental as it is, is not the end of the story. Our new relationship to sin is one that we must appropriate and live out. Although we are "dead to sin," as Paul has said (v. 2), we still need to view ourselves in that light (v. 11); and once we see ourselves this way, we then can break the reign of sin in practice (v. 12). The "indicative" of what God has done for us does not render unnecessary the "imperative" of what we are to do; rather, it stimulates it and makes it possible. Paul continues to employ metaphors drawn from the world of rulership as he calls on us in verse 13 not to "offer" ourselves to sin but, rather, to "offer" ourselves to God. The verb translated "offer" in the NIV (*paristēmi*) can have the connotation "dedicate in service to a king" (e.g., 1 Kgs 10:8, in the Greek Old Testament).[6] God is our new ruler, and we are to present ourselves to him daily for whatever service he demands.

Paul concludes the passage with a last reminder of the new position we enjoy in Christ. He promises, "Sin will not be your master." The text uses the verbal form of *kyrios*, "lord": sin will not lord itself over you anymore. And the reason it will no longer dominate us is that we "are not under law, but under grace." Some Christians have taken this well-known claim to mean that believers are no longer obliged to any set of commandments. But again, Paul is talking about *the* law—the law of Moses—and not *any* law in general. Many interpreters think that this claim relates to the forgiveness of sins: the law no longer has power to condemn us because we are protected under the grace of God in Christ.[7] But "under law" elsewhere in Paul's writings has a broader sense (see esp. Gal 4:4, where Paul claims that Christ was born "under the law"). In keeping with his rulership language, being "under the law" means to be dominated by the law, to be part of the old era of salvation history over which the *torah* held sway. To be "under grace," on the other hand, means to be living in the new era, in which God's grace in Christ now reigns supreme (see Rom 5:2, 21). John said much the same thing in the prologue to his Gospel: "For the law was given through Moses; grace and truth came through Jesus Christ" (Jn 1:17).

Freed from Sin, Enslaved to God (6:15–23)

The second part of Romans 6 seems almost to be a repeat of the first part. Paul again begins by asking whether the overwhelming experience of God's grace means that sin does not matter any more (v. 15). He responds by asserting again that we have been set free from sin and thus are to live new lives of righteousness. Repetition there certainly is. Paul clearly wants us to get the point he is making. There is also, however, a new focus. As we have seen, Paul uses the imagery of a "transfer of realm" to make his point about our new status. In verses 1–14, he focuses on the negative side of that transfer: release from the tyranny of sin; in verses 15–23, on the other hand, he develops in more detail the positive side of the transfer: the rule of God and the demand for obedience and righteousness.

As in 6:1, where he picked up the language of 5:20, Paul formulates his initial question with the language he has just used in verse 14. Someone might misunderstand the claim that believers are not under law but under grace as an invitation to sin. Again echoing the beginning of chapter 6, Paul emphatically rejects any such inference: "By no means!" His explanation of that rejection in verse 16 focuses on a key reality: people are always enslaved to something. Absolute freedom, Paul implies, is a chimera. No one is ever free in that sense. And so the question becomes, "To whom or to what do you want to be enslaved?" To sin, reaping eternal death as the consequence? Or to obedience, which brings righteousness? To continue to live a life of sin would be to reveal that we were still slaves to sin. The only alternative is to obey God and thereby reveal that he is now truly our master. In verses 17–18, Paul reminds us that the life of obedience that he calls for is both mandated and made possible by our transfer from the old realm of sin and death into the new realm of righteousness and life. At one time we were slaves of sin, but in placing our faith in Christ, we have committed ourselves to a new "form of teaching"—the gospel. And the gospel demands that we acknowledge Jesus as our Lord and live out the implications of that lordship.

Verse 19 is the center of verses 15–23. Paul leads up to it with reminders of the new situation we are in as a result of God's grace (vv. 17–18), and he follows on after it with similar emphases (vv. 20–23). But here, in verse 19, he repeats the basic command of verse 13: recognizing the new realm in which we live, we are to offer ourselves as slaves to righteousness and holiness. Paul acknowledges the limitations of his metaphor at the beginning of the verse ("I put this in human terms"), for to call believers "slaves" could imply that we have been forced into an onerous service, whereas to serve Christ is a high and joyful privilege. But the point of that analogy is that believers really have no choice in whether they will serve God or how they will serve

him. God demands that his people obey him, and he has laid down in his word just how we are to obey him. Interestingly, Paul suggests that our new obedience is to mirror the old obedience. If at one time we were dedicated to serving money, or striving for status, now we are to employ those same energies in serving God and righteousness. As unbelievers and slaves to sin, Paul reminds us in verse 20, we were quite free from the control of righteousness. Here at least is one freedom that unbelievers enjoy: freedom from any ultimate ability to live lives of righteousness. Therefore, people who live in the realm of sin have a certain freedom, but it is an unenviable freedom. Also, they produce "fruit" (*karpos*; "benefit" in the NIV), but it is an undesirable fruit because it leads to death. Paul uses the imagery of fruit to describe the characteristic behavior of unbelievers. As slaves of sin, unbelievers produce attitudes and patterns of life that lead to condemnation and are the source of shame for Christians. In contrast (v. 22), believers, the slaves of God, are able to produce fruit that leads to holiness and to eternal life. The good works that believers do as a result of their new relationship to Christ form an overall pattern of life that Paul calls "holiness." This word (*hagiasmos*) comes from an important biblical word group that denotes the character of God and, derivatively, the character that his people are to exhibit. "Be holy as I am holy" is a well-known summary of this matter, echoed throughout the Old and New Testaments (e.g., Lv 11:45; 1 Pt 1:16). In the new realm, set free from sin and enslaved to God, believers can obey this summons to a holy life.

Many of us know by heart the words of verse 23. We often hear it quoted in isolation as the essence of the Christian gospel. But now we are in a position to see how well it fits its context. Paul has been warning us throughout Romans 6, especially in verses 15–22, that the lifestyle of sin leads to eternal death and condemnation. Believers who have "died to sin" will no longer lead that kind of life. But still we can treat sin too cavalierly, as

Study Questions

1. What does Paul mean when he says that believers have "died to sin," and what are the practical ramifications?

2. Why does Paul use the language of baptism in verses 3–4? What do these verses suggest about our practice of baptism?

3. How does the idea of "realm transfer" help us to understand the nature of the Christian life?

4. What does Paul's teaching in verses 15–23 suggest about the way we often use the language of "freedom" in the modern world?

if it did not really matter now that we are saved and destined for heaven. Paul's warning, therefore, is just as much for us who believe as for the non-Christian. And the positive side is an encouragement also to us who believe: God's gift is eternal life in Christ Jesus our Lord. As D. M. Lloyd-Jones notes, this verse uses three contrasts that are basic to Paul's teaching in this part of Romans:

1. the master served (sin vs. God)
2. the outcome of that service (death vs. eternal life)
3. how that outcome is reached (a wage earned vs. a gift received).[8]

11 Freedom from the Law

Romans 7:1–25

Objectives

After reading this chapter, you should be able to

1. Explain the implications of the believer's release from bondage to the Mosaic law.
2. List and evaluate three common interpretations of the experience described in 7:7–25.
3. Explain the contribution of Romans 7 to our understanding of the Christian life, particularly in relationship to the law and to the continuing power of sin.

Under the old covenant, sacrifices were offered on altars like this one. (John McRay)

Who am I? Few questions are more important. Your answer to that question will dictate your values, your lifestyle, your future. If I decide, for instance, that I am an NBA prospect, then I may decide it is well worth it for me to quit my day job and concentrate on basketball and conditioning. If I decide, under the influence of certain psychological schools, that I am determined by my environment and heredity, then I will not spend much time wondering what actions to take and whether they are right or wrong. If, on the other hand, I decide that I am a child of God, created in his image and redeemed from sin through his Son, then I will think quite differently about how I should go about my life. I assume that most, if not all, people reading this book have already made this last decision. But if we answer the question "Who am I?" with the response "a Christian," we still leave a lot unsettled. What does it mean to be a Christian? What is a Christian supposed to be like? And it is here that Romans 7 enters the picture.

Few passages of Scripture have been more influential in shaping how Christians think about themselves. Yet, I submit, most Christians have been wrong in the conclusions they have drawn from this chapter. If my own informal survey is a reliable indicator, most believers think that Paul in Romans 7 (esp. in vv. 15–20) is describing the experience of a "normal Christian." And so they conclude that constant struggle with sin and even defeat by sin is the norm in the Christian life. Now it is clear that Christians do struggle with sin. Indeed, I think that Paul

teaches that our struggle with sin will not end until our bodies themselves are transformed. I do not think, however, that Romans 7 describes this struggle. And I do not think that the negative outcome of that struggle depicted in Romans 7 should be typical of the Christian life. I will explain these points and try to justify them as this chapter unfolds. But it is important to get off on the right foot, and to do that we need to establish the basic topic of Romans 7.

Romans 7 is not about the Christian life; it is about the law, the *torah*. As Paul develops his case for the certainty of Christian hope, the overall topic of Romans 5–8, he pauses in chapters 6 and 7 to deal with two key threats to that hope: sin and the Mosaic law. Sin is an obvious threat. But why include the Mosaic law? The reasons will become clearer as the chapter unfolds. But recall that Paul already in Romans has cast the law in a very negative role in salvation history. It brings "knowledge of sin" (3:20), it cannot justify (3:28), it stirs up wrath (4:15), it increases the trespass (5:20), and it is contrary to grace (6:14, 15). The first paragraph in Romans 7, verses 1–6, brings this negative theme to a crescendo. Then Paul, ever aware of how people will respond to his teaching, backs off to consider the inevitable question: if the law has done all those bad things, is it, in itself, an evil thing? Paul answers this question in verses 7–25. So, again, Romans 7 is about the law of Moses: why Christians need to be released from its bondage, why it nevertheless is God's good and holy law, and why, finally, it lacks the power to overcome the problem of sin and death.

Released from Bondage to the Law through the Death of Christ (7:1–6)

Verse 4 is the center of this brief paragraph: Christians are released from bondage to the law through the death of

The Law and the Christian

One pressing theological and practical matter is raised by Paul's teaching in Romans 7:4, 6 (see also 6:14, 15): what role does the Mosaic law play in the life of the believer? Modern evangelical theology owes a great deal to the stream of teaching descending from Calvin through the Puritans. In this teaching, a fundamental distinction is made between the Mosaic law as a "covenant of works" and the Mosaic law as a "rule of life." The former, the demand that we follow the law in order to receive God's approval, is abolished in Christ. Advocates of this tradition insist that this is what Paul is referring to in Romans 7:4.[1] But it is doubtful that we can make this distinction. Any power that the law has to condemn is tied to its binding power. If one is "under the law," then one is separated from grace and is a helpless victim of sin (see Rom 6:14). And being "under the law," as 1 Corinthians 9:19–21 makes clear, is to be under its commanding power. I think it preferable, then, to interpret Romans 7:4 (and 6:14, 15) as teaching that the believer is set free from the immediate binding authority of the Mosaic law. No part of that law remains as an independent source of moral direction, not even the Ten Commandments. The believer has been transferred from the realm over which the law rules into the realm over which Christ rules. We therefore are subject directly to the "law of Christ" (Gal 6:2), not to the law of Moses. To put it in terms of historical theology, I side with Luther in rejecting the typical Reformed teaching about the "third use of the law"—the use of the law as a rule of life for the believer.

What difference does such a view make? In practice, not much. Two points are especially important here. First, whatever most Christians would identify as eternal "moral" law in the law of Moses clearly is taken up by Christ and the apostles and made part of the "law of Christ," under which we live. Of the Ten Commandments, only the Sabbath command is not repeated virtually verbatim in the New Testament. (This is why the nature and meaning of the Sabbath has been a matter of such controversy.) Second, Paul is *not* saying (as some have wrongly interpreted him to say) that Christians no longer are bound by any specific commandments at all. He says precisely the reverse (see 1 Cor 7:19b). The point of Romans 7:4, and of similar texts, is that we are not bound to the law *of Moses*. But we are bound to a law—the law of Christ (Gal 6:2; 1 Cor 7:19–21).[2]

1. See Calvin's *Institutes* 2.11.9; see also Patrick Fairbairn, *The Revelation of Law in Scripture* (1869; reprint, Grand Rapids: Zondervan, 1957), 429–30.
2. For an exploration from several viewpoints of this whole issue, see W. A. VanGemeren et al., *The Law, the Gospel, and the Modern Christian: Five Views* (Grand Rapids: Zondervan, 1993).

Christ. Verse 1 states a principle, which verses 2–3 illustrate, as a way of leading up to this main point. Verses 5–6 then elaborate on the reason why this release had to take place and the outcome of that release.

As my preceding comments have made clear, the "law" (*nomos*) that Paul is talking about throughout Romans 7 is the Mosaic law, the *torah*. This probably is also the case in verse 1. But by addressing his readers as "men who know the law," is Paul signaling a shift in audience? That is, is he now narrowing his focus from Christians in Rome in general to those who are Jewish? This interpretation is possible, but probably it is not correct. For one thing, Paul ties his discussion in this chapter too closely to his general argument for us to isolate this section as devoted to a narrower audience. For another, it is likely that almost all the Christians in Rome, Jewish or not, "knew the law." Many of the Gentile converts

Synagogue in Capernaum built on the foundations of the synagogue in which Christ probably taught. (Jim Yancey)

probably had been "God-fearers," who attended synagogue and read the Scriptures before their conversion to Christ. And what these people would know from the law itself is that its power over people ends at death. Paul illustrates this principle in verses 2–3. Quite a number of commentators have tried to find an elaborate allegory in these verses. For instance, they identify the wife with the believer, the first husband with the "old man," and the second husband with the "new man." But neither this nor any of the other allegorical schemes work very well. We would do better simply to view the story as an illustration of a simple truth: a death must take place if one is to be released from the authority of the law. The woman, as long as her husband is alive, is prevented by the law from marrying another man. But once the husband dies, she is free from the law pertaining to marriage and adultery. She can marry again without fear of penalty or criticism.

So also it is, Paul concludes in verse 4, with Christians. We, too, have had to experience a death so that we could be free from the law and be joined to Christ. We should not miss the parallel at this point between Romans 6 and Romans 7. If, according to Romans 6, Christians have "died to sin" (e.g., v. 3), so also, according to Romans 7, have we "died to the law." The theological concept in both cases is the same. In the old era we lived under the domination of sin and the law. Both, though for very different reasons (see vv. 7–12), exercised a baleful influence on us. Coming to Christ means, in effect, to experience a totally new change of status with respect to sin and the law. Neither has the power to dominate believers any longer. Neither determines our destiny. We are "free" from both, and this freedom was won through the work of Christ. The focus in chapter 6 is on our union with Christ in his death, burial, and resurrection. Paul may hint at a similar corporate idea by using the language of "the body of Christ," but his focus is on the body of Christ given up for us in his death. Finally, as chapter 6 portrays our death to sin as resulting in a new life and fruit leading to holiness (see v. 22), so 7:4

indicates that our death to the law has led to our being joined to Christ, with the ultimate purpose that we should "bear fruit for God." We have been transferred from the realm of sin and the law into the realm of Christ, holiness, and life.

Why did we need to be released from the law? Verse 5 offers a brief explanation. Essentially, Paul claims that the law became the instrument that sin was able to use to produce death. Just how the law aroused these "sinful passions" Paul does not say here. The idea, as he elaborates it elsewhere (see 4:15; 5:13–14; 7:7–12), seems to be that the coming of the law both stimulated rebellion in sinful human creatures and increased the penalty for sin. We all are familiar with the notion of "forbidden fruits": forbidding an activity is the best possible way to increase its popularity. If I tell my children that on no account are they to play in mud puddles after a rainstorm, they will have a very difficult time not doing so, even if my prohibition was the first time they ever heard of the idea. And, as we have seen earlier in Romans, Paul clearly believes that the coming of the law made the human situation worse by turning sin into "transgression": disobedience of a definite command of the Lord. So we needed to be released from the law because it had become allied with sin in producing death in us. If verse 5 describes the situation from which we are released, verse 6 describes the new situation we enjoy as a result of that release. Freedom from the law does not mean the end of God's claim on us. That claim is exerted in a new and powerful way through his Spirit. No longer do we serve in "the old way of the written code." "Written code" translates *gramma*, "letter," a word that Paul uses to denote the Mosaic covenant as being fundamentally an external demand (see comments on 2:28–29). In contrast is the Spirit, the gift of the new realm that God gives to all who come to him in faith. Paul has not said much about the Spirit thus far in Romans (though, again, see the comments on 2:28–29). Here he briefly touches on the Spirit as a hint at the larger development to come in Romans 8.

The Coming of the Law (7:7–12)

Paul's purpose in this paragraph is twofold. First, he wants to vindicate the law from the charge that it is itself evil. One can imagine why someone might make this charge. Has not Paul himself claimed that the law has aroused sin (v. 5) and that Christians need to be released from it (vv. 4, 6)? Paul clearly rejects this charge (v. 7), concluding that "the law is holy, and the commandment is holy, righteous and good" (v. 12). Second, Paul wants to delve more deeply into the exact relationship among sin, the law, and death. He denies that the law is in the same category as sin, but he does not back down from his insistence that there is a relationship between them. Sin, Paul teaches, is the culprit: it has used the law to bring death.

In making these basic points, Paul reverts to a narrative style. He portrays the experience, apparently, of an individual: "I." Who is this "I"? Here, many readers might think that I am raising a ridiculous question, because it is obvious that the

Parallels between Romans 6 and Romans 7:4

Romans 6	Romans 7:4
"We died to sin" (v. 2)	"You died to the law
through union with Christ (vv. 4–5)	through the body of Christ,
slaves of righteousness and of God (vv. 18, 22)	that you might belong to another, to him who was raised from the dead,
"the benefit [fruit] you reap leads to holiness" (v. 22)	in order that we might bear fruit to God."

"I" is the author of Romans writing about personal experience. Paul is the author, and the experience is his. What more need be said? I am sympathetic to such objections: scholars sometimes pursue pointless issues that abandon the plain meaning of the text. But I do not think that such an accusation would be just in this case. The fact is, as we will see, that there are elements in the experience described in verses 7–25 that only with great difficulty can be attributed to Paul. Moreover, we must reckon with differences between our culture and Paul's. We might think that a narrative using the pronoun "I" can mean only one thing. But in the first-century Jewish world, this was not so clear. Recall my comments on Adam in Romans 5: Jews had a lively sense of corporate identity. To a degree quite foreign to most of us, they could identify themselves with other people.

With these general observations in place, we now can examine quickly three main interpretations of the "I" in Romans 7:7–12.

1. "I" is Paul. He describes his own experience, either (a) when he came of age and took on full responsibility for the law,[1] or (b) when he came to Christ and recognized his sin for the first time.[2]
2. "I" is Adam. Paul speaks as a human being, caught up in Adam's representative transgression of God's law and its terrible consequences.[3]
3. "I" is Israel. Paul speaks of the history of his people, for whom the coming of the law meant not life but death.[4]

Each of these views has strong arguments in its favor and capable defenders. The strengths and weaknesses can be assessed by focusing on a key narrative development within verses 8b–9:

Apart from the law	When the commandment came
sin is dead	sin sprang to life
I was alive	I died

The problem with thinking that Paul simply is describing his own experience is that he had never lived "apart from the law," nor did he "die" when the commandment came. As a Jew, he had always lived under the law; furthermore, he was born under sentence of death because of Adam's sin. Herein lies the attraction of the Adamic interpretation, for Adam and Eve alone of all human beings were "alive" (spiritually) before law was given. They alone "died" (spiritually) when the commandment (not to eat the fruit of the one tree) came. But this view suffers from a fatal objection. Paul is talking in this context about the law of Moses, which, obviously, did not exist when Adam and Eve were alive. The best option, then, is a combination of the first and third interpretations. Taking his usual salvation-historical perspective, Paul is reflecting on the impact of the law of Moses on the people of Israel; at the same time, however, using typical first-century corporate perspective, he identifies himself with the experience of his people Israel. It is helpful at this point to remember that Jews celebrated the Passover by thinking of themselves as being present during the great events of the exodus. Paul does the same kind of thing, thinking of himself, as a typical Jew, as being present when the Mosaic law first was given to Israel.

With this overall perspective in place, we can glance at some of the details in the paragraph. As in 3:20, Paul claims that knowledge of sin came through the law. As he explains further in verse 13, this probably means that the law first revealed sin in its true colors. By disobeying the law that God himself gave the people of Israel, the Jews became aware that their sin was flagrant rebellion against God. Paul illustrates by citing the last of the Ten Commandments, "Do not covet" (v. 7). Some interpreters think that Paul chooses this commandment because he personally had a particularly difficult struggle with "coveting" or "desire" (possibly, sexual sin). More likely, however, is that Paul follows Jewish precedent in citing the commandment as representative of the law as a whole.[5]

Paul's claim that "sin was dead" and then, when the commandment came, "sprang to life" (vv. 8b–9) reflects his teaching about the Mosaic law elsewhere in Romans. As we have seen, he repeatedly suggests that the coming of the law turned sin into transgression and therefore increased both the number and the seriousness of sins (4:15; 5:13–15, 20; 7:5). So it could be said that Israel "died" when the commandment came. To be sure, the people of Israel were already "dead," as are all descendants of Adam. But certain Jewish traditions presented the giving of the law as the time when Israel, alone of all the nations on the earth, awoke to true spiritual life. Paul therefore exaggerates for polemical effect, claiming that the coming of the law did not mean "life" for Israel, but "death." By affixing clear, unequivocal responsibility for the obedience of fixed commands on Israel, the law sealed the death of the people. All this is to illustrate Paul's main point: sin used the law to bring death (v. 11). The law was the occasion of sin. As good and holy as it was, the law of God made severe demands upon Israel without granting them the renewed heart and mind necessary for obeying it. Sin, which Paul virtually personifies here, then could stand up and say, in effect, "See, you have not obeyed the law God gave you. You continue to follow me. Therefore, your death clearly is deserved."

Life under the Law (7:13–25)

Verse 13 is transitional, as Paul moves from a description of the coming of the law (vv. 7–12) to a description of the law's continuing effects (vv. 14–25). Note, therefore, that while we find English past tenses in verses 7–12, English present tenses are used throughout verses 14–25. Once again, we have to establish a broad perspective on this passage as a whole before we can understand any of its details.

We simplify a bit by introducing three main options.

1. Paul describes his experience as an unconverted Jew under the law.[6]
2. Paul describes his experience, perhaps shortly after his conversion, as he sought sanctification through the law.[7]
3. Paul describes his experience as a mature Christian.[8]

Debate over Romans 7 is so lively precisely because each view has some points in the text in its favor. There is no "slam dunk" in the interpretive game here. So the best interpretation will be the one that produces the best overall fit with all the evidence. I think that the first of these options best satisfies this requirement. But before I explain why I come to this conclusion, let's get a sense of the debate by noting two key arguments for the first and the third views. The argument in favor of Paul referring to his pre-Christian experience (the first view) is that (1) he claims to be "unspiritual, sold as a slave to sin" (v. 14), an impossible state for any believer (see Romans 6); and (2) he claims to be "a prisoner of the law of sin" (v. 23), which contradicts the situation of all Christians, who have been "set free from the law of sin and death" (8:2). The argument in favor of Paul referring to his mature Christian experience (the third view) is that (1) he writes in the present tense; and (2) he concludes the passage, *after* expressing thanks for deliverance through Christ, with a statement of his divided being.

The main argument for the second, "immature Christian," view is, of course, that the arguments for the first and third views both carry weight, and so the only way to reconcile all the data is with a mediating view. Paul is a Christian (explaining the data in the third-view argument), but a Christian who finds himself frustrated because he is trying to live by the law (explaining the data in the first-view argument). But the problem with this mediating view, and the reason I finally think that the passage describes an unregenerate person, is that the data in

Applying Romans 7

I have argued that in Romans 7:14–25, Paul describes the failure of Jews to obey the law, the *torah*, that God gave to them. How can most of us, who are not Jews and have never been under the *torah*, apply these verses to ourselves? We must begin by recognizing that Israel's experience with the law plays a paradigmatic role in Paul's writings. Israel's experience, in other words, is typical. It shows what happens when sinful human beings meet up with the will of God. As the Old Testament so eloquently shows, here we have a people who saw firsthand God's mighty acts on their behalf. He brought them out of Egypt, gave them a good and productive land, and promised to give them permanent rest in that land. All he asked was that they obey the law that he gave to them through Moses. Yet, as we all know, the history of Old Testament Israel is largely a history of their failure to keep that law. Judgment came in the form of removal from their land. Israel's failure revealed that the human heart itself had to be changed; thus, God promised to initiate a new covenant with his people that would accomplish precisely that.

Writing in the context of the first century, with deep concerns about Jews and Gentiles, Paul naturally speaks often about this history—as he does, I think, in Romans 7. But he gives many hints that this history is one that is representative of all people confronted with "law" in any form. If Old Testament Israel, with all their advantages, could not keep God's law, how much less will any other person or nation be able to keep whatever "law" it might be trying to live up to? Romans 7 ultimately is about the inevitable failure of "law" in general to deliver people from the problem of sin. Therefore, while I do not think that Paul is describing Christian experience in Romans 7, that chapter nonetheless holds important lessons for Christians. For we, too, must be careful not to fall into the dangerous habit of thinking that our laws, or rules, can be the source of true holiness. We indeed may need laws and rules to guide us in this life—the New Testament gives us plenty!—but never should we regard them as ends in themselves or think that we can become holy simply by following them.

the argument for the first view involve an objective state, not a subjective feeling. Paul does not say that he feels as if he were a slave of sin or that he feels as if he were a prisoner of the law of sin; rather, he states such as the reality of his situation. However, that situation is, by definition, one that no Christian can ever experience. As Paul has taught at some length in Romans 6, every believer, united with Christ in death and resurrection, has been "set free from sin" (see 6:6, 14, 18, 22). And Romans 8:2 makes it clear that the Spirit sets every believer free from the law of sin and death. For me, then, the decisive point is simply put: the assertions made in verses 14–25 cannot be true of a believer, and thus cannot be referring to Paul. That is why I think that Paul is describing what it was like to live as an unregenerate Jew under the law.

Before moving on, let me make three quick, but vital, points about my position. First, I again admit that other views can cite good evidence in their favor. I do not ignore this evidence, but I do conclude that it is not as decisive as the evidence in favor of my own interpretation. Second, I emphasize that Paul writes about Jewish experience. Verses 14–25 therefore follow on naturally from verses 7–12. If in his previous paragraph he wrote about the effect of the coming of the law on the Jewish people, he now writes about the continuing consequences of that law on the Jewish people. Third, I admit that verses 15–20, taken on their own, could describe the struggle with sin that even the best Christians continue to have. But what we must recognize is that the struggle depicted in these verses issues in defeat: imprisoned by the law of sin. This is

The Translator as Traitor: "Sinful Nature" in the NIV

In Romans 7:5, for the first time in the letter, we meet in the NIV translation the phrase "sinful nature." We meet the same rendering later in the chapter (see vv. 18, 25) and especially often in Romans 8 (see vv. 3, 4, 5, 8, 9, 12, 13). Behind this phrase, as the NIV footnote points out, is the Greek word *sarx*, "flesh." The NIV translators frequently have been criticized for this rendering. Why avoid a "literal" rendering and choose a phrase that might give rise to all kinds of unfortunate speculation, e.g., where is this "sinful nature" that we supposedly have? I raised precisely this question some years ago. Then, probably in very just irony, I was appointed to the NIV translation committee and asked to come up with a better rendering of this word in English. Only when I put myself in the seat of the translator did I begin to see the real issues. Two things need to be said.

First, we must understand better the nature of the translator's task. Many Christians think that translators go through a kind of mechanical "cut and paste" procedure, whereby we simply put the right English word in the place of the Greek word.

Anyone who has translated from one language into another knows how futile such a procedure would be. Words simply do not have the same spread of meaning in each language. A word in one language may have several distinct meanings, each of which is best represented with an individual word in another language. (A good example is the many Eskimo words for "snow.") Or one language may have a word for which another language simply does not have a good one-word equivalent. The point is that translation requires numerous difficult decisions. And while we can be confident that our modern English versions are generally accurate representations of the originals, none of them comes close to the "real thing," which is why scholars, pastors, and even some laypeople still learn Hebrew and Greek. Every translator, therefore, is something of a "traitor" to the original, making decisions that he or she knows cannot bring over the exact nuance of meaning.

Second, then, on "flesh." The New Testament uses the Greek word *sarx* to refer to the meat on the bones of a person or animal, human life or experience as such, and the

tendency to sin that is part of fallen human experience. The English "flesh" is a good equivalent to the first meaning (see, e.g., 1 Cor 15:39). But is it a good equivalent for the second two? The NIV translation committee doubts it. We think that people will tend to think of the first meaning when they see the English word "flesh." So when they read, for instance, "the flesh desires what is contrary to the Spirit" (Gal 5:17, in a literal rendering), we are concerned that they will think that it is only the physical body that is the problem. They may even narrow the idea down to sexual sin. This would not convey at all accurately the intention of Paul. So, faced with a decision to render *sarx* in places like this "flesh" (and thus possibly give a wrong impression about the nature of sin) or "sinful nature" (and give rise to unfortunate speculation about "natures"), the NIV committee opted for the latter. But the English reader should recognize that a difficult decision had to be made, and that behind "sinful nature" stands the Greek *sarx*, with a set of associations that might be important in getting at Paul's intention.

not the outcome of the Christian's struggle with sin.

As we saw, verse 13 is transitional. Verse 14 then establishes the fundamental contrast that Paul describes in these verses: the good law of God versus the sinful human being. The struggle that marks this contrast is described in verses 15–20 before Paul wraps up the narrative with a look back at the general state of affairs (vv. 21–25).

Paul has claimed that the law is "good" (v. 12), but he has not explained yet how something good could have been used by sin to produce death. This he will do in verses 14–25. His basic answer is that the law, though good and holy, was given to people who were not. Because people were under sin's power, the law could not be obeyed. And so it was that the law revealed sin for what it really is, turning even the good law of God into an instrument of death (v. 13). Paul neatly summarizes this situation in verse 14. The law may be "spiritual" (i.e., a divinely given, authoritative word), but "I" am "unspiritual, sold as a slave to sin." Interpreters who think that Paul describes his Christian experience in these verses argue that these words simply state the biblical and experiential truth that Christians, still under the influence of the old realm, continue to be attracted to sin. But the language is stronger than this. It implies a slavery to sin such as no Christian any longer experiences (see Romans 6).

In verses 15–20, Paul movingly depicts the effect of this tension in the life of sincere, torah-loving Jews. Jews agree that "the law is good" (v. 16). They want to obey it, but they find themselves constantly falling short of its demands. Of course, Paul does not mean that Jews always failed to do the law. Many of them lived exemplary lives, carrying out many of the law's demands even in difficult circumstances. But his point is that the obedience always falls short. No Jew has ever "done" the law perfectly. Every Jew who was at all sensitive to spiritual things sensed frustration at the failure to live up fully to the law's demands. Although not with respect to every command, nevertheless far too frequently, they saw all too clearly that their "doing" did not match their "willing." How can this difference be explained? It must be the effect of "sin living in me" (v. 17b). Paul again pictures sin as a power that holds sway over people outside of Christ. By claiming that it "lives in me," Paul may imply that sin is in a dominant position in this person's life. He says roughly the same thing at the end of verse 20: "It is no longer I who do it, but it is sin living in me that does it." This is not an attempt to avoid blame ("The devil made me do it!"). Rather, it is simply the recognition that there must be some explanation for the constant failure to do what one wills. That explanation is the power of sin. As we saw, verses 15–20, taken on their own, could describe the frustration of the Christian, alive to God and seeking to do his will yet constantly falling short of perfect conformity to that will. Paul makes very clear elsewhere that in this life believers will never be fully free of that struggle. And this is probably also the way we should explain verse 18a: "Nothing good lives in me, that is, in my sinful nature." "Sinful nature" is the NIV rendering of sarx, "flesh." But why does Paul qualify his absolute claim with this

Study Questions

1. Why does Paul describe God's law as an agent of sin?

2. What might Paul mean when he claims that believers have been "released from the law" (v. 6)? How have theologians explained this release?

3. What experience does Paul describe in verses 7–12? Describe and analyze three different possibilities.

4. What specific ways might we apply Paul's teaching about the law in Romans 7? Cite specific examples from your own experience.

reference to "flesh"? Some scholars claim that this addition shows that Paul is describing a Christian. He wants to make clear that the believer is subject to sin's influence only in the sinful nature that still remains. This could make sense of the text, but it is also possible that Paul wants to explain why "nothing good" dwells in this person: he or she is still dominated by the flesh.

If verses 15–20 might apply to the Christian, the same cannot be said of verses 21–25. In these verses Paul draws a conclusion from the struggle that he has depicted in these earlier verses. That conclusion is that the person undergoing that struggle finally is defeated by sin and can be rescued only by Jesus Christ. Paul begins by citing a "law": "When I want to do good, evil is right there with me" (v. 21). This is one of the few places in Romans that Paul uses the word *nomos* to mean something other than the law of Moses. Here it must mean something like "rule" or "principle." The principle neatly summarizes what Paul has described in verses 15–20. Verses 22–23 elaborate. Paul contrasts two "laws" that govern the situation: the "law of God," which Paul further describes as the "law of his mind"; and the "law of sin," the law "at work within my members." Scholars debate the nuance of the word "law" in these verses. All agree that the "law of God" in verse 22 is the Mosaic law or, perhaps, divine law in general. And almost all also think that the "law of the mind" in verse 23 is but another way of describing this law. As Paul has made clear, the person he describes in these verses knows God's law to be good and seeks to do it. His or her "mind" is fully committed to the law of God. The debate centers on the identity of the other, contrasting, law. More and

more interpreters in recent years are attracted to the idea that this "law of sin" might also be the law of Moses. Paul would call it the law of sin because it has been used by sin to produce death (see vv. 7–12).[9] But I think that this interpretation is unlikely. The most natural way to interpret Paul's reference to "another law" is that he refers to a law different from the law of Moses, not to the same law from a different perspective. So it is better to think of the "law of sin" as a rhetorical play on words. Opposed to God's law, the claim he exerts on his people, is another "law," a claim exerted on us by sin. These laws oppose one another. But God's law, Paul concludes, is unable to overcome this law of sin. The result? "I . . . am a prisoner of the law of sin."

This objective conclusion is a key reason why I think that the "I" Paul describes here cannot be a Christian. Believers are no longer held captive by "the law of sin" (Rom 8:2). They have been delivered from sin's authority and death-dealing power through Jesus Christ. It is this deliverance that Paul celebrates in verses 24–25a. Apart from Christ, he is "wretched," but God has delivered him from that state of dejection and defeat through Jesus Christ the Lord. Paul, looking back on his past life and reflecting on its struggles and tensions, cannot restrain himself from celebrating the victory he has experienced in Christ. Verse 25a is an interruption in the narrative, a skipping ahead to the victory that Paul knows has already been won. In verse 25b, then, he reverts back to his main line of thought, summarizing the dividedness that he has depicted so movingly in this passage. The mind stands in tension with the "flesh" ("sinful nature" in the NIV). The one follows God's law, the other the law of sin.

12 Life and Hope through the Spirit

Romans 8:1–39

Outline

- The Spirit of Life (8:1–13)
- The Spirit of Adoption (8:14–17)
- The Spirit of Glory (8:18–30)
- Response: Celebration of Our Security in Christ (8:31–39)

Objectives

After reading this chapter, you should be able to

1. Explain the contribution that Romans 8 makes to Paul's presentation of the gospel in Romans.
2. Appreciate the benefits conferred on the believer by the ministry of the Spirit.
3. Identify and explain three key sources of support given to us by God in our time of anticipation.
4. Rejoice in the security provided for the believer by God in Christ.

Conspicuous by absence so far in Romans has been the Spirit of God. Paul mentions the Spirit only four times before chapter 8 (1:4; 2:29; 5:5; 7:6), but he now makes up for that absence. He uses the word "spirit" (*pneuma*) twenty-one times in Romans 8, and all but two (vv. 15a, 16b) refer to the Holy Spirit. However, the Spirit, although the constant motif in Romans 8, is not really Paul's topic. That is, Paul does not actually tell us much about the Spirit as such; he tells us about what the Spirit does. And what the Spirit does is mediate to Christians the life and hope that have been the key themes since Romans 5. The Spirit applies the work of God in Christ to us so that we can enjoy life, both new spiritual life in the present and resurrection life in the future (vv. 1–13). The Spirit makes us aware that we are God's own children and that as his children we can expect a wonderful inheritance some day (vv. 14–17). And the Spirit causes us to groan at the present time, manifesting our frustration at not yet experiencing the glory to which we are infallibly destined (vv. 18–30). This work of the Spirit is an elaboration of 7:6, where Paul briefly introduced the life of the Spirit before launching into his excursus about the law. As 7:7–25 elaborates the situation that Paul has described in 7:5—controlled by the sinful nature, with the law arousing sinful passions—so 8:1–30 depicts the status of the believer as one who serves "in the new way of the Spirit" (7:6).

The Spirit of Life (8:1–13)

Paul refers to the "Spirit of life" in verse 2, and this title points to the theme of these verses. Through the Spirit we enjoy new spiritual life, having been rescued from the condemnation due our sin in Adam (vv. 1–4); through the Spirit we learn to live in ways pleasing to him and to God (vv. 5–8); through the Spirit God will raise our bodies from the dead (vv. 9–11); and through the Spirit we are to kill off the lifestyle of sin so that we can enjoy the

life of God forever (vv. 12–13). In contrast to the divisions found in some Bibles and commentaries, then, verses 12–13 should be kept with verses 1–11. Verses 12–13 bring the section on the Spirit of life to a fitting conclusion by reminding us that God's gift of the Spirit must be appropriated and used if we truly are to enjoy the life brought by the Spirit.

Verses 1–4 restate and elaborate the central truth of Romans 5:12–21 in light of chapter 7. In Romans 5:12–21, Paul has taught that believers belong to Jesus Christ and therefore are rescued from the condemnation that all people suffer in Adam. So, in 8:1, Paul proclaims that "those who are in Christ Jesus" need not fear condemnation.[1] Paul explains why this is so by referring to the believer's freedom from "the law of sin and death" (v. 2)—an unmistakable reference to the situation that Paul has delineated in 7:7–25. As is the case in 7:22–23, Paul's use of "law" language in 8:2 has stimulated vigorous debate. "The law of sin and death" at the end of the verse could well refer to the law of Moses, for it is precisely in these terms that Paul has described the law in Romans 7. Sin has used the law to bring death (cf. 7:5). But in 7:23, the phrase "law of sin" refers to a power or authority exercised by sin. That probably is what Paul means here as well. "The law of sin and death" is the immutable divine "rule" that those who sin must die. We are set free from that law by "the law of the Spirit of life." Again, this could refer to the Mosaic law, as it functions in the realm of the Spirit.[2] But Paul does not present the law as a liberating force, and the contrast between Spirit and law in texts such as 2:28–29 and 7:6 also makes it difficult to think that he associates them here. Probably, then, this first "law" also means "rule" or "principle."

In verse 3, however, "what the law was powerless to do in that it was weakened by the sinful nature" certainly refers to the law of Moses. The phrase is a tidy summary of the basic message of Romans 7. Despite its divine origin and innate goodness, the law of Moses could not rescue human beings from the nexus of sin and death, because human beings are helpless captives to the power of this world. So another way to redeem human beings must be found, and God has found that way through his Son. He sent him "in the likeness of sinful man." This phrase neatly balances two important facets of the incarnate Son. First, Jesus became fully human. He did not just "appear" to be a man (the "docetic" heresy); he truly was man. Paul therefore emphasizes that Jesus took on the likeness of *sinful man*. Second, Jesus never sinned. Paul therefore says that Jesus took on the *likeness* of sinful man. But not only did God send Jesus to earth as a man; he also sent him as a "sin offering."[3] Jesus was given over to death as a sacrifice to take care of our sin problem. To paraphrase an ancient theological truth: Jesus became what we are so that we might become what he is. God condemned sin in Jesus (v. 3) so that we would not have to be condemned (v. 1).

The upshot of God's work in Christ is that the "righteous requirement of the law might be fully met in us" (v. 4). I have deliberately modified the NIV here to bring out what I think is the sense of this phrase. The Greek behind "righteous requirement" is a singular noun *(dikaiōma)*, so the NIV's "righteous requirements" is an interpretive paraphrase. Paul chooses the singular word to stress that the totality of the law's demands is fulfilled in us when we come to Christ. Probably lying behind his statement is again the idea of Christ as our substitute. He fulfilled the law perfectly. When we are in him, therefore, God views us also as having fulfilled the law perfectly. No longer can we be condemned for failing to do the law; in Christ, we have done it. This passage is not only a wonderful summary of the work of God on our behalf, but also one of those many New Testament passages that hint at the doctrine of the Trinity. Note how each of the persons of the Godhead is involved in securing our redemption from sin: God the Father sends the Son, whose work is applied to our lives by the Holy Spirit.

At the end of verse 4, Paul introduces a contrast that dominates verses 5–9: the Holy Spirit versus the flesh. (The NIV again paraphrases *sarx*, "flesh," with "sinful nature.") When I first read these verses many years ago in another version of the Bible, I thought that Paul was contrasting my own flesh, my material side, with my spirit, that part of me open to the spiritual realm. This idea of a division between two parts of the human being ("anthropological dualism") has a long history in Western culture. But certainly this text is not talking about any kind of division within human beings. As all modern English versions recognize by capitalizing "Spirit," Paul is referring not to some part of the human being but to God's Holy Spirit. And even the "flesh" is not so much a part of us as an influence or force. Hence, Paul can describe Christians as people who are no longer "in the flesh" (a literal rendering of v. 9a). So the contrast in these verses is between two different influences. People apart from Christ, Paul claims, are dominated by the flesh, while believers are dominated by the Spirit. He expresses this point in three contrasts, which move from the sphere of "position" to "mind-set" to "lifestyle":

> Position: being "in the flesh" versus being "in the Spirit" (vv. 8–9a)
> Mind-set: the mind of the flesh versus the mind of the Spirit (vv. 5b–7)
> Lifestyle: living according to the flesh versus living according to the Spirit (vv. 4b–5a)

A progression is obvious. All believers are "in the Spirit" (NIV: "controlled" by the Spirit in v. 9). Anyone who belongs to Christ has the Spirit of God dwelling in him or her. And the person in whom the Spirit dwells—in a startling shift of the metaphor—is "in the Spirit." These are two ways of saying the same thing: the Christian is one who is now dominated by God's Spirit. To use the salvation-historical imagery that is so basic to Romans 5–8: we have been transferred from the realm of the flesh and put into the realm of the Spirit. As people who now belong to that realm, we need to mold our thinking in accordance with our identity.

First-century tomb with the stone rolled away. (John McRay)

We need to cultivate the "mind" or, better, "mind-set" of the Spirit. And once we do that, Paul suggests, our behavior will follow as a matter of course. A mind focused on the Spirit's values will inevitably produce a lifestyle that pleases the Spirit. As he does so often (see, e.g., Rom 12:1–2), Paul highlights the cultivation of a Christ-centered, Spirit-filled mind as the critical step in holy living.

The Spirit creates in us new spiritual existence (vv. 1–4a), leads us into a new lifestyle (vv. 4b–9), and ultimately will raise our bodies from the dead (vv. 10–11). Paul acknowledges a reality at the beginning of verse 10 that he never ignores for long in his discussion of the Christian life: the incomplete nature of God's work in history and in us. With Christ's death and resurrection and the coming of the Spirit, the new age of salvation has begun. However, since the old age of sin and death has not yet been ended, we believers live in the "overlap" of the ages. We belong to the new age, and our futures now are determined by that fact, but we

are still influenced by the old age, and we still must face physical death. Nevertheless, though the body still is "dead because of sin," "the Spirit is life because of righteousness." Again I depart from the NIV (cf. the NRSV), which takes *pneuma* here to refer to our own spirit. But it is better, in a paragraph full of references to the Holy Spirit, to maintain that meaning if possible.[4] And indeed, the passage makes better sense this way. For it is the Holy Spirit, according to verse 11, through whom God will raise our bodies from the dead. It would be quite natural, then, for Paul to refer to this same Spirit in verse 10 as the animating power that now resides within us. Our bodies must die, but the power of that Spirit within us will not let the body remain dead.

As we noted, many Bibles and commentaries do not include verses 12–13 with verses 1–11. This is a mistake, because these verses strike an appropriate balance with the focus of verses 1–11. These first eleven verses have stressed what God through the Spirit has done for

Final Salvation and Christian Obedience

What Paul says in Romans 8:12–13 might disturb some believers because, as I have interpreted those verses, Paul claims that we will be saved in the last day ("you will live") only if we use God's Spirit to conquer sins. Does not this make obedience, or "works," necessary for salvation? And does not this emphasis also undercut any belief in eternal security? Those who hold to **Arminianism,** of course, would have no problem if the latter were true. They stress that our eventual salvation is not certain, that it depends on our will to remain in the grace of God. But how would those who hold to **Calvinism,** believing in eternal security, handle these verses? And what do we do about the focus on "works"?

As both a Calvinist and someone who believes that we are saved by faith alone, let me suggest answers to these questions. First, we should distinguish, as theologians usually do, between an "effective" cause and an "instrumental" cause. We are saved on the basis of God's work in Christ; this is the only ultimate basis for our salvation. Our faith effectively applies the benefits of that work to us. But works, as James so eloquently stresses (Jas 2:14–26), are the inevitable fruit of true faith. Works do not save us; nor, strictly speaking, does our faith. God saves us in Christ. But faith is the instrumental means by which we appropriate God's salvation, and works, since they must follow faith, also can be said to be a condition (if not, strictly, a cause) of our salvation. What Paul says here, then, about the need for believers to put sin to death if we are to live is in keeping with what the New Testament teaches elsewhere and fits the standard orthodox Christian view of salvation.

Where Arminians and Calvinists differ is on whether the genuine Christian will inevitably produce these saving works. Arminians insist that believers still have the will to resist the work of God's Spirit. They therefore might decide to abandon God's grace and thus never produce those works that lead to eternal life. Calvinists, on the other hand, think that God's Spirit has become so powerful in the believer's life that the Christian cannot ultimately thwart the Spirit's intention to produce fruit pleasing to God. But the Calvinist would want to add quickly that this certainly takes nothing from the need for Christians to be active in using the Spirit to put sin to death. As a Calvinist, I believe in the "perseverance of the saints," but I believe equally that it is the saints who will persevere. We manifest our status as saints by actively advancing in Godlikeness through the help of the Spirit.

Arminianism

Calvinism

us. Now Paul will conclude by reminding us that we still have to respond through that same Spirit. We find here again, in other words, the balance between "indicative" and "imperative" that we noticed in chapter 6. Certainly Paul wants to encourage us by reminding us of all that God has done for us and all that God will do for us. We are secure in him and have a certain hope for the future. Yet Paul never wants that security to breed complacency. He does not want believers to sit back and rest, thinking that God has taken care of it all. Response on our part is still necessary. And so, while he can proclaim the "life" that the Spirit has won for us, Paul now reminds us that we will never experience that life unless we are growing in holiness. We are to use the Spirit to "put to death" the continuing sinful patterns of behavior from the old life. Only as we do so will we find life.

The Spirit of Adoption (8:14–17)

These four brief verses provide an effective transition from the believer's pres-

Coin depicting the emperor Augustus, who was adopted by Julius Caesar. (Ben Witherington III)

ent (vv. 1–13) to his or her future (vv. 18–30). Following a pattern that he uses elsewhere (cf. esp. Gal 4:3–7), Paul connects the Christian's past redemption from the penalty of the law to his or her future joy in heaven by means of status as a child of God. Being a child of God, Paul argues, also means being God's heir. God adopts people from the world and puts them in a new relationship to himself. God has not yet, however, given us everything he is planning to give us. A wonderful inheritance has been promised us. Again, then, Paul highlights the tension in which we Christians live: redeemed, justified, adopted, but not yet glorified.

Verse 14 can be connected quite directly to verse 13 (as in the NIV), but the shift of focus from "life" (the dominant motif in vv. 1–13) to "adoption"/"sons of God" (vv. 14–17) suggests, rather, a paragraph break between verses 13 and 14. The idea of adoption is taken from the Greco-Roman world. Greeks and especially Romans made adoption an important legal institution. A person could adopt a child, and that child would become the legal heir to everything that the adopting person owned. The Roman emperor Julius Caesar, for instance, adopted a young man named Octavian, who became by that act the heir to the Roman Empire. Eventually he became emperor, changing his name to Augustus. In a similar manner, Paul suggests, God, the ruler of this universe, has adopted us as his heirs. But we should not miss another set of background echoes in this

passage. The Old Testament frequently describes Israel, God's chosen people, as his "son(s)" or children (Ex 4:22; Dt 14:1; Is 43:6; Jer 3:19; Hos 1:10; 11:1). So, when Paul says that believers who are led by God's Spirit are God's sons, he is also saying that believers are now God's people. They become what Israel used to be. One begins to see why Paul has to clarify the situation of Israel, as he does in Romans 9–11.

The Spirit, of course, continues to be a dominant element in Paul's argument. Those who belong to the Spirit are God's sons (v. 14). And the Spirit also makes us actively aware of the status as God's children that we believers enjoy (vv. 15–16). The Spirit we have received is not one who leads to slavery or fear. The Spirit of God witnesses to us that we are indeed the children of God. Thus, we can follow Jesus in crying out spontaneously to God, "Abba, Father" (see Mk 14:36). "Abba" is the Aramaic word for "father," or "dad." Contrary to the claim of some scholars, Jews occasionally did use this title to refer to God. But it was not common. The title had enough intimate family associations (some paraphrase it as "daddy") that it was the perfect way to convey the believer's new intimate relationship to God. But Paul ends the paragraph by reminding us again that this relationship has not yet been consummated. As heirs of God, we are destined for the glory that is particularly his (v. 17; cf. 3:23; 5:2). In order to attain that glory, however, we must walk the same road that our forerunner, Christ, walked. He did not attain the glory of resurrection until he had suffered. So also is it for us who belong to him. We cannot expect to share in his glory if we do not share in his suffering. As participants in the new age, we look forward confidently to the glory that awaits us, but still we live out our lives in the old age of sin, sickness, and death. Suffering of various kinds is therefore bound to come our way. Only by carrying the cross will we win the crown.

inclusio

The Spirit of Glory (8:18–30)

Verse 17 has introduced the topic of verses 18–30: the glory that one day will be ours. Paul begins the passage by drawing our gaze to the "glory that will be revealed in us" (v. 18); he ends it with a similar emphasis: "those he justified, he also glorified" (v. 30). These statements form an **inclusio.** That is, Paul implies that the material "included" between these assertions is all oriented to the glory destined for believers. Paul makes two basic points about this glory. First, it is the climax of God's plan for the world and for his people (vv. 18–25). Second, God provides the means for us to attain that glory (vv. 26–30).

Paul begins by picking up the theme of verse 17. Believers must suffer with Christ if they are to share his glory. But now Paul brings these two into perspective with one another. However severe and prolonged that suffering might be, it cannot compare with the glory that is to come. As I noted in the introduction to chapters 5–8, the beginning and ending of these chapters have a lot in common. Both 5:1–11 and 8:18–39 focus on the believer's hope for glory, and they both indicate that our hope for glory springs from God's work in Christ, his love for us, and the power of the Holy Spirit. However, both passages also are realistic about the difficulties that believers will have to face before they reach that glory. In 5:3–4, Paul reminded us that God has a purpose in the suffering he allows into our lives. Here he simply puts that suffering into perspective. And we gain even more perspective on the overwhelming prospect of glory when we realize that the entire created world will be caught up in the glory that God one day will give us. To be sure, some interpreters doubt that Paul refers to the created world in verses 19–21. They note that Paul uses language about "creation" that does not apply very well to the nonhuman creation: it "waits," "was subjected to frustration," and "groans." So, it is argued, Paul must be referring to willful creatures—either angels or human beings or both.[5] But "creation" (ktisis) is not a normal way of referring to human beings, and there is good precedent for such language being applied to the subhuman creation in the Old Testament. The psalms, for instance, speak of hills, meadows, and valleys "shouting and singing together for joy" (Ps 65:12–13). Paul effectively uses this literary device to portray the "fall" and anticipated "redemption" of what we would call nature. As Paul reminds us (v. 20), the earth itself was subject to a curse when Adam and Eve fell into sin (Gn 3:17–18). It was "subject to frustration": it did not reach its original created goal of being a place where people could dwell securely and with minimal labor. This frustration, however, was not its own fault, but the fault of "the one who subjected it"—almost certainly God, who uttered the sentence of the curse.[6] Because of this frustration, therefore, nature eagerly awaits the day when the children of God will be glorified, for on that day, it will share in that glory (vv. 19, 21). What Paul says in these verses is important for our theology of nature (see the sidebar "How 'Green' Was Paul?"). But his overall purpose in this context is to show how wonderful is the grace that believers one day will enjoy.

Paul has another purpose as well, and this purpose, hinted at in verse 19, emerges clearly in verses 22–23. In verse 19, Paul claimed that nature "waits in eager expectation." Here the NIV tries to capture some of the power of Paul's Greek, in which he speaks of nature "craning its neck" to see what might be coming next. Verse 22 returns to this theme in light of nature's "frustration" and "bondage" (vv. 20, 21). Creation, because of its longing for liberation, "groans as in the pains of childbirth." The pain of an expectant mother is a natural and common biblical metaphor for hope (see Mk 13:8; Jn 16:20–22), for the pain of childbirth has a joyful outcome. "Groaning" captures this dual notion. It expresses both the pain of suffering and the longing for deliverance. In verse 23, then, we reach the main point: Christians also "groan." For they are in a situation just like the one that the whole created world is in: suffering at the present time and longing for the deliverance yet to come. Significantly, here Paul also brings the Spirit back into the picture. Paul often pictures the Spirit as the bridge between the believer's present and future, between initial salvation and final salvation. As Paul has made clear, Christians have already been made children of God (vv. 14–17). Yet now he can claim that we "wait eagerly for our adoption as sons." No better expression of the typical New

How "Green" Was Paul?

Few movements have had as strong an impact on modern society as environmentalism. Yet Christians have had difficulty coming to grips with the movement and are only now beginning to develop a better theological approach to the subject. Undoubtedly, one of the reasons Christians have responded rather uncertainly to environmentalism is that the New Testament simply does not have much to say about the natural world. Thus, quite a lot of attention has been given to Romans 8:19–21, because it is one of the few New Testament passages that says anything at all about nature. What can we conclude from these verses?

Two points of relevance to this matter might be noted. First, Paul accords significance to nature as such. The natural world, he says, is destined for glory. It has a future and therefore is clearly important in its own right. Second, the future of nature illustrates and is in some sense subordinate to the future of Christians. Nature will share in the freedom from bondage that will characterize the people of God in glory. These two points suggest that

Paul would steer something of a middle course between two extremes often found in current attitudes about environmental issues. At the one extreme are those who make nature equal in importance to human beings. Edward Abbey, one of the most famous of the radical environmentalists, once claimed that he would rather kill a human being than a snake. Indeed, powerful voices in our culture suggest that we have no reason to think that the human species is more important than any other. Paul, however, reflects in these verses the biblical perspective that human beings, and they only, were created in God's image. We have a right, based on Scripture, to give precedence to human beings.

Sadly, however, this legitimate biblical insight is used by some Christians to justify the other extreme: dismissing or downplaying concern for nature. God's charge to our human parents to "subdue" the earth (Gn 1:28) is taken to mean that we have the right to use the world of nature in any way we choose. The

upshot is that some Christians teach that human needs and wants take precedence over the good of the natural world. We have a right, they argue, to exploit nature for our own good—defined quite broadly to include a high standard of living, with its demand for cheap energy and the comforts of big cars, big houses, and easy access to wilderness. But such an attitude stands in basic tension with the biblical emphasis, reflected here by Paul, that nature was created by God and has value in its own right. Our attitude toward nature should not be one of exploitation but of stewardship. Paul, I am convinced, was a lot "greener" than many Christians have recognized.[1]

1. See F. van Dyke et al., *Redeeming Creation: The Biblical Basis for Environmental Stewardship* (Downers Grove, Ill.: InterVarsity, 1996). For a helpful taxonomy of Christian attitudes toward the environment, see R. E. Grizzle, P. E. Rothrock, and C. B. Barrett, "Evangelicals and Environmentalism: Past, Present, and Future," *Trinity Journal* 19 (1998): 3–27.

Testament tension between the "already" and the "not yet" could be found. We are already God's children, adopted into his family, but we are not yet his children in the full sense. We do not yet perfectly manifest our Father's character or share in all the blessings he bestows on his family. This means that we have to wait. The blessings that we already enjoy make the wait, in one sense at least, even more difficult. Here Paul calls the Spirit the "first-fruits," implying that the Spirit is the pledge of many more blessings to come. Experiencing some of those blessings makes us eager for more of them. Paul reminds us that as Christians, we never should be feeling at home here on earth. We are pilgrims here, passing through on the way to our true homeland, heaven (see Phil 3:20–21). While God in his common grace gives us many delightful experiences here on earth, our lives always will be marred by the many remaining effects of the fall: ruptured relationships, difficult work, disease, death. Furthermore, for believers, our time here also will be marred by a sense of futility at not living up to the goals that God has set for us.

In brief, Paul has been saying, "We live in hope," and it is on this note that he concludes this paragraph (vv. 24–25). We were saved "in hope." By this Paul apparently means that hope has been a part of what our salvation involves from the beginning. Salvation always is a two-part experience: coming to Christ is the first and decisive stage, but ultimate deliverance from sin and death is the second stage (see 5:9–10), and that, of course, does not come until the return of Christ in glory. Thus, hope is not merely an option for the believer; it is a necessary part of what it means to be a Christian. We are people who are always looking forward to what is yet to come. But, Paul concludes, we are to "wait patiently." The Greek underlying the word "patiently" (di' hypomonēs) contains the idea of endurance. We need to learn to bear up under the suffering that will be ours in this life.

In verses 26–30, Paul tells us three things that God is doing to support us in our time of patient waiting. We might summarize these (somewhat homiletically) as (1) prayer (vv. 26–27), (2) providence (v. 28), and (3) predestination (vv. 29–30).

"In the same way" might suggest that we should connect verses 26–27 with verses 22–23: as creation "groans" (v. 22) and Christians "groan" (v. 23), so also the Spirit "groans" (v. 26).[7] There is, however, no real parallel between the groaning of the Spirit and that of creation and believers. So it is better to draw a connection between verses 24–25 and verses 26–27: as hope sustains Christians in their waiting, so also does the Spirit. How does the Spirit help us? By interceding for us in prayer when we do not know how to pray. One of our limitations in this life is our inability always to know what the will of God might be. We are not sure what major to pursue, or what job to take, or whom to marry. How can we pray? What should we pray for? In such situations, Paul teaches, the Spirit comes to our aid. The Spirit intercedes for us "with groans that words cannot express." The NIV nicely preserves the ambiguity of the original. Are the "groans" of the Holy Spirit inaudible, or are they simply incapable of being put into normal human words? In the former case, Paul might be teaching that the intercession of the Spirit goes on in our hearts, without our even knowing it. In the latter case, the Spirit's intercession might take the form of utterances as we pray. Some have thought of speaking in tongues,[8] but Paul's implication that all believers experience this intercessory ministry of the Spirit weighs against that idea. More likely, if the groans are audible, Paul thinks of the way in which we sometimes will moan as we pray, uncertain of what words to use as we try to formulate our prayers out loud. Whatever the exact mechanism, the Spirit's intercession is an extremely valuable resource. While we always should seek to know God's will and pray accordingly, we do not have to be worried that we always do so perfectly. As we

election

pray, not knowing just what to ask for, God's Spirit is there, praying for us. And even when we pray for the wrong thing, we are assured that the Spirit is praying for us and that the Spirit's prayer is in perfect accord with the will of God (v. 27).

The promise of verse 28 is one of the most well known in the Bible, and rightly so. The verse beautifully expresses the providential care of God for his children. But we need to look carefully at the verse to determine precisely what this promise is, and what it is not. Four issues need to be tackled. First, who is it that is "working for the good"? The NIV makes God the subject, but the word "God" is not in the best manuscripts, and so other options are possible. The Revised English Bible makes the Spirit the subject—a good option in light of the emphasis on the Spirit throughout this chapter. The NRSV translates, "all things work together for good." While a decision is not easy, this last rendering probably is best. But, of course, "all things work together for good" only because God, by his Spirit, so directs them.

A second issue is the exact meaning of the word translated "work" in the NIV. As the NRSV rendering reveals, the verb also can be translated "work together." In this case, some suggest, the promise in this verse relates to the way God brings various circumstances together in our lives to produce good. But this nuance is doubtful, and so we probably should go with the NIV rendering.

Third, what is the "good" toward which all things are working? Given the context, Paul undoubtedly thinks of our final salvation (see vv. 18, 30). However, we should probably not limit the good to our final glory only; it will also include the many blessings that God wants to give us in this life. Having said that, we must be very careful not to interpret "good" in a selfish or even material fashion. Although all things that touch the life of a Christian are used by God for our good, that good will often be an ultimate spiritual good. So God might allow us to lose a good job in order to create the "good" of a deeper commitment to him. He might

allow us to suffer a physical disability in a car accident so that we learn to depend on him more than ever. The verse does not promise a better job or restored health.

Fourth, for whom is this promise valid? For "those who love him, who have been called according to his purpose." This is a way of describing Christians from both the divine vantage point (God calls us) and the human vantage point (we love God). The "call" here is God's own irresistible summons to enter into the salvation won for us by Christ.

The final support Paul mentions in our period of patient waiting is predestination. While the notion is quite controversial, the word "predestination" in its general sense simply means that God has destined us beforehand for a certain end. That end, as the climax of verses 29–30 reveals, is glory. All the other things that God does for us that Paul mentions in these verses lead up to this final stage of glory. A certain sequence is obvious. God's activity on our behalf begins with his "foreknowing." As is usually the case with this kind of language in Scripture, the reference is to God's decision to enter into intimate fellowship with someone (see Acts 2:23; Rom 11:2; 1 Pt 1:2, 1:20). When God "knows" a person, he does not learn some information about that person; rather, he comes into relationship with that person. Note, for instance, Amos 3:2: "You only have I chosen ['known' in the Hebrew and the Greek] of all the families of the earth." "Foreknowing" is another way, then, of speaking of God's choosing, or **election.** Paul therefore is elaborating the notion of God's "call" that he mentioned at the end of verse 28. "Foreknowing" leads to "predestining." This word, as I suggested, emphasizes the purpose or result of God's choosing. In this case, that end is that we should be "conformed to the image of [God's] son." In this context, that refers to our being glorified with Christ (see vv. 17, 30). God's predestining leads to his calling (see v. 28), his calling to his justifying, and his justifying to his glorifying. These verses are justly famous for their theological teaching. Calvinists especially use them to buttress two of their key doctrines: God's unconditional election and eternal security. Although these verses do imply those two doctrines, the key point, as I have emphasized, comes at the end: God is determined to bring all those who belong to him to glory. He has decided it; we can depend on it. What stronger support for our confident hope could we ever find?

Response: Celebration of Our Security in Christ (8:31–39)

This renowned reminder of God's enduring love and faithfulness is a fitting conclusion to Romans 5–8. In these chapters Paul hammers home the truth that believers have absolute assurance for the future. God has transferred us from the realm of Adam, sin, and death into the realm of Christ, righteousness, and life. Although the old realm has not been eradicated and still has the power to attract us away from the path to righteousness and life, nothing can stand in the way of our ultimate salvation. We have a "hope of glory" (5:2) that can withstand any challenge. Most of us associate the language of 8:31–39 with funerals. While the reminder that nothing can separate us from God's love for us in Christ is certainly appropriate when we are dealing with the death of a loved one or friend, this same reminder is equally important at every juncture of life. Facing the doubts, uncertainties, and difficulties of a world hostile to God and his values, we constantly need the reassurance that "God is for us."

The question that opens this paragraph—"What, then, shall we say in response to this?"—relates to the whole of Romans 5–8. Paul now invites us to sit back and contemplate the spiritual implications of the theology he has taught in these chapters. He divides his response into two parts: verses 31–34 focus on God's work for us in Christ; verses 35–39

focus on God's love for us in Christ. Judicial language dominates verses 31–34, as Paul brings before us a law court scene. Accusations are being brought against us. The prosecuting attorney is bringing charges against us (v. 33), seeking to condemn us (v. 34). But standing in defense is God himself. He has chosen us; he has justified us (v. 33; cf. v. 30). Nobody can overcome such a defense. Paul builds this teaching on a passage from Isaiah:

> He who vindicates me is near.
>> Who then will bring charges
>>> against me?
>> Let us face each other!
> Who is my accuser?
>> Let him confront me!
> It is the sovereign Lord who helps
>> me.
>> Who is he that will condemn
>>> me? (Is 50:8–9a)

Paul, of course, knows that both Satan and some human beings will be "against us." His point is that no one can stand against us successfully. As Chrysostom, one of the greatest preachers in the early church, comments,

> Yet those that be against us, so far are they from thwarting us at all, that even without their will they become to us the causes of crowns, and procurers of countless blessings, so that God's wisdom turns their plots unto our salvation and glory. See how really no one is against us![9]

And not only do we have God to defend us; we also have Jesus Christ to intercede on our behalf (v. 34). God demonstrates his commitment to us in sending his own Son to die for us (v. 32). If he has done that, surely we can depend on him to provide all that is necessary to bring us to glory (note the parallel here with 5:9–10). Christ has died as a sacrifice for our sins and been raised to enter a new and powerful mode of existence. He stands ever ready to intercede for God's people.

In verses 35–39, the focus turns to God's love for us in Christ. At the beginning of this paragraph Paul asks, "Who shall sep-

141

arate us from the love of Christ?" At the end of the paragraph he answers the question: nothing "will be able to separate us from the love of God that is in Christ Jesus our Lord." As he has done throughout Romans 5–8, Paul takes a very realistic view of the difficulties that believers will have to face in this life. He specifically refers to "trouble," "hardship," "persecution," "famine," "nakedness," "danger," and the "sword" (v. 35). This list is somewhat similar to lists of difficulties that Paul himself faced during his apostolic ministry (see 2 Cor 11:23–27; 12:10). Paul speaks from experience. He has suffered many of the hardships he mentions here, and he can confidently claim that they will be unable to take the believer away from God's love

Key Terms

Arminianism

Calvinism

inclusio

election

in Christ. Indeed, through Christ, "the one who loved us," we can be "more than conquerors" (v. 37). Just to make sure that we get the point, Paul concludes by listing a wide variety of possible challenges to our love relationship with God. The two states of existence, death and life, cannot interfere with that relationship. Nor can any spiritual power disrupt the union of the believer with Christ. "Angels and demons" summarize the whole spiritual realm. "Demons" in the NIV translates *archai* ("rulers"), a word that Paul uses to describe evil spiritual beings (cf. Eph 6:12; Col 2:15). But why mention angels as a possible threat to God's love for us? Perhaps because Paul knows that Christians can be distracted from their allegiance and worship of God by a preoccupation with other spiritual beings (such a situation seems to have existed in Colossae [see Col 2:6–23]). "Powers" (*dynameis*) later in the verse also refers to spiritual beings. "Present" and "future" cover, of course, the temporal realm. "Height" and "depth" in verse 39 also might refer to various spiritual beings, considered by ancient people to inhabit the regions above and below the horizon. But Paul's usage elsewhere (Eph 3:18) suggests that he uses the terms with a simple spatial reference. Paul mentions every possible sphere of existence in order to make absolutely clear that nothing in all creation can interfere with God's love for us in Christ.

Study Questions

1. Explain the relationship between Romans 8 and the argument of the letter up to this point.

2. List and contemplate the blessings that the Spirit bestows on the believer, according to Romans 8.

3. How can Paul say both that we are now children of God (vv. 14–17) and that we still wait for adoption as God's children (v. 23)? What does this teach us about the New Testament theological perspective? What significance should this perspective have for our understanding of the Christian life?

4. How do verses 19–21 contribute to our theology of nature?

5. Why do Calvinists like Romans 8:29–30? What conclusions do they draw from these verses? How might one respond to their claims about these verses?

Part

5

Encountering the Relationship between Israel and the Gospel

Romans 9:1–11:36

13 Israel and the Plan of God

Romans 9:1–29

Outline

- **The Problem: The Conflict between God's Promises and Israel's Plight (9:1–5)**
- **The Nature of God's Promise to Israel (9:6–29)**

    God's Call and the Patriarchs (9:6–13)

    Excursus: The Justice of God (9:14–23)

    God's Call and the Prophets (9:24–29)

Objectives

After reading this chapter, you should be able to

1. Explain Paul's purpose in Romans 9–11 and relate that purpose to the theme and development of the letter.
2. Appreciate afresh the sovereignty of God in working out his plans in the world.
3. Identify at least two different ways that we can relate Paul's argument about God's call of Israel to God's election of individuals to salvation.
4. Explain your own position (however tentative) on the issue mentioned in no. 3.

Memorial sculpture expressing the suffering Jews endured during the Holocaust. (Chris Miller)

bicovenantalism

Sonderweg

The Holocaust—the Nazi slaughter of Jews during World War II—has left a lasting legacy. The world is still coming to grips with this shattering reminder of humankind's ability to act inhumanely. For Christians, the Holocaust presents special problems. Some Jews and some Christians claim that the Holocaust is a natural, albeit extreme, outcome of traditional Christian theology, for Christians historically have taught that they have taken the place of the Jews as the chosen people of God. The Jews disenfranchised themselves by refusing to acknowledge Jesus as the Messiah. Indeed, they hounded him to death. By denying that Jews can claim to be God's people any more, therefore, Christian theology opens the door to anti-Semitism and even persecution. Christian theologians have reacted in three ways to this analysis. Some see it as accurate and think that the only way forward is to reject those streams of New Testament teaching that disenfranchise the Jews.[1] Others emphasize that the New Testament, while anti-Judaistic, is not anti-Semitic. In other words, while the early Christians did believe that the Jewish religion was no longer a way to reach God, they had nothing at all against the Jewish people. Indeed, most of the New Testament authors were themselves Jews and sought in love to win them to the gospel.[2] Finally, other theologians have argued that some passages in the New Testament teach that the Jewish faith is still a valid way of salvation. Alongside faith in Jesus—the Gentile way of salvation—we need to keep a place for the *torah* covenant as the Jewish way of salvation. This view is sometimes called **bicovenantalism.** Its advocates claim that a "special way" (German, *Sonderweg*) exists for Jewish salvation.[3]

In all these debates, Romans 9–11 is the center of attention. Indeed, the *Sonderweg* view is based almost entirely on these chapters. What this means is that we need to approach Paul's teaching in this part of Romans with special care. We need to clear away misconceptions and prejudices, trying to find out exactly what Paul does teach about Israel. In the comments that follow, I will argue basically for the second view described above. Salvation is to be found in Jesus alone, for both Gentiles and Jews. That position, however, does not make Paul anti-Semitic. He agonizes over the failure of so many of his fellow Jews to respond to the gospel (9:1–2; 10:1), and one of his greatest motivations in evangelizing Gentiles is the hope that his own people will by this means come to Christ (11:13–14). How much hope does

Paul hold out for a conversion of his fellow Jews? That question will have to wait until we look at Romans 11.

Before we become immersed in the issue of Israel and its future, we need to back up and take a broader view of Romans 9–11. Israel is not, finally, the main topic of these chapters. The main topic is the integrity of God. By the time Paul wrote Romans, the general makeup of the early church had become clear. It was composed of many Gentiles and relatively few Jews. We are so accustomed to this situation that it creates no surprise or shock. But this simple fact was one of the most difficult theological issues that the early church had to face. The Old Testament appears to promise that the messianic salvation will be for Jews, with some Gentiles allowed in. Paul and the other early Christians proclaim that the messianic salvation has come through Jesus of Nazareth. Why, then, is Israel not being redeemed, as the Old Testament promised? Why is the church a mainly Gentile body? Such questions cut right to the heart of the gospel, for if the gospel could not truly be seen as the continuation of God's plan from the Old Testament, then it would cease to be the "gospel of God" (cf. 1:2). God would seem to have changed his mind or gone back on his promises. In Romans 9–11, Paul tackles this key theological issue. He argues that the situation in his day is quite in keeping with the Old Testament promises of God—when those promises are rightly interpreted. Along the way, he develops a theology that has enduring importance for our understanding of the ways of God with the world and a perspective on history that should challenge and excite us.

The Problem: The Conflict between God's Promises and Israel's Plight (9:1–5)

With the marvelous celebration of God's unshakable love for us in Christ (8:31–39), we might think that the doctrinal part of Romans is at an end—time for Paul to move on to the practical ramifications of that doctrine. Of course, he does precisely that in chapter 12. But what are we to think about this long section in between, chapters 9–11? What is its purpose? Augustine, and many others after him, thought that Paul used this material to elaborate the theology he had developed earlier in the letter: predestination (see 8:29–30) or justification by faith. Other interpreters have suggested that the chapters are a kind of personal excursus, as Paul the Jew expresses concern for his kinfolk. But when we remember the overall purpose of Romans, these chapters fit quite naturally into the argument of the letter. Paul is presenting his gospel. He especially wants to show how it embraces Gentiles without breaking continuity with the Old Testament. The relatively small number of Jews that have become Christians is a severe challenge to this continuity. God seems to have abandoned the people he chose and made promises to in the Old Testament in favor of a new people. If this were so, then the connection between Old Testament and New Testament would be broken, and God would be revealed as capricious and undependable. The reader of Romans who is attuned to Old Testament imagery could be forgiven for raising this objection, for Paul himself applies to the church language that was applied to Israel in the Old Testament. The church is the "seed of Abraham" (4:16), the children of God (8:14–17), and the recipient of God's glory (8:30). Has Israel, then, been abandoned? Has the church replaced Israel and God reneged on his promises to Israel? These are the questions that motivate chapters 9–11. Verses 1–5 introduce these questions.

In this paragraph, Paul contrasts the current plight of Israel (vv. 1–3) with the promises God made to Israel (vv. 4–5). Paul does not state Israel's plight in so many words. He expresses deep and sincere concern for them (vv. 1–2) and even offers to put himself under a curse on their behalf (v. 3). Paul's offer resembles the response of Moses when he found the people of Israel fashioning a golden calf and worshiping it:

> The next day Moses said to the people, "You have committed a great sin. But now I will go up to the Lord; perhaps I can make atonement for your sin." So Moses went back to the Lord and said, "Oh, what a great sin these people have committed! They have made themselves gods of gold. But now, please forgive their sin—but if not, then blot me out of the book you have written." (Ex 32:30–32)

But Paul goes further than Moses, asking that the curse earned by Israel fall on him so that the people might be forgiven. Of course, Paul knows that he cannot become, and the Lord never would accept, such a curse. Paul speaks emotionally and hyperbolically to make his point. Nevertheless, the fact that he states the matter in this way reveals that the problem of Israel is its failure to embrace the salvation offered in Christ. By turning their backs on Christ, the Israelites have placed themselves under the curse that comes on all those who are not saved.[4]

As I have emphasized, Israel's failure to accept Jesus is not simply a matter of Paul's personal anguish. Far from it. The list of blessings and promises granted Israel by God in verses 4–5 makes clear that Israel's failure creates an acute theological problem. How can the people to whom God gave so much now be cut off from the eschatological salvation? Israel has received the "adoption as sons." By choosing Israel from all the nations of the earth to be his own people, God adopted this nation as his own. Strikingly, Paul has just applied this language to Christians in Romans 8 (vv. 16, 23), fueling the tension that Paul deals with in these chapters. Israel also was given the glory (the presence of God among them), the covenants (e.g., the Abrahamic, the Mosaic, the Davidic), the law, the temple worship, and the promises. To them also belong the patriarchs, who naturally are mentioned along with the promises because Paul believes that God's promises to Abraham, Isaac, and Jacob are foun-

dational to salvation history and bear continuing significance for the future of Israel (see 11:28). Finally, and climactically, the Messiah also belongs to Israel, at least in terms of his "human ancestry" (*sarx*, "flesh" [again the NIV paraphrases]). As John puts it, the Messiah came to "his own" (Jn 1:11). But the Messiah's human descent is not all that is to be said about him. In a pattern that he follows elsewhere (see esp. Rom 1:3–4), Paul also reminds us of another side of the Messiah's nature: he is "God over all, forever praised." Here we find one of the few verses in the New Testament that directly applies to Jesus the title "God" (*theos*). Or do we? The RSV translates the end of verse 5 this way: "Of their race, according to the flesh, is the Christ. God who is over all be blessed forever. Amen." The difference, as you can see, is a matter of punctuation. Should we put a comma after "Christ" (NIV; KJV; NRSV; NASB)? Or should we put a period there (RSV)? The earliest Greek manuscripts had no punctuation, so the decision is a matter of exegesis, not textual history. Although scholars are divided over the point, a growing consensus sees the comma as the better alternative (note the shift between the RSV and the NRSV).[5] The general NIV rendering is probably correct, then. Here Paul calls Jesus "God."

The Nature of God's Promise to Israel (9:6–29)

Paul has implicitly set before us this question: how can the present state of the church be reconciled with God's promises to Israel? He answers in three stages. In 9:6–29, Paul uses the Old Testament itself to define the promise. Then, after a bit of an excursus in 9:30–10:21, he reminds us that God is continuing to manifest his grace to Israel by calling Jews to be saved (11:1–10). Finally, he holds out hope for a greater bestowal of grace on Israel in the future (11:11–36).

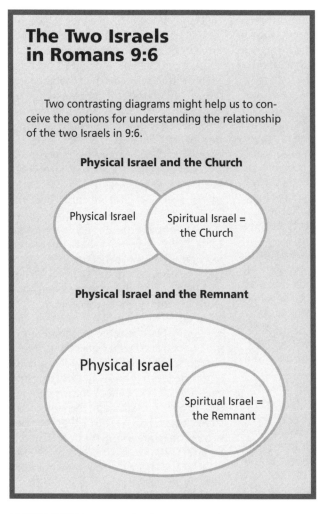

The Two Israels in Romans 9:6

Two contrasting diagrams might help us to conceive the options for understanding the relationship of the two Israels in 9:6.

Physical Israel and the Church

Physical Israel

Spiritual Israel = the Church

Physical Israel and the Remnant

Physical Israel

Spiritual Israel = the Remnant

---

patriarchs

not delivered what he promised. And so Paul begins by showing just what it was that God had promised.

Verse 6b states the leading idea of verses 6–13—indeed, of all of verses 6–29. Here Paul makes a basic distinction between "Israel" and "Israel." Not all the physical members of the nation of Israel, Paul claims, belong to "Israel" in the spiritual sense. A very important concept is now introduced: spiritual Israel. Just what is this spiritual Israel? A long and distinguished line of interpretation holds that the New Testament writers "transfer" the title Israel from the nation to the church. Scholars have engaged in strenuous debate over this matter in recent years. Suffice it to say that I think at least one New Testament verse, Galatians 6:16, does use the word "Israel" this way.[6] And so the second "Israel" in verse 6 might also be a reference to the church in general, composed of both Jews and Gentiles. But the application of the word "Israel" to the church is rare in the New Testament, and the immediate context here focuses not on the church but on the way in which God selected a spiritual nucleus from *within* the larger national entity of Israel. Probably, then, Paul's point here is that there exists within physical Israel a spiritual Israel or, to use the language Paul introduces later, a "remnant."

Paul demonstrates his contention about an Israel within an Israel with two key illustrations from the history of the **patriarchs:** the choice of Isaac over Ishmael (vv. 7–9) and the choice of Jacob over Esau (vv. 10–13). Both choices prove that God has not simply guaranteed his blessing to all the physical descendants of Abraham. Receiving the blessing of that promise has always been a matter of God's own choosing. It is, as N. T. Wright succinctly puts it, a matter of "grace, not race." Abraham, we recall, had two sons: Ishmael, whose mother was Hagar, a slave in his household, and Isaac, whose mother was his wife, Sarah. God makes clear that it is through Isaac that Abraham's "offspring will be reckoned" (v. 7, quoting Gn 21:12). The meaning is that only the descendants of Isaac would be

Paul's first answer focuses on the nature of God's "call" to Israel. This word is prominent in both verses 6–13 and verses 24–29, where Paul makes his basic point. Verses 14–23 are a slight detour from that argument, as Paul pauses to answer objections to his emphasis on the divine initiative in Israel's history.

God's Call and the Patriarchs (9:6–13)

Verse 6a summarizes the basic theological issue in Romans 9–11: the integrity of God's promises. "It is not as though God's word had failed" reveals Paul's deepest concern in Israel's present dilemma: God himself would be charged with failure. It might seem that God had

"counted" as those who would receive the promised blessing from God. Ishmael and his children would have no part in those special blessings. They would not be considered to be part of the nation that God was creating. So, Paul concludes, God's children are not the "natural children" but the "children of promise," those whom God chooses to be the recipients of his promise.

However, someone might object, the status of Abraham's children is complicated by their different parentage. Isaac and Ishmael had different mothers, so perhaps it is this difference in their physical origin that accounts for their contrasting spiritual states. To counter this objection, Paul takes us down one generation in the patriarchal family tree. Isaac also had two sons, but his sons were born to one woman, Rebekah. And not only that. These two sons were born at the same time—they were twins (vv. 10–11). Nothing in their physical origins distinguished Jacob from Esau. Indeed, if we remember the story in Genesis, Esau was the older of the two, and yet God promised Rebekah, "The older will serve the younger" (v. 12, quoting Gn 25:23). It would be Jacob who would inherit God's promise and become the father of the nation of Israel. His name, in fact, was changed to "Israel." Paul summarizes the contrasting states of Jacob and Esau with a quotation from Malachi 1:2–3: "Jacob I loved, but Esau I hated." The language of love and hate reflects the idea of election: God chose Jacob for special blessing, but he rejected Esau from having any part in that blessing. The example of Jacob and Esau, Paul concludes, reveals particularly clearly that election is a matter of God's choosing and not of human birthright or decision. Jacob and Esau had done nothing at all when God promised Rebekah that Jacob would have the preeminence. They had not even been born yet.

The theological implications of this paragraph are hotly contested. Calvinists traditionally have found in these verses important support for the notion of unconditional election. This notion holds that God chooses, from eternity past, the people who are to be saved. His choice is "unconditional" in the sense that it is not conditioned by anything apart from his own hidden will. He does not base his choice on anything he knows about us, such as, for instance, whether we will believe or not. For our believing is itself a product of God's choice. We believe because God chooses us. (Arminians argue, by contrast, that God chooses those whom he foresees as believing.) However, many interpreters are not so sure that the Calvinists can use verses 6–13 to prove this theological point. They note that Malachi 1:2–3, the text that Paul quotes in verse 13, uses "Jacob" and "Esau" to refer, respectively, to the nations of Israel and Edom. And the other passages that Paul cites from Genesis do not refer to the spiritual destiny of individuals; they refer to the way God used these individuals in salvation history. So Romans 9:6–13 is not about the salvation of individuals at all, but rather, about the way God has sovereignly selected nations to carry out his plan in history.[7] Although these objectors have a point, I do not think that they can succeed in overturning the usual Calvinist interpretation of these verses. While the passages from Genesis may not refer directly to the salvation of individuals, Paul applies them to the question of who belongs in the spiritual Israel (v. 6). In other words, the ultimate concern is to show how God has determined who belongs to his people. That means that the issue is, finally, about the salvation of individuals.[8]

Excursus: The Justice of God (9:14–23)

Paul again reveals his sensitivity to the way his teaching will be understood. He well knows that what he has said about God's sovereignty in election will cause many readers to raise questions about God's justice and fairness. Indeed, one of the arguments in favor of the view that Paul is talking about unconditional election in verses 6–13 is that he himself raises just the objections that we tend to have

Thus, we might rephrase the question: "Has God acted according to his revealed character and will?" Once we refine the question in this way, we can see how Paul does indeed answer the question in the verses that follow.

Paul's answer takes the form of two parallel arguments from Scripture (vv. 15–16 and vv. 17–18). In each, Paul quotes Scripture and then draws a conclusion ("therefore") from it. These quotations reveal the two sides of God's sovereign decision making. On the one side we find God's mercy. When Moses asks God to reveal his glory to him, God causes his goodness to pass before Moses, proclaims his name, the Lord, and then asserts his freedom in bestowing mercy on whomever he chooses (v. 15; Ex 33:19). The principle to be derived from this quotation, claims Paul, is that God's mercy cannot be earned by a human being (v. 16). Nothing we will and nothing we do can force God to be merciful to us. Recall Paul's emphasis in Romans 4:3–5 on the grace of God. The very nature of God is to be gracious. This means that he must remain absolutely free to act as he chooses. His mercy always is a gift to be gratefully received, never a "wage" that we are owed. The other side of God's decision making is his "hardening" (see v. 18). Though Paul does not use this word in verse 17, the passage he quotes from Exodus 9:16 refers to the idea. The "hardening" of Pharaoh, or of Pharaoh's heart, is mentioned almost forty times in Exodus 4–14. It was by the stubborn disobedience of Pharaoh that God displayed his power and glory through him. By refusing to let the people of Israel go at Moses' bidding, Pharaoh forced God to display miracle after miracle until he agreed to God's purpose. Paul therefore uses Pharaoh as an example of the contrary side of God's mercy. As God bestows mercy on whomever he wants to, so also he hardens whomever he wants to harden (v. 18). Sometimes the initiative of God in his hardening is questioned because of the many times in Exodus that Pharaoh is said to harden his own heart (e.g., Ex 8:32, 9:34). So, some interpreters conclude, God's hardening of Pharaoh

Headpiece of Tutankhamen, a pharaoh who probably ruled Egypt shortly after the exodus. (Jim Yancey)

when we hear about this doctrine: Is God unjust (v. 14)? How can God still blame people (v. 19)? Paul must have heard such objections many times over a lifetime of gospel preaching. He pauses in his main argument to answer them before gradually turning back to his main line of teaching in verse 24.

Lurking in Paul's opening, apparently straightforward question—"Is God unjust?"—is an issue critical to our approach to this section. In asking whether someone or something is "unjust," we presume a standard of "justness," or right, that we can use to judge that person or action. What standard do we apply when we ask whether God is unjust? The minute we ask that question, the answer becomes obvious: we finite and sinful human beings can measure God only by the standards that he himself has revealed to us. Imposing our own standards of "right" on the God who created us and stands so far above us would be the height of folly and presumption.

God's Decisions and Ours

Romans 9 teaches the absolute sovereignty of God in the decisions he makes about the ultimate fate of human beings. That teaching naturally raises questions in our minds. As we have seen, Paul does not really try to answer these questions—at least from our perspective. For him it is enough to know that God has revealed himself as the one who determines these matters. We have no right to stand in judgment of what God does. We can judge him only by the standard of his own revelation, and by that standard, God certainly is "just."

Nevertheless, Paul plainly believes in the reality of human decisions. We are not puppets or robots. Our decisions matter, and we are responsible to make the right ones—to accept Christ, to live holy lives, to love one another, and so forth. How can our decisions *really* matter if God decides everything? Theologians and philosophers have debated this issue for centuries. They have discovered no neat logical solution to the problem. We must be willing at this point to live with what we call an "antinomy," an unresolved tension between two clear truths. God determines what happens; I am responsible for what happens. Scripture teaches both, and therefore I am compelled to believe both, even if ultimately I can't explain their relationship. Many who have written on this topic use the term "compatibilism" for this general viewpoint. The term refers to the belief that absolute sovereignty and genuine responsibility are not contradictory but "compatible" with one another.[1] I think that this comes closest to the teaching of Paul in Romans and to the witness of the Bible in general.

1. See J. Feinberg, "God Ordains All Things," in *Predestination and Free Will*, ed. D. and R. Basinger (Downers Grove, Ill.: InterVarsity, 1986), 17–43; D. A. Carson, *Divine Sovereignty and Human Responsibility* (Atlanta: Knox, 1981), 201–22.

simply comes in response to Pharaoh's prior decision to harden his own heart.[9] But this is not clear. Before Pharaoh is said to harden his own heart, that hardening is predicted by God (Ex 4:21; 7:3), and there are five references to Pharaoh's being hardened (Ex 7:13, 14, 22; 8:11, 15 in the Septuagint). It is therefore more likely that Pharaoh hardens his heart as a response to God's prior decision to harden him.[10]

Do these verses therefore teach what we call "double predestination"? God predestines, "decides beforehand," who will receive his mercy. Does he also decide beforehand who will suffer wrath? This text, along with verses 22–23, would seem to suggest this idea, but we must voice two reservations before accepting it. First, Paul teaches in Romans 11 that God can remove his hardening. We cannot be certain, then, that the hardening he describes here is a permanent condition. Second, God's hardening, while not determined by a person's own decisions, nevertheless is a response to the general condition of human sinfulness. God bestows mercy on people who have done nothing and can do nothing to earn that mercy. He hardens people who have already determined (in the sin of Adam) to rebel against God and to go their own way.

Far from "answering" our concern about God's "justness," verses 15–18 would seem to have exacerbated the matter. And so Paul raises the issue one more time, from a related angle: how can God blame human beings if they act in accordance with the decisions that God himself has made about them (v. 19)? Once again, Paul offers us no logically compelling response. We want to know how God's sovereign decision making can be squared with meaningful human decision making. Paul, however, simply reasserts the sovereign power of God. Alluding to several Old Testament passages (Is 29:16; 45:9; Jer 18:6–10; cf. Wis 15:7), Paul compares God to the potter, who works clay into whatever form he chooses (vv. 20–21). Why does Paul not try to explain how God legitimately can blame people who do what he decides they will do? To answer that question, we have to recall our starting point in this section (v. 14). Paul is not explaining how God's actions might correspond to *our* sense of justice. Indeed, I suspect that he would reject any idea that God could be judged by our standards. It is by God's standards that he must be judged. And Scripture, where we discover those standards, reveals that God does act in accordance with his character (vv. 15–18), and that he is the one who has the right to do with human beings whatever he might want to do (vv. 20–21). The search for philosophical/theological explanations of the relation between God's sovereign decision making and human responsibility is not wrong, but we must begin where Paul and the Bible begin: a vision of a God who is absolutely free to make whatever decision he wants about his creation. Paul would be the last to deny the importance of human decisions. His repeated pleas to people to believe in Christ and to reject sin reveal his belief in real human responsibility. Paul's purpose, however, is not to offer an explanation of how God's sovereignty and human responsibility fit together. He affirms both without resolving the tension between them. And perhaps this might offer a clue that they cannot finally be neatly resolved at all (see the sidebar "God's Decisions and Ours").

To conclude this excursus on God's right as the Creator to deal with his crea-

tures in any way he pleases, Paul turns back to the central issue in this passage: God's activity in creating his own people by accepting some and rejecting others. Verses 22 and 23 ask questions that Paul does not answer. The implication is that we are to supply the answer from verses 20–21. "What if" God has acted in such-and-such a way? That gives us no basis to criticize the potter, does it? Verse 22 focuses on God's patience in refusing to bring his wrath upon people who disobey him. Why does God display such patience? Paul gives no clear answer. Some think that God waits for those who disobey to repent. Others think that God waits in order to manifest his full power and glory in the judgment of the wicked in the end. No matter how we answer that question, the most important reason for God's patience becomes clear in verse 23: his desire to make known his glory to "the objects of his mercy," those whom he has chosen to be his people. God is at work in history to create a people for himself. To do so, he must choose some and reject others. And those who are rejected are, ultimately, judged. But we must remember again that people are judged, finally, because, in Adam, they have chosen to reject God. We never will fully understand the ways of God in moving history along to its intended goal, but always we can trust God to act in complete integrity as he does so.

God's Call and the Prophets (9:24–29)

Verse 24 is an extension of verse 23: the "objects of mercy" of verse 23 are defined in verse 24 as those whom God has called, both Jews and Gentiles. It would seem, then, that verse 24 should be kept in the same paragraph as verse 23. But Paul's syntax in verses 22–24 is very hard to unravel; and, at least in subject matter, verse 24 returns to the main theme of verses 6–13: God's sovereign "calling" (see v. 12 especially). But if verses 6–13 focused on the story of the patriarchs, verses 24–29 concentrate on the predictions of the prophets. Paul wants to show that the prophets agree with the patriarchal history in confining the true people of God to those whom he has specially called. The new element is the extension of that call to the Gentiles. In verse 24 Paul claims that God calls his people from among both Jews and Gentiles. Then, in verses 25–29, he elaborates on each group, in reverse order. Verses 25–26 quote the prophet Hosea to show that God planned to invite Gentiles to be part of his people (Hos 2:23; 1:10). Through the preaching of the gospel, what Hosea predicted has come true: those who were not God's people have become God's people, "sons of the living God." Those familiar with the Old Testament might wonder at Paul's application of these prophecies from Hosea to Gentiles, for Hosea was predicting the return of the ten northern tribes of Israel, not the conversion of the Gentiles. This is one example of the many places in which Paul does not seem to

Key Terms

bicovenantalism

Sonderweg

patriarchs

quote the Old Testament in accordance with its original meaning. Many scholars have explored this problem and offered all kinds of solutions. All that we can say here is that we must always remember that Paul quotes any part of the Old Testament in light of its fulfillment. What God has done in Christ sheds light on the ultimate significance of many Old Testament passages. Thus, while Hosea referred to the northern tribes as the "not my people," his prophecy finds its final salvation-historical application in God's acceptance of the "not my people" par excellence: the Gentiles.

Finally, Paul turns back to Israel. In verses 27–28, he quotes from one of the fundamental "remnant" texts in the Old Testament. The prophets saw very clearly in their day that not all the people of Israel were faithful to God's covenant. And so they began insisting that God's promises of blessing ultimately would apply not to all Israel, but only to those Israelites who were faithful to God. This teaching naturally suits Paul's purposes very well. The fact that so many Jews in Paul's day had not accepted Christ does not mean that God's word had failed (cf. v. 6). For God's word itself reveals that "only the remnant will be saved" (v. 27). Unfaithful Israelites will be judged (v. 28), but God is faithful to his people in preserving a "seed," descendants, who would carry on the heritage of Israel's blessings and mission (v. 29, quoting Is 1:9).

Study Questions

1. What is Paul's purpose in Romans 9–11? How does that purpose fit into the purpose and argument of the letter as a whole?

2. Why would Paul call Christ "God" in this context (v. 5)?

3. What two different issues might Paul ultimately be talking about in verses 6–13? Explain the significance of each option and try to settle in your own mind which option you prefer.

4. What concept of "justness" does Paul operate with in verses 14–23?

5. How does Paul's reference to the inclusion of Gentiles in the people of God (vv. 24–26) fit into his purposes in this part of Romans?

14 Israel, the Gentiles, and the Righteousness of God

Romans 9:30–10:21

Outline

- God's Righteousness versus "Their Own" Righteousness (9:30–10:13)
- Israel's Failure to Believe (10:14–21)

Objectives

After reading this chapter, you should be able to

1. Understand that God's sovereign election does not negate human responsibility to believe.
2. Describe two different interpretations of the way that Christ "ends" the Mosaic law and their theological implications.
3. Explain why Israel failed to recognize the revelation of God's righteousness in Christ.

We will never be able to put together in a neat package the biblical truth that God determines everything that happens with the equally biblical truth that human beings are fully responsible for their actions. The relationship between Romans 9 and Romans 10 mirrors this tension. In Romans 9, Paul teaches that the existence of only a remnant of Jewish believers is because God chose only certain Jews to belong to his true spiritual people. But in Romans 10, he teaches that the Jewish people themselves were at fault for refusing to recognize and submit to God's righteousness in Christ. Paul says nothing about how these two perspectives are to be integrated. Some interpreters think that Romans 10 explains Romans 9: God does not choose certain Jews for his people because they already have refused God's offer of salvation in Christ. Others exactly reverse the relationship: the reason that so many Jews have not accepted Christ is because God has not chosen them. I think that the latter is closer to the truth. But perhaps it is better simply to respect the way that Paul has allowed these two perspectives to stand side by side without resolving them. Jews (and Gentiles) belong to God's people because God has chosen them; Jews (and Gentiles) belong to God's people because they have chosen God.

God's Righteousness versus "Their Own" Righteousness (9:30–10:13)

The early editors of the Bible placed the chapter break where they did because Paul's personal comment in 10:1, matching 9:1–2, seems to initiate a new section. But a more important break occurs between 9:29 and 9:30. The question that Paul raises in verse 30 signals a break in the argument; and, with verse 30, Paul introduces a new set of key terminology. Dominating all of 9:30–10:13 is a contrast between two kinds of righteousness:

"Righteousness that is by faith" (9:30) versus "a law of righteousness" (9:31)

"God's righteousness" versus "their own righteousness" (10:3)

"The righteousness that is by faith" (10:6) versus "the righteousness that is by the law" (10:5)

Paul uses these contrasts to explain from another angle why salvation history has taken such a surprising turn. Jews, who had so many blessings and to whom so many promises were made, make up a small percentage of the people of God in the gospel era. Gentiles, on the other hand, have responded to the gospel in significant numbers. Although Paul mentions the Gentiles, his main concern in 9:30–10:21 is to explain why Israel in general has been excluded from the messianic people of God. Paul reverts to basic gospel language in helping us to understand this surprising state of affairs. In 1:16–17, the statement of the letter's theme, Paul explains that the gospel brings salvation because "the righteousness of God" is revealed in it for everyone who believes. We find these same points reiterated and applied to Jews and Gentiles in 9:30–10:13. Christ has come, the climax of the law, bringing the possibility of righteousness for everyone who believes (10:4). God blesses anyone, Jew or Gentile, who calls on Christ in faith (10:9–13). Gentiles have been included in the new people of God because they responded to the message of the gospel by receiving God's righteousness in faith (9:30). Jews, however, have stumbled over Christ (9:32b–33). Though God revealed himself to them, and they were zealous for God (10:2), they did not comprehend that Christ was bringing God's righteousness (10:3). Their preoccupation with the law kept them from seeing that Jesus of Nazareth was the climax of God's plan of redemption (9:31–32a; 10:5–8).

Paul begins the section by contrasting Gentiles, who obtained righteousness even though they were not pursuing it, with Israel, who pursued but did not obtain (vv. 30–31). Using the device of inclusio, Paul returns to the same basic

Modern-day Jew wearing a prayer shawl and phylacteries while reading at the Wailing Wall. (Jim Yancey)

teousness" but did not attain it because Israel pursued it "not by faith but as if it were by works." What is this "law of righteousness"? "Law" (*nomos*) could simply mean "principle."[1] In that case, we could almost ignore the word. Israel's pursuit and failure to attain righteousness would be the point. But Paul says too much about the Mosaic law in this context to let us think that we could water down the word in this way here. Almost certainly he means "the Mosaic law in its connection with righteousness." And if so, Paul might be saying something very significant about that law here: true pursuit of the law must take place by faith and not by works.[2] However, such a connection between the law and faith would be most unusual in Paul. He of course would not deny that God's basic requirement always has been to believe, and that this was true in the Mosaic era as in any other. But generally, Paul uses the word "law" in a very specific way: to refer to the commandments that God gave his people through Moses. And commandments, by their very nature, are not to be believed, but carried out. Note, for instance, how Paul can say in Galatians 3:12 that "the law is not of faith." Consistency with Pauline usage makes it difficult to think, then, that he would be faulting Israel here for failing to "believe" the law. I suggest that confusion arises because Paul is trying to make two points at the same time: (1) Israel failed to achieve righteousness because they sought that righteousness through works; and (2) Israel got hung up with works because they put too much emphasis on the law. Paul's "law of righteousness" is his attempt to combine these ideas.[3]

The second reason that Israel failed to achieve righteousness was because they stumbled over "the stumbling stone" (vv. 32b–33). Paul combines two prophecies about "stones" from Isaiah (8:14; 28:16) and applies them to Christ. For those who put their trust in Christ, he becomes a foundation stone, a stone on which to build a spiritual life. Others, not recognizing who he really is, trip over him and fall. This is what has happened to Israel.

point at the end of this larger section (10:20–21): Gentiles who were not seeking the Lord have found him, while Israel, God's chosen people, are "disobedient and obstinate." The language of "pursuing" and "obtaining" in 9:30–32 is race imagery, and the idea of Christ being a stone over which people stumble (vv. 32b–33) continues this imagery. Israel is pictured as a runner who is trying to overtake righteousness—a right standing with God. Israel, however, fails to achieve the goal of righteousness. Why? Paul gives two answers in verses 31–33.

First, Israel failed because they were trying to achieve their goal through works (vv. 31–32a). Because of his introduction of the law at this point, Paul's intention here is not easy to discern. He says that Israel was pursuing "the law of righ-

157

In 10:1–4, Paul describes the failure of Israel from a slightly different perspective. In 9:30–33, Israel's fall is attributed to the failure to believe. In this new paragraph, it is a failure to understand that leads to Israel's downfall. Israel's insight into God's plan does not match its zeal (v. 2). The Jews do not lack passion for God; indeed, they exhibit their commitment to him by following the prescriptions of *torah* in the midst of a Gentile society. Nevertheless, their passion for God is misdirected. Their very passion for the law blinds them to the larger plan of God. Their myopic, tunnel-vision focus on the law and its requirements keeps them from seeing the larger picture. Thus, they do not submit to the righteousness of God revealed in Christ but instead keep seeking to establish "their own righteousness." Some interpreters think that "their own" connotes a corporate idea. The Jews cling to their beloved status as God's people, refusing to concede any place for Gentiles within that people. "Their own righteousness" is a "national righteousness," a right standing with God that is exclusively for the people of Israel.[4] Paul certainly is concerned with "national" issues in this context, as he emphasizes how God's work in Christ is "for all who believe" (v. 4b; cf. vv. 9–13). However, Paul's

Inscription warning Gentiles not to enter the temple if they value their lives. (Chris Miller)

use of very similar language in Philippians 3 suggests a more individual focus. In that chapter, Paul claims that in his preconversion state he had "a righteousness of my own that comes from the law" (Phil 3:9). As a Jew, Paul thought that his right standing with God needed to be validated through his adherence to the law. It is this same preoccupation with the law that Paul now attributes in Romans 10:3 to Israel as a whole.

Verse 4 explains why Israel was wrong to focus so intently on the law. The law was never intended by God to be his final word. All along it was anticipating something greater to come. Now, that something greater has come: Christ. He is the *telos* of the law. This little Greek word has stimulated an amazing amount of discussion and debate. Does it mean "end," in the sense of termination (see, e.g., 1 Cor 15:24)? Or does it mean "goal" (see, e.g., 1 Tim 1:5)? Does Christ bring the law to an end? Or is he the inner meaning of the law? Perhaps the best way to answer this question is to go back to the race imagery that Paul has been using in this context. We might picture the law as the race itself. Christ is the finish line. As Israel runs the race of the law, they should always, of course, have their eyes fixed on the finish line. Instead, Paul has been suggest-

Jesus as Yahweh

In Romans 9:5, I argued, Paul calls Jesus "God." This verse probably should be added to several others where the name "God" is applied to Jesus (see Jn 1:1; 1:18; 20:28; Ti 2:13; Heb 1:8; 2 Pt 1:1). These passages obviously provide us with the most direct evidence for the deity of Christ.[1] But just as compelling, if not as direct, are many other verses in which Jesus is pictured as doing something that only God can do, or is worshiped, or where Old Testament language reserved for God is applied to Jesus. Romans 10:13 falls into this last category. Joel 2:32 promises that everyone who "calls on the name of the Lord" will be saved. "The Lord" in Joel translates the Hebrew *Yahweh*, the most common name applied to God in the Old Testament. Paul quotes this verse from Joel, using the Greek *kyrios* (as did the Septuagint [Greek Old Testament] translators) for "Lord." In the New Testament, this title can refer either to God the Father or to Jesus. But in Romans 10:13, "Lord" must refer to Jesus. Paul identifies Jesus as "the Lord" in verse 9. He then refers to him in verses 9b and 11 with the third person pronoun: "God raised *him*," "anyone who trusts in *him* will never be put to shame" (quoting Is 28:16). In verse 12, Paul again refers to the Lord; he is the same for both Jew and Gentile, blessing all who call on him. Again, from verse 9 it is evident that this "Lord" is Jesus. But the Lord on whom people "call" in verse 13 must be the same Lord on whom they "call" in verse 12—Jesus. Paul therefore almost unobtrusively associates Jesus with Yahweh (or Jehovah) of the Old Testament. The verse therefore testifies to the way that early Christians, by A.D. 57, were thinking of Jesus as divine. Although neither Paul nor any other early Christian had worked out the doctrine of the Trinity, already they were operating with implicit trinitarian ideas. (See my comments on Romans 8:2–4.)

1. On these texts, see M. J. Harris, *Jesus as God: The New Testament Use of Theos in Reference to Jesus* (Grand Rapids: Baker, 1992).

ing, Israel concentrated so exclusively on the race that they forgot about the finish line. With the coming of Christ, that finish line has been reached, but Israel does not recognize it. With this imagery in mind, *telos* has the sense of "climax" or "culmination." Christ does "end" the law in the sense that his arrival means that the era of *torah* is over. But also, Christ is the law's goal, as the law was instituted by God for a set time and a set purpose. It prepared Israel for the coming of the Messiah. Now that the Messiah has come, righteousness is available for everyone who believes.[5]

Paul has contrasted the righteousness by faith that Gentiles discovered with "the law of righteousness" that Israel pursued (9:30–33). He has contrasted "God's righteousness" with "their own righteousness" (10:1–4). Now he contrasts the "righteousness that is by the law" (v. 5) with "the righteousness that is by faith" (v. 6). Paul describes each kind of righteousness by referring to the Old Testament. The righteousness that is by the law is unpacked through Leviticus 18:5: "The man who does these things will live by them." This verse had become almost a slogan among the Jews to describe the nature of the law. Paul picks it up to make clear that legal righteousness involves *doing*. He is not teaching, as some have thought, that the Old Testament taught that a person could attain eternal life by doing the law. The "life" in Leviticus 18:5

refers to the blessings that the people of Israel would experience if they followed the law that God gave them. It does not mean that an individual Jew could be saved on the basis of doing the law. For Paul, the point of the verse simply is that any righteousness based on law is based on human works; and works, as Paul has made clear earlier in the letter, never can justify us before God, because we are locked up under sin and never can produce enough works to satisfy God (1:18–3:20). To explain the opposite kind of righteousness, the kind that comes by faith, Paul cites language drawn from Deuteronomy 30:12–14 (vv. 6–8). He quotes lines from that text and then applies them to Christ or to the gospel. In Deuteronomy 30, however, Moses is talking about the law of God. He urges the Israelites to recognize that God has made his will available to the people. They don't have go up into heaven to find it or to descend into the deep (the abyss). God's word, his law, is near them, in their mouths and hearts. The application of these words to Christ and the gospel makes good sense. People do not have to struggle to accomplish a certain level of obedience to please God. Christ has come down from heaven and been raised from the dead to provide all that we need for salvation. All we need to do now is believe the word that has come near to us in the preaching of the gospel. But if the application of this language to the gospel makes sense in one way, it creates difficulties in another way. How can Paul take words from the Old Testament that refer to the law and apply them to Christ and the gospel? This question has been discussed for many years, as scholars have tried to justify Paul's hermeneutical procedure. Some think that Paul does not really quote the Old Testament but just borrows its language. Others think that he is influenced by certain Jewish traditions. The best option is that Paul uses the language from Deuteronomy because it expresses very well the grace of God in his covenant dealings. God makes his word known; he takes the initiative. He did so in the old covenant, as Moses points out.

Now, Paul insists, that same grace of God is available in the word of Christ.[6] Deuteronomy 30:14 says that God's word is in the "mouth" and in the "heart." In verses 9–10, Paul applies both these to the word of the gospel, in reverse (chiastic) order. If people confess with the mouth that "Jesus is Lord" and believe in the heart that God raised him from the dead, they will be saved.

In the final verses of this section (vv. 11–13), Paul makes the point that this opportunity to confess and to believe is open to everyone. Paul's main concern in this section, as we have seen, is to show why Israel fell short of the goal of right standing with God. A subsidiary purpose is to show how the Gentiles have now found that right standing. The coming of Christ, "ending" the law (v. 4) opens up God's grace to the Gentiles in a new way. Now, as the Old Testament teaches, "anyone" who trusts in Christ will "never be put to shame" (v. 11, quoting Is 28:16; cf. 9:33). "Everybody" who calls on Christ's name can be saved (v. 13; quoting Jl 2:32). And in verse 12, Paul makes quite clear that this "anyone" and "everybody" refers especially to Jew and Gentile. The new age is a time when God opens wide the doors of salvation to all people. No longer is his plan focused on one people, Israel.

Israel's Failure to Believe (10:14–21)

Many of us probably are familiar with verses 14–15 in this section because of missionary sermons. Paul's insistence that people must be sent so that the message about Christ can be proclaimed and believed provides a natural launchpad for an appeal to serve Christ in missions. Although I don't question that the text can be used in this way, we should note that stimulating interest in missions is not Paul's purpose here. The paragraph as a whole focuses on the situation of Israel. Paul has said in verse 2 of this chapter that Israel's zeal for God was not accompanied by "knowledge." But could Israel

The Many Uses of Quotations

We have encountered several places in Romans where Paul does not seem to apply the Old Testament in quite the way the original Old Testament context would seem to validate. This creates a theological problem. How can a New Testament writer use the Old Testament to claim that something is true when the Old Testament does not even teach what he claims it does? Such a procedure would be like our trying to prove a doctrine from a text that we have misunderstood. Understandably, we would convince few people. Answers to this problem, which theologians have discussed for years, are not simple. In fact, each of the texts has to be taken on its own, because they present different kinds of problems. But one part of the solution is to recognize that New Testament writers sometimes use the Old Testament not to prove a point but to borrow its language and ethos. An illustration will make the point.

When I was young, and my sons were even younger, we often played basketball out on the driveway together. Then I, and they, grew. I became weaker and slower; they became bigger, stronger, and faster. Foolishly, I kept trying to compete. One day, I was playing one-on-one with my third son, Lukas. He had grown to about six feet six inches and 240 pounds, and was a very strong, highly skilled basketball player. I warned him, "Watch out, Luke, I'm going to take the ball to the basket on you!" He shot back, "Go ahead, Dad, make my day." He was "quoting" the lines of the character Dirty Harry from the movie starring Clint Eastwood. Eastwood, portraying a cop, uses these words to dare a criminal to draw his gun on him. Luke did not have a gun; he was not threatening to shoot me. He did not intend to quote the author's "original intention," nor did I think that he was doing so. The language was a striking way of making a point: if I was foolish enough to try to take the ball to the basket on Luke, I could very well suffer the violence that Dirty Harry's bad guy suffered in the movie. The quotation worked because we both knew the movie; it therefore communicated the point very well. So Paul and other New Testament writers often use Old Testament language. They know that their readers will understand it, and the application of the language often helps them to perceive a situation in a new light. Thus, in Romans 10:18, for instance, Paul quotes Psalm 19:4 not because he thinks that this text speaks directly about the preaching of the gospel to Israel; rather, he quotes it because the words would awaken echoes in his readers' minds that would lend force to his assertion.[1]

1. On this use of the Old Testament in Paul, see R. Hays, *Echoes of Scripture in the Letters of Paul* (New Haven: Yale University Press, 1989).

be faulted for not knowing what God was doing in Christ? Had they been given the opportunity to learn God's purposes and so respond properly to them? Yes, Paul answers in verses 14–21. These verses show that Israel had heard about God's purposes and indeed had understood something about them. Thus, the Jews are culpable when they don't respond. In a sentence: they knew but did not believe.

The so-called chain of evangelism in verses 14–15 is a general statement that

Study Questions

1. Why is it a problem to think that Paul might be scolding Israel for not pursuing the law by faith (9:31–32)?

2. Some interpreters think that Paul is claiming in Romans 10:4 that "Christ is the end of the law as a way of righteousness." What is the problem with this view in light of Paul's teaching elsewhere?

3. How does Paul's insistence that salvation is open to "anyone" who believes (10:9–13) function in his argument? What implications does his language have today?

4. What does Paul's argument in 10:16–21 suggest about the importance of hearing and understanding?

sets up Paul's discussion of Israel's situation in verses 16–21. In verse 13, quoting Joel 2:32, Paul affirms that salvation depends on "calling on the Lord." Paul works back from this requirement. To call on the Lord, one must believe. But to believe, one must hear the message. And to hear the message, one must proclaim that message. And proclaiming the message only happens if people are sent to proclaim it. Again, Paul's point here is not that people need to get involved in preaching the gospel—as true as that may be. His point is that God has sent people to preach. This first and vital step in the process that leads to salvation has been taken. Paul quotes Isaiah 52:7 to make this point: "How beautiful are the feet of those who bring good news." God has sent a constant stream of prophets and apostles proclaiming God's purpose and inviting response. Paul and his fellow evangelists represent the latest phase in this great task of proclamation. Nevertheless, according to Paul himself, it goes

back at least as far as Abraham (see Gal 3:8).

So the problem is not with God; it is with Israel. As Paul puts it in verse 16, "not all the Israelites accepted the good news." ("Israelites" is the NIV interpretation of the vague "they" of the Greek text, and appears to be justified.) That good news, the message about Christ, is the necessary condition for faith (v. 17), but Israel has not, in general, responded in faith. Isaiah, in his fourth and greatest Servant Song, wondered if anyone would believe the message (Is 53:1, quoted in v. 16b). Israel should have believed, because Israel has heard (v. 18) and understood (v. 19). Paul quotes Psalm 19:4 to buttress the former point. What is interesting about this quotation is that Psalm 19 is about God's natural revelation to the entire world. We need to realize that Paul does not always quote the Old Testament to "prove" a theological point (see the sidebar "The Many Uses of Quotations"). He sometimes uses the language of the Old Testament to express a new truth. Here he borrows language about God's universal revelation in nature to assert that God has revealed his special purpose in the gospel to Israel in general. But God has done more than that. Ever since the time of Moses, Paul suggests, God also has been making clear his ultimate intention to bring blessing to people outside the nation of Israel. Deuteronomy 32:21 predicted that God would use Gentiles to make the Israelites envious and stir up their anger (v. 19). Isaiah also prophesied that people who were not seeking God (the Gentiles; cf. 9:30) would find him (v. 20). And the Old Testament predicts not only the inclusion of Gentiles but also the setting aside of many Israelites. Paul therefore appropriately concludes this passage with a quotation (from Is 65:2) that sounds notes of both judgment and grace. Israel is "disobedient and obstinate," but God still holds out his hands to them.

The Future of Israel

Romans 11:1–36

Outline

- God's Continuing Faithfulness to Israel: The Remnant (11:1–10)
- God's Continuing Faithfulness to Israel: "All Israel Will Be Saved" (11:11–32)
- Response: The Wonderful Plan of God (11:33–36)

Objectives

After reading this chapter, you should be able to

1. Explain how God's promises to Israel are being fulfilled in the present and will be fulfilled in the future.
2. Understand how the theological argument of Romans 11 advances Paul's purposes in writing to the Roman Christians.
3. List and briefly analyze at least three prominent interpretations of the promise in Romans 11:26, "All Israel will be saved."
4. Explain and offer a response to the "bicovenantal" theological position.

Israeli tanks in the Negev. (Chris Miller)

At few points do biblical teaching and contemporary news stories intersect so directly as on the status of the State of Israel. The Jews' tenacious hold on the homeland they finally won back in 1948 has been challenged repeatedly by Arab countries and by the Palestinian movement. Violence seems to be a way of life in the Middle East, and Christians are often at a loss to understand the rights and wrongs of the situation. What should we learn from our Bibles about the stance we should take toward the nation of Israel? Some Christians think that the current State of Israel is a fulfillment of God's promise to his people. These Christians tend to support Israel unconditionally and blame the Arabs for almost all of the Middle East's problems. Other Christians, however, are not so sure about the relationship between biblical prophecy and the current State of Israel. Either they don't think that the Bible promises that the people of Israel will return to their homeland or they are not convinced that this particular State of Israel fulfills that promise. Such Christians generally do not assume that Israel is always in the right, and they want to assess the conflict in the same terms as they would any international conflict.

Romans 11 will not answer all these questions. Indeed, it will provide decisive answers to none of them. Nevertheless, as the New Testament text bearing most directly on the question of Israel's future, it must be our starting point in all our discussions of these questions. In this chapter, Paul returns to the main line of his argument. He has asked whether Israel's failure to respond to Christ jeopardizes God's faithfulness to his promises to Israel (9:6). His first answer came in 9:6–29. God's promises to Israel never included all the biological descendants of Abraham. His blessing always was given only to those whom he specifically chose to bless. So the unbelief of so many Jews does not, in itself, challenge God's faithfulness. After an elaboration of the situation of Israel and the Gentiles in chapter 10, his second and third answers now come in chapter 11. God is faithful to his promise to Israel, Paul argues, because

(1) he is preserving at the present time a remnant of Jewish believers (vv. 1–10); and (2) he will bring "all Israel" to salvation in the future (vv. 11–32).

God's Continuing Faithfulness to Israel: The Remnant (11:1–10)

In the immediately preceding section of the letter, Paul has charged Israel with stumbling over the "stumbling stone" (9:32–33), failing to submit to God's righteousness (10:3), and refusing to believe the good news (10:16). Israel is, in short, "a disobedient and obstinate people" (10:21). No wonder Paul asks, "Did God reject his people?" But his answer is clear: "By no means! . . . God did not reject his people, whom he foreknew" (11:1–2). Paul spends the rest of chapter 11 elaborating this answer. Two initial observations about Paul's answer are in order. First, "his people" refers to national Israel. This is clear from the connection between 11:1–2 and 10:21, where "people" is identified with Israel. Second, as the NIV punctuation rightly recognizes, "whom he foreknew" is a nonrestrictive clause. In other words, this phrase does not restrict the meaning of "his people" to a particular group. If that had been Paul's meaning, we would have to eliminate the comma: "God did not reject his people whom he foreknew." This sentence means that God did not reject the "foreknown" people or persons. It leaves open the possibility that he might have rejected other people whom he did *not* foreknow. Verse 2 therefore would be claiming simply that God has not rejected the Israel within an Israel that he has specifically chosen to be his spiritual people.[1] This view misses Paul's corporate focus. He begins with the general: Israel, that people whom God foreknew, or "chose ahead of time," has not been rejected.

Exactly what that means Paul will explain in the rest of the chapter.

Paul's first explanation picks up the idea of the remnant, which he introduced in 9:27–29. Isaiah predicted that "the remnant will be saved" (9:27, quoting Is 10:22). That remnant of faithful Jewish believers continues to exist in Paul's day. "At the present time there is a remnant chosen by grace" (v. 5). Here is the central claim of verses 1–10. Paul buttresses that claim by citing his own example: "I am an Israelite myself, a descendant of Abraham, from the tribe of Benjamin" (v. 1b). In other words, Paul is thoroughly Jewish—a point we tend to forget—and yet also a Christian. God cannot have rejected his people, then, as Jewish believers like Paul prove. Paul illustrates his claim about a remnant by reminding us of one of the most critical periods in Israel's history. King Ahab had taken up the worship of Baal and embarked on a persecution of the followers of the Lord. Elijah the prophet was the most prominent of those who continued to fear the Lord. Because he opposed Ahab and especially his wife Jezebel, he became a special object of their hatred. In fear of his life, he fled into the desert. Paul records Elijah's lament (v. 3, quoting 1 Kgs 19:10, 14) in the desert and the Lord's assurance that he does not stand alone: God has "reserved for himself" seven thousand who are faithful to the Lord (v. 4, quoting 1 Kgs 19:18). Similarly, Paul does not stand alone. Joining with him are many Jews, all across the Mediterranean basin, who also have come to accept Jesus as the Messiah.

Yet these Jewish believers are what they are, Paul reminds us, because of God's grace. Here again Paul picks up a prominent motif from 9:6–29. As in this earlier text, Paul insists that those Jews who believe do so because God chose them. It is "the elect" who have obtained God's righteousness (v. 7; cf. 9:30–31; and, on God's election, 9:12–13, 22–23). Those Jews who have not believed have been hardened by God (9:18; cf. 9:12–13, 22–23). The overriding principle of God's grace, his absolute freedom to act

Monument celebrating Elijah's victory over the prophets of Baal. (Jim Yancey)

whom he foresees as exercising faith? Arminians claim that it does, but I am not so sure. At any point along the way, Paul easily could have defused the charge that he was turning human beings into robots by reminding us that God's choice is based on our faith (see esp. 9:14–23). He never does so. His silence, although not conclusive, is suggestive. Coupled with Paul's insistence in chapter 9 that it is God's decision that determines the destiny of human beings, this silence seems to remove any human contribution from the basis for election.

Perhaps even more controversial is the "dark side of election": God's hardening of people. To be sure, Paul does not claim explicitly in this passage that God hardens people. He simply asserts that they "were hardened" (v. 7). But the Old Testament passage that he goes on to cite casts God in the active role: he is the one who gives "the spirit of stupor" (v. 8, quoting Dt 29:4; Is 29:10). Thus, as in 9:18, the state of hardening, or spiritual insensitivity, comes from God. Again, however, we must note that Paul predicts a time limit on God's hardening (11:25; cf. 11:11–12). How we factor this into our conclusions about the theological issue of "double predestination" is unclear. Perhaps Paul is speaking corporately about the nation of Israel in verses 11–12 and verse 25, while verse 7 refers to the hardening he brings on individuals. In that case, this hardening may very well be a permanent sentence of damnation. However, even if we conclude that Paul teaches a duality in predestination, such that God both elects to salvation and "hardens" to damnation, we must remember one critical difference: God hardens people who have already chosen their own destiny via their sin in Adam. When God elects us to be saved, he gives us a gift that we do not deserve and never could deserve. When he hardens, he confirms the sentence that people deserve and have already chosen for themselves.

as he wishes without any creaturely constraint, is seen here again (see my comments on 4:4–6). God's grace means that those who become his people owe nothing to their own accomplishments or works and everything to God. Theologians debate how far we should take this point. Paul clearly removes what we do from having any place in our election to God's favor (v. 6). But does he exclude faith also? Does the passage allow room for us to think that God elects those

God's Continuing Faithfulness to Israel: "All Israel Will Be Saved" (11:11–32)

In verses 1–10, Paul teaches that the rejection of Israel is not total—a remnant exists. Now, in verses 11–32, he teaches that the rejection of Israel is not final. As he so often does in Romans, Paul launches into his new topic by means of a question: "Did they stumble so as to fall beyond recovery?" The "they" in this question might be hardened Israelites but probably refers to Israel in general (v. 7). Israel has not obtained what it so earnestly sought. Is Israel's condition permanent? Will God's people continue to include only a small number of Jewish believers, as it now does? Or is there hope for a change in the situation of Israel? Paul's answer is debated among scholars. All agree that the key verse is 11:26: "All Israel will be saved." But the identity of "Israel" and the manner and time of its salvation are contested. I think that Paul here predicts that a significant number of Jews will turn to Christ and be saved at the time of Christ's return in glory, and in the comments that follow I will try to show why I think that this is the best option. But before we look at some of the details, an overview of the argument will orient us.

The entire section is built on the framework of a series of events in salvation history. These events involve God using Jews and Gentiles to accomplish his plan of salvation. The passage features a repeated pattern of oscillation between the two groups (see the sidebar "Jews and Gentiles in Romans 11"). God has set Israel aside so that Gentiles might be saved, but the salvation of the Gentiles stimulates Israel to jealousy. That jealousy, Paul suggests, brings Jews again into the kingdom, and the coming of Jews into the kingdom will mean "greater riches" (v. 12) and "life from the dead" (v. 15). A key issue is whether Paul envisions this sequence as a repeated historical pattern or as a single movement spanning the course of salvation history. I think that the latter is more likely. The salvation of Israel for which Paul hopes is a future, eschatological event.

The pastoral purpose of this theology is very clear. In this section Paul addresses especially Gentile Christians (v. 13). He warns them against arrogance and pride

Jews and Gentiles in Romans 11

- v. 11: because of their transgression → salvation has come to the Gentiles → to make Israel envious

- v. 12: their transgression → riches for the world
    their loss → riches for the Gentiles
    their fullness → greater riches

- v. 15: their rejection → reconciliation of the world
    their acceptance → life from the dead

- vv. 17–23: some of the branches have been broken off → you, though a wild olive shoot, have been grafted in → God is able to graft them in again

- vv. 25–26: Israel has experienced a hardening in part → until the full number of the Gentiles has come in → and so all Israel will be saved

- vv. 30–31: as a result of their disobedience → you who once were disobedient now have received mercy as a result of God's mercy to you → they who have now become disobedient now too may receive mercy in relationship to Jews and Jewish Christians (v. 25). This warning becomes particularly clear in the section that features the olive tree analogy (vv. 17–24). Gentile Christians should not delude themselves by thinking that they have taken the place of Israel in God's plan. God has brought salvation to Gentiles, but they have no cause to brag about it, because it happened through the grace of God. And their own salvation is being used by God to influence the Jews. One of the key pastoral concerns in Paul's letter to the Romans emerges here. He writes to a church that has undergone a shift from a Jewish majority to a Gentile majority, and this shift has led some of the Gentiles to take too much credit for their status and to look with disdain on their Jewish-Christian brothers and sisters. Of course, the Jewish Christians are not without fault in the matter. Paul will rebuke both sides in chapters 14–15. For now, however, his concern is with the Gentiles. Romans 11 affords a great example of a pattern found throughout the New Testament: theology with a practical concern.

As I have suggested, Paul's question "Did they stumble so as to fall beyond recovery?" probably applies to Israel as a whole. Paul, in effect, renews the question he asked at the beginning of the chapter: has God abandoned Israel? And again Paul responds with a resounding negative. He then grounds that negative by showing that Israel's "transgression," its failure to respond to God's salvation in Christ, has a purpose. God has initiated a process through which he is accomplishing his plan of salvation for the world. That plan required that Israel refuse God's offer so that the Gentiles might be included. We discover a microcosm of that plan in the Book of Acts. Paul and his fellow evangelists would frequently enter a city and preach to Jews in the synagogue. A few Jews would believe, but most would refuse God's offer. Paul would then turn to the Gentiles. The next stage in this pattern is not evident in the Book of Acts but is very important for Romans 11. The salvation of the Gentiles, Paul claims, is "to make Israel envious."

The immediate allusion is to Deuteronomy 32:21, quoted by Paul in 10:19: "I will make you envious by those who are not a nation; I will make you angry by a nation that has no understanding." The Gentiles' enjoyment of the blessings promised first of all to Israel will make the Jews desire those blessings for themselves. Verse 12 restates and elaborates that process. Israel has suffered a "loss" or "diminution" (hēttēma) that opens the way for God's riches to be bestowed on the Gentile world. And if that is so, think what wonderful blessings will come because of Israel's "fullness." This "fullness" (plērōma) may refer to a great number of Jews who come to salvation, but the word more naturally has a qualitative force, referring to the full experience of kingdom blessing that the Jews one day will experience.[2] Here Paul hints early on at what verse 26 asserts more clearly: a day is coming when "all Israel will be saved."

As we saw, Paul has a specific pastoral purpose in what he writes in Romans 11, and he makes it clear in verses 13–14. God chose Paul to be his "point man" in bringing salvation to Gentiles. On three great missionary trips Paul opened up the Gentile world to the gospel. He gained the reputation of being the "apostle to the Gentiles." Both Gentile and Jewish Christians alike may well have gained the impression that Paul had abandoned all interest in his own people to focus on the Gentiles. Paul now rejects any such misguided thinking. His ministry to Gentiles, in light of the salvation-historical plan he has just outlined, is designed to bring blessing to Israel. By saving Gentiles, Paul hopes to make his own people jealous and so save them as well. Gentile Christians need to know that they cannot use Paul's ministry to the Gentiles as an excuse for their own anti-Jewish attitudes, and Jewish Christians need to know that Paul has not abandoned the people of Israel. Again Paul reminds us of the overall plan of God of which his ministry is a part (v. 15). Israel's "rejection" means that the message of reconciliation comes to the world; Israel's "acceptance" will mean "life from the dead." This last phrase marks something of a turning point in interpretations of the sequence that makes up the framework of this chapter. If it refers to physical resurrection from the dead, then we would have evidence that the final step in the sequence, the acceptance of Israel, is an eschatological event. The return of Israel to the Lord would mean that the day of resurrection is upon us.[3] But the phrase also could refer to renewed spiritual life. Paul simply could be saying that Israel's acceptance of God's offer of salvation will mean that Israel has become spiritually alive once again.[4] Although there is some evidence in the New Testament that the phrase could have a spiritual meaning (see esp. Rom 6:12), the bulk of New Testament usage points to the physical meaning.

Verse 16 effects a transition from Paul's initial statement of the sequence of salvation history (vv. 11–15) to the olive tree

Balanced between Toleration and Spiritual Pride

When I was in college, we debated about which religion was "true." My children now in college discuss the truth of the different religions. A postmodern approach refuses to label any religion as being true in any absolute sense. Thus, debate about which one might be true is out. All that we can do is share what truth we have found in our own religious experience. This new context opens up possibilities for Christian witness. As my children who attended secular colleges discovered, fellow students and professors had to tolerate their beliefs. Along with that tolerance, however, came resistance to any notion of conversion. Why? Because conversion implies that one religion might be false and another one true. The culture in which we live always poses threats to the integrity of Christian thinking and living. One of those threats in our day is the lure of toleration. Familiarity with the world's religions makes it more difficult for Christians to believe that their faith really is superior to that of other people, and so various universalistic approaches are becoming more and more popular. Probably, few Christians will come to believe that their religion is no better than anyone else's. Nevertheless, the concept of toleration has affected many of us, sapping our eagerness to witness to others because we may think, down deep inside, that other people really might not need the gospel.

Contrast Paul's attitude in Romans 11. He knows that his people, the Jews, have been given many great blessings from God. But he also knows that without faith in Christ those blessings go for naught. So he dedicates himself tirelessly to evangelism, seeking to bring Gentiles to salvation so that ultimately he also might win his own people. Paul is under no illusions about the "equal truth" of Judaism and Christianity. Jews need Christ.

Paul, however, also warns us against the opposing danger. At the other end of the spectrum from tolerance is spiritual pride. Paul rebukes the Gentile Christians of his day for thinking too much of themselves and looking down on other people. In our effort to avoid tolerance of any viewpoint, we must be careful not to become proud and boastful. We need to witness to others, but to witness to them in the humility that comes from recognizing that all we have comes as a gift from God. We want to convince people of the truth of Christianity, but to do so in a way that makes the life of Christianity attractive to them. Balance in the Christian life always is difficult to achieve; Satan likes to tip us over one way or the other. But effective witness to the gospel of Christ demands such a balance, as we combine unshakable confidence in the truth of Christ with a gracious humility in presenting Christ to others.

imagery of verses 17–24. The existence of a remnant of Jewish believers at the present time (the "dough offered as firstfruits") creates an expectation of greater blessing to come. The "root" also could stand for the remnant, but Jewish authors referred to the patriarchs as the "root" (e.g., *1 Enoch* 93.5, 8; Philo, *Who Is the Heir?* 279), and Paul himself bases Israel's hope for the future on the patriarchs (Rom 9:5; 11:28). God's promises to the patriarchs cannot be taken back; they will be fulfilled in a renewed Israel. The idea of the root becomes the full-fledged metaphor of the olive tree in verses 17–24. Paul uses the metaphor to illustrate the relationship between Jewish and Gentile Christians. Jewish Christians, by virtue of their ethnic origin, are "natural branches." They belong to the olive tree, which represents the true people of God, by birth. But God has grafted "wild olive branches" into the tree: he has called Gentiles, who had no stake in Israel by birth, to become part of his people. Paul draws two important lessons from this analogy. First, Gentiles have no basis for pride or presumption. Their spiritual existence depends entirely on the root—God's promises to Jewish patriarchs (v. 18). They have nothing to brag about. Only by God's kindness and grace are Gentiles able to have any part in God's salvific plans. Furthermore, they must not presume on that grace. God can remove wild branches just as easily as he grafted them in (vv. 21–22). Second, Jews have hope for the future. God has grafted wild olive branches into the tree—a procedure "contrary to nature" (v. 24). If God can do that, how much more is he able to graft natural branches back into the tree again. The olive tree illustration does not perfectly capture every aspect of the way God has worked to form a people for his name. No illustration perfectly mirrors its spiritual truth. But the illustration does serve to make one point very clear: ultimately there is only one people of God. Gentile believers and Jewish believers belong to the same tree. One root—God's promises to the patriarchs—nourishes them all. God's kindness in election is the basis for his grafting all branches into the tree. And one condition—faith—keeps Jews and Gentiles alike in the tree.

Paul signals the importance of what he says next with an interruption to get our attention: "I do not want you to be ignorant of this mystery, brothers" (v. 25). "Mystery" *(mystērion)* refers to a complex cluster of theological ideas in Paul's writings. Generally, it has the sense of a purpose of God that previously has not been revealed. What is the mystery here? It might be the hardening that Israel is experiencing.[5] It might be the promise that "all Israel will be saved" (v. 26).[6] But probably it refers to the process of Jewish hardening followed by Gentile salvation followed by Jewish salvation that he has been talking about throughout this section.[7] Paul succinctly states this process in verses 25b–26a. The "hardening in part" that Israel is experiencing repeats the idea of Israel's "transgression" (vv. 11–12), "loss" (v. 12), "rejection" (v. 15), the natural branches that are cut off from the olive tree (v. 17). This hardening will last "until the full number of the Gentiles has come in." "Full number" translates the same Greek word we encountered in verse 12, *plērōma*. As I argued there, the word usually has a qualitative meaning, and so a more literal translation would be "fullness." But since that fullness is achieved by numerical addition, the NIV's "full number" is probably accurate enough. Paul looks for Israel's hardening to last only until the destined number of Gentiles to be saved has entered into the kingdom. It is "in this way" that "all Israel will be saved." I think that this refers to a significant number of Jews who will be saved in the last day, after the full number of Gentiles has been saved. After this era, during which God is saving many Gentiles and Jews, he will turn afresh to Israel, increasing the size of the remnant. This interpretation of verse 26 is the most popular among recent commentators on Romans. It explains the "until" of verse 25b, fits in well with the sequence that Paul has rehearsed several times in this chapter, and makes sense of the reference to the coming of Christ in glory that follows in verse 26b. But other interpretations are possible, and three should be noted.

The first is not, in my opinion, a viable option, but deserves to be mentioned. In the introduction to chapters 9–11, I referred to a notion that recently has gained popularity in some quarters: bicovenantalism. This view holds that there are two covenants, two ways to salvation: the Christ covenant for Gentiles and the *torah* covenant for Jews. Advocates of this view usually cite verse 26 in support of the *torah* covenant. "All Israel," they insist, must refer to the people of Israel as a whole, over the course of history. Paul makes no reference to Christ here, grounding the salvation of all Israel rather in the promise of God to the patriarchs (v. 28). Thus, all Jews are saved because of the eternal validity of God's covenant with the nation of Israel. But clearly, this interpretation is not right. Paul has defined what he means by "being saved" in Romans and argues that it happens only through Christ (see esp. 10:8–13). When Paul uses "saved" in verse 26, we must assume that it means there what it has meant throughout the letter. Neither Paul nor any other New Testament author teaches any route to salvation other than Christ. Jew or Gentile, slave or free, male or female—all must come through Christ to be saved.[8]

In contrast to this first view, the other two alternative views have been taught by orthodox theologians and have some basis in the text. Most of the Reformers and a few modern authors have taught that "all Israel" refers to the church as a whole.[9] The process that Paul has described in this chapter—Jews hardened, Gentiles saved, Jews made jealous and brought to new spiritual life—is the way in which God intends to bring all his elect to salvation. The problem with this view is that it must give "Israel" in verse 26 a meaning different from that which it has in the rest of the chapter. Everywhere else in chapter 11 "Israel" means ethnic Israel, and we must assume that it has that same meaning in verse 26. The third alternative view agrees, interpreting "all Israel" to refer to ethnic Israel, but advocates of this view suggest that it refers to all elect

Jews throughout the course of church history. In contrast to the view that I prefer, then, "all Israel" does not refer to a significant group of Jews living in the end time; rather, it refers to elect Jews at all times. In a cycle continually repeated, God brings elect Jews to salvation by causing them to be jealous of the salvation he has granted the Gentiles.[10] This view has much to be said for it but does not do justice to the indications that Paul sees the salvation of all Israel as an end-time event. "Life from the dead" in verse 15 points in this direction, as does the Old Testament quotation in verse 26b, which seems to refer to the second coming.

To summarize and conclude this discussion: I think that verse 26a predicts the conversion of a significant number of Jews at the time of Christ's return in glory, and I am deliberately vague about the timing. When will this conversion take place with respect to the rapture? Will it happen when Christ appears at the end of the tribulation? Paul does not give us the detail we would need to be this specific. One might also wonder how I can interpret "all Israel" to mean "a significant number of Jews." But a look at the way that the Old Testament uses the phrase "all Israel" shows that the phrase almost never refers to every single Israelite; rather, it refers to a representative collection of Israelites. Note, for example, 2 Samuel 16:22: "So they pitched a tent for Absalom on the roof, and he lay with his father's concubines in the sight of all Israel." Did every single Israelite alive at that time witness Absalom's sexual sin? Obviously not. The text suggests that a representative number did.[11] So, in the last days, I believe, God will turn again in his grace to Israel, saving a representative number in fulfillment of his promises to the people.

These promises are the focus of verses 26b–29. Paul quotes Isaiah 59:20–21 and 27:9 (with a possible allusion to Jer 31:31–34) to show that the Old Testament promises forgiveness of sins for Israel in accordance with the covenant when "the deliverer will come." A few scholars think that this deliverer might be God, but Paul is probably referring to Christ's return in glory. Verse 28 captures the essential tension that drives the argument of Romans 9–11. Israel's failure to respond to the gospel has made them "enemies" of God; they stand condemned under his wrath for refusing to believe in Christ. However, the word of judgment is not God's last word about Israel, for Israel remains beloved of God because of his promise to them in the patriarchs. God's gifts and calling are irrevocable. The promises that God has made to his people imply an increase in Jewish converts in the last days. Paul one last time sketches the course of events (vv. 30–31): as Gentiles have now received mercy through Jewish disobe-dience, so eventually the Jews also will receive mercy through God's kindness to the Gentiles. God has imprisoned all people in disobedience that ultimately he might have mercy on all people (v. 32). This verse does not teach universalism, that all people eventually will be saved. In this context, as is often the case in the Bible, "all" means "all kinds." God is working in salvation history to bring all kinds of people to salvation—Jews and Gentiles alike.

Response: The Wonderful Plan of God (11:33–36)

As Paul ended Romans 5–8 celebrating God's unshakable love for his people, so he ends Romans 9–11 celebrating God's marvelous plan for humankind. God's wisdom and knowledge, his plans and his purposes, are ultimately quite beyond the capacity of any human being to figure out. How does his unconditional election mesh with the demand that human beings believe and obey? How does God remain fair and impartial even as he promises salvation in the future to a significant number of Jews? How can he work in the lives of individuals to accomplish his plans? We have every right to ask such questions, but we must be cautious about demanding clear and logical answers. We cannot penetrate the mind of God. He does not need to consult us before he decides what he is going to do. At a certain point, we must stop questioning and demanding answers and simply believe and worship.

Study Questions

1. How does Paul's claim about the existence of a remnant of Jewish believers (vv. 1–10) fit in with his overall argument in Romans 9–11?

2 Does Romans 11:7–10 teach double predestination? Why or why not?

3. Sketch the four basic steps in the sequence of salvation history that Paul outlines in Romans 11:11–32. What are two basic ways of understanding this sequence?

4. When and how will "all Israel be saved" (v. 26)?

5. Does Romans 11:32 teach that all people will receive mercy? If not, what does it teach?

Part

6

Encountering the Transforming Power of the Gospel

Romans 12:1–15:13

16 The Christian Mind-Set

Romans 12:1–21

Objectives

After reading this chapter, you should be able to

1. Explain how the "practical" advice in Romans 12:1–15:13 fits into the theological argument of Romans.
2. Explain the relationship of the teaching in these chapters to what Paul teaches elsewhere in his letters.
3. Describe briefly the kind of worship that pleases God.
4. Understand the way Christians are to relate to each other in the body of Christ.
5. Appreciate how Christian love should affect our relationship to those within and outside the church.

Romans is justly famous for its theology. Christians have spent an incredible amount of time over the years debating the significance of the theological issues that Paul presents in chapters 1–11. Sadly, we have not always spent enough time reading and appropriating the teaching in chapters 12–16. These chapters are not an "add-on," an afterthought of miscellaneous pieces of practical advice. They are an integral part of Romans and the theology that it teaches. The New Testament knows nothing about a theology that remains on the theoretical level. All theology, all teaching about God, has implications for life, for when we learn about God, we learn about ultimate reality. And we cannot simply sit back and contemplate that reality; it changes the way we think about ourselves, our place in the world, our purpose for being. Theology, in other words, includes in its nature an implicit call to transform one's life, to adjust our thinking and our acting in accordance with the truth of God in Christ. The gospel not only saves us from God's wrath but also transforms us into the image of Christ. Paul has made this element of his theological teaching clear throughout Romans, but now, in chapter 12, he turns more directly to these implications of theology for life.

The well-known verses 12:1–2 issue the basic call for a transformed life. They stand as a heading over all of 12:1–15:13. In 12:3–13:14, Paul tackles several general aspects of that transformed life. He talks about how believers should relate to the body of Christ (12:3–8), how we should reveal the sincerity of our love (12:9–21), how we should relate to the governing authorities (13:1–7), how we fulfill the law by our love for others (13:8–10), and how we are to live in light of the day of the Lord (13:11–14). He then turns to a specific problem that was plaguing the Roman church: the dispute between Jewish and Gentile believers over the importance of certain demands of the Old Testament law (14:1–15:13). Clearly, therefore, we find a contrast between 12:1–13:14, which offers very general advice, and 14:1–15:13, which focuses

directly on the Roman Christians. Indeed, this first section is so general that some scholars think that Paul is summarizing his basic moral teaching.[1] The topics that he treats in chapters 12–13, however, are selected with at least one eye on the situation of the Roman Christians.[2] He chooses the topics of these chapters because they are especially relevant to the problems of the Roman community, although Romans 12–13 indeed addresses every Christian quite directly. But even the more focused teaching about the "strong" and the "weak" in 14:1–15:13 is relevant for us, for Paul uses the occasion of the specific dispute in the Roman church to teach enduring principles about how Christians who disagree should relate to one another.

The Basic Requirement: Total Transformation (12:1–2)

The moral life of the Christian grows directly out of the theology of the gospel. Paul makes this clear by exhorting believers "in view of the mercy of God." The NIV obscures the fact that the word translated as "mercy" is plural in Greek (oiktirmōn). Paul uses the plural form to emphasize the many aspects of God's mercy that he has highlighted in Romans. All these blessings should stimulate believers to give themselves in dedicated service to God and to his will. The central demand of verses 1–2 is that we offer our bodies as living sacrifices. By using the word "body" (sōma), Paul of course does not mean that we are to offer to God only our physical faculties. "Body" in Paul's teaching does not refer to a part of the human being, but to the whole person in relationship to the world. It includes our thoughts, our emotions, and our wills. All are to be given over to God in his service. This, Paul concludes, is our "spiritual act of worship." The Greek behind "spiritual" (logikēn) can also be translated as "reasonable" (KJV) or "rational" (cf. J. B. Phillips's "intelligent"). This sense might give the better translation. Paul is picking up an important strand of teaching from the world of his day that emphasized the need for human beings to offer God the worship appropriate for them. Animals might be slaughtered in sacrificial worship, but people worship God by using their God-given intelligence to honor him. The Jewish philosopher Philo puts it like this: "That which is precious in the sight of God is not the number of victims immolated but the true purity of a rational spirit *[pneuma logikon]* in him who makes the sacrifice" (*Special Laws* 1.277; cf. 1.272; see also *Testament of Levi* 3.6).

Verse 2 elaborates verse 1 by telling us how we can offer ourselves to God. We do it by avoiding the pattern of thinking and behaving characteristic of this world and aligning ourselves with the values of the world to come. That world has already dawned in the redemption accomplished by Christ. Believers enter that world and must realize that it, not this world, is now their true home. What Paul calls on us to do, then, is to live out the reality of our true, spiritual existence. But how do we take on board the values of the new age to which we belong? By "renewing the mind." This is a key idea in Paul's conception of the Christian life (see also Eph 4:21–25). Our minds are fallen; they have been corrupted through sin (see Rom 1:28–29). When we come to Christ, we are transferred into a new realm of righteousness and life (see Rom 5–8). Nevertheless, our minds are not imme-

Worship

Christians are sharply divided over worship these days. Some insist that God can be honored only through traditional hymns sung to organ accompaniment. Others cannot worship God without guitars, amplifiers, drums, and a worship team. Which style does the Bible mandate? Neither, of course. The Bible says almost nothing about the style of our worship. But it does say a great deal about other elements of our worship. Romans 12:1–2 makes two important points about our worship.

First, worship is not merely, or even mainly, what we do on Sunday morning. Worship is a "24/7" matter. We worship God when we give ourselves to him in service. We worship God when we show love to others, when we do our jobs faithfully and with integrity, when we play with our kids and nurture our families. God wants us always to be bringing glory to him by the way we live. A worship "service" is quite appropriate, even

mandated by Scripture. But we delude ourselves badly if we think that God is interested in our worship only during that service.

Second, worship that God honors involves the mind. I don't think that God much cares whether the songs we sing to him are accompanied by an organ or by a guitar. But I am sure that he cares about the words that we sing to him. The words that we sing should not only stir our emotions but also engage our minds. Our worship songs should reflect that fact that we are creatures endowed by God with reason. He wants us to *think* about him as the foundation for true worship. The best worship songs will remind us of some truth about God, Christ, or the Spirit, or about God's plan and purpose. As we sing to ourselves and to each other, we will be taught, and that teaching will be the stimulus for praise, confession, and thanksgiving.

An early Christian baptism, representing new spiritual life.

different parts with different functions, so too the church has people who are very different and serve that church in different ways (vv. 6–8). This means that each of us needs carefully to understand our role in the church and not to think more of ourselves than we should (vv. 3–4). What Paul says in these verses is highly relevant to any church, for we are always tempted to put on airs and forget our place in the community. But he may include it here in Romans because he knows that the Roman Christians are struggling with this very issue (cf. 11:25; 14:1–15:13).

Paul reminds us that he speaks as one who has been given a special grace from God: he is an apostle, with the right to address us with God's own authority. His central command, asserted at the end of verse 3, plays on the word "think" (the root *phron-* in Greek). We are not to "think" too highly of ourselves but to "think" in a "realistic-thinking" kind of way (an attempt to bring out the underlying Greek). Paul urges us soberly and deliberately to recognize what kind of people we are—what gifts we have been given, what weaknesses we have. He says to do this "in accordance with the measure of faith God has given you." The NIV rendering suggests that this "measure of faith" is an individual matter, that we are to consider how much faith God has given each of us and appraise ourselves accordingly.[3] But "measure of faith" also could be an objective standard that all Christians have in common: the faith itself, Christian truth. This is the yardstick by which we all measure ourselves.[4] Both interpretations make sense, but the second, because it supplies a clear and objective standard, might be slightly better.

We are not sure why Paul uses the imagery of the body to describe the church. It simply might have been an apt analogy, and Paul was not the first to use it.[5] Paul, however, sometimes expands the phrase to "the body of Christ" (e.g., 1 Cor 12:27; Eph 4:12), suggesting that he may think of the church as an extension of Christ himself, who gave his

diately changed; our thinking still tends to follow the well-worn ruts of the old way of life. Thus, we are called to engage in the lifelong process of changing the way we think, and by changing the way we think, we change the way we live. As Paul indicates at the end of the verse, the person transformed by the renewing of the mind is able to discern and put into practice the will of God.

Finding Our Place in the Body of Christ (12:3–8)

In this short paragraph, Paul touches briefly on themes that he has developed more fully in 1 Corinthians 12. The church, Paul explains, is like the human body. All Christians are part of that one body (vv. 4–5). But just as the body has

body in death in order to bring the church into being. However that may be, Paul's emphasis in this context is on the fact that Christians are unavoidably tied to each other in that one body, the church. We must view ourselves not as isolated individuals but as parts of one organism. If we view ourselves that way and truly make the health of that organism a priority, then it will be much more difficult for us to think too highly of ourselves. We will think, rather, how best we can fit in with the other members of the body and carry out effectively whatever function we might have in that body. In verses 6–8 Paul briefly mentions some of those functions. As he does elsewhere (see esp. 1 Cor 12–14; Eph 4:11–12), he uses the language of "gifts" *(charismata)*. Paul implies that all believers have been given at least one gift from God that they are to use in serving the body of Christ. Believers might, of course, have more than one gift, and Paul never provides an exhaustive list of all the available gifts. What he does, as here in Romans 12, is illustrate his point with a few selected gifts. That Paul would begin here with "prophesying" is natural, since he estimates this gift very highly (see 1 Cor 14). The New Testament prophet does not have the same authority as the Old Testament prophet, for the New Testament prophet's utterances are subject to scrutiny and assessment (1 Cor 14:29). But, like the Old Testament prophets, the New Testament prophet passes on to the community "revelation" from God (1 Cor 14:30–31). The prophet communicates to the church information that otherwise it could not have known. This information sometimes might be about the future (Acts 11:27–28; 21:10–11) but perhaps more often takes the form of exhortation or encouragement. Whatever word the prophet brings, he or she must be sure to prophesy "in proportion to faith." Again, as with the similar phrase in verse 3, this might refer to the degree of the prophet's own faith, but more likely refers to the faith in general as the standard by which the prophecy must be measured (cf. the NIV margin, "in agreement with the faith," with the NIV text, "in proportion to his faith").

"Serving" (v. 7) is, of course, something that all Christians are to do. But Paul probably has in mind here a more specific gift—perhaps the ministry of the "deacons," who serve the church by administering the affairs of the community, visiting the sick, and so forth (see 1 Tm 3:8–13; Rom 16:1; Phil 1:1; cf. Acts 6:1–6). Those who are gifted and called to this ministry are to give themselves to it. Indeed, this is Paul's emphasis throughout verses 7–8. He urges Christians to use the gifts they have been given. Teaching is the communicating of Christian truth to the community. All Christians teach each other to some extent (see Col 3:16), but certain believers are given a special gift in this area. They are the preachers and teachers of our day. The word translated as "encouraging" *(parakaleō)* in verse 8 can also be translated as "exhorting." Paul is probably thinking of believers who encourage others to live out the truth of the gospel. Probably, not many of us think of giving as a gift, but Paul names it as such here. Again, while all Christians are, of course, called to share their resources with the community, some believers, perhaps because they are wealthier than others, have a special ability to give. Such people are to give "generously," or "with a single will" (as *haplotēti* might imply). Those called to be leaders in the community should lead "diligently"; those who are good at showing mercy should do so "cheerfully." As one scrutinizes this list, it becomes clear that although some of the gifts, such as prophecy, can come only as special endowments from God, most of them do not require a supernatural touch. Serving, leading, teaching, encouraging, and showing mercy are functions that might reflect abilities that we have quite naturally. "Gifts," therefore, may take the form of natural abilities that a person already had before coming to Christ, which God then uses through that person in serving the church.

179

The Many Manifestations of Love (12:9–21)

These verses seem to be a hodgepodge of various teachings. Little structure or sequence of thought can be discerned. This should not bother us. There are times when a rapid-fire, somewhat random list of commands can be very effective in getting our attention. Paul does, however, pursue a persistent theme in these verses: the need for a humble and peaceable attitude toward others, whether fellow Christians (vv. 10, 13, 16) or non-Christians (vv. 14, 17–21). But this motif is subordinated to another that Paul announces at the beginning of the passage: sincere love (v. 9a). English translations usually insert a verb in this verse (e.g., the NIV: "Love must be sincere"). The Greek, however, has no verb. Paul therefore might intend the words to function as the heading or title of what follows: "sincere love" will look like this. "Sincere" translates a word (anypokritos) that means "not playing a part." Our love for others should not be faked or merely external. It should reflect the attitude of our heart.

Love, Paul suggests first of all, has a moral dimension (v. 9b). We tend to think of love as an emotion that we have little control over. We "fall" into it; we "drift" out of it. But in the Bible, love is a matter of the will. We determine to love. And true love will be directed to the good and will shun evil. We are in control. We are to choose to love what God values, what God loves. We are not to love those things that are wrong. Sleeping with another person before marriage is not an example of "love" in any biblical sense. Biblical love does not lead us to do anything contrary to the will of God. The command at the beginning of verse 10 uses two words from the Greek phil- root. Words from this root were used especially to denote the affection of family members for one another. The church, Paul implies, is to be a kind of extended family, in which believers have natural affection for one

another. And the result of such an attitude will be that we want what is best for others, honoring them above ourselves. Here Paul touches on the positive side of what he has warned us against in verse 3. Instead of thinking too much of ourselves, we are to think well of others.

The six commands in verses 11–12 do not seem to have much relationship to each other. Note, however, that they all use the same grammatical structure in the Greek. Most of the commands are quite straightforward, but two deserve some comment. "Keep your spiritual fervor" (v. 11b [NIV]) translates a phrase that also can be translated "be set on fire by the Spirit." Since Paul refers to the "Lord" in the next command, which is parallel to this one, a reference to the Holy Spirit is likely. Paul views the Spirit as the agent who creates enthusiasm within us for the things of the Lord. But the use of a command here indicates that the Spirit does not do this work automatically. We need to allow the Spirit to inflame our passions for Christ, his will, and his people. The second command that requires a brief note is the very next one. Most English translations have something like what we find in the NIV: "serving the Lord." An interesting textual variant has the word "time" (kairos) in place of "Lord" (kyrios). "Serving the time" would stand parallel to Paul's commands elsewhere to "redeem the time" (Eph 5:16; Col 4:5). In other words, he would be urging us to use the time that God gives us effectively in God's service.[6] The variant, however, is probably not original, and so the NIV should be followed.

Verse 13 returns to the theme of verse 10a. Our family affection for brothers and sisters in Christ should motivate us to share with those of them who are in need and to provide hospitality to those who require it. Putting up travelers for the night and providing them with a meal was a very important service in a culture without many hotels. Such inns as did exist were often hotbeds of crime. Thus, believers would depend on fellow Christians, their extended spiritual family, for hospitality.

Paul and Jesus on Enemies

Romans 12:14
"Bless those who persecute you; bless and do not curse."

Matthew 5:44
"But I tell you: Love your enemies and pray for those who persecute you."

Luke 6:27–28
"But I tell you who hear me: Love your enemies, do good to those who hate you, bless those who curse you, pray for those who mistreat you."

With verse 14 Paul introduces a very different dimension of sincere Christian love. We are not only to treat with affection our brothers and sisters in Christ, but also to extend love to people outside the community. As a reflection of that love, we are to bless our persecutors and not curse them. Anyone familiar with the teaching of Jesus cannot help but note the similarity between verse 14 and Jesus' own command in Matthew 5:44 and Luke 6:27–28. Indeed, Paul alludes to the teaching of Jesus more often in this part of Romans than in any other place in his letters. We cannot be sure why he does so, but perhaps he is again concerned to establish common ground with a Christian church that he had never visited by referring to teaching that he knew they would be familiar with. Although the Gospels had not been written yet (with the possible exception of Mark), Jesus' teaching had been passed down in the church orally by the apostles.

In verses 17–21, Paul will expand on the way that our sincere love should be manifested to people outside the faith, but first he turns back one last time to the Christian community (vv. 15–16). Again he urges us to identify with the needs of others and not to focus so much on ourselves. We should be willing genuinely to rejoice when things go well for others. A selfish, sinful reaction is to be jealous of the good that others experience. How often we feel that temptation! Love should lead us to look beyond ourselves and to join in the joy that others feel. In the same way, we should share the sorrow of those who mourn. This kind of identification with others can be difficult and painful. By opening ourselves up to others, we run the risk of emotional exhaustion and strenuous commitments of time, but after all, this is the nature of family life. "Live in harmony with one another" (v. 16a) summarizes the overall thrust of Paul's commands as they apply to our fellow Christians. Since the greatest barrier to that unity is our own pride, it is natural that Paul follows up with a warning about pride (see the similar sequence in Phil 2:1–4). In contrast to pride, Paul urges us to "associate with people of low position." "People of low position" also can be translated as "menial tasks" (see Today's English Version). In that case, Paul would be encouraging us to be willing to take on the jobs in the church that are not prestigious and perhaps get little recognition.

The final elaboration of "sincere love" returns to the issue of how we react to people who persecute us. The first Christians, of course, suffered a lot of persecution—although, at the time Romans was written, it consisted mainly of social ostracism and economic deprivation rather than physical abuse or legal measures. Therefore, the persecution that they suffered is somewhat analogous to what many of us face: scorn from those who

Study Questions

1. How does Paul's demand in Romans 12 that we live a transformed life fit with his teaching about the Christian life in Romans 6?

2. What standard can we use to gauge our significance in the church?

3. What is the unifying idea behind verses 9–21?

do not share our faith and cannot (or will not) understand it; the loss of jobs because we are not willing to go along with immoral bosses; petty slights and putdowns from people who are offended at our beliefs. The requirement of sincere love in these circumstances is clear: we are to avoid retaliation and instead seek to overcome with good the evil done to us. Paul again reflects key motifs from the teaching of Jesus (see esp. Mt 5:38, 43; cf. Lk 6:27, 29–30). And perhaps he also alludes to the example of Jesus, for Jesus not only taught the need to overcome evil with good, but also lived it. As Peter reminds us, "When they hurled their insults at him, he did not retaliate; when he suffered, he made no threats" (1 Pt 2:23). Echoing another theme of 1 Peter, Paul calls on us to continue doing good even when under the pressure of persecution. Indeed, we should seek to live at peace with everyone (v. 18). However, Paul's qualification, "if it is possible," reminds us that peace with others sometimes will not be possible. Paul would not have us compromise our morals or our integrity for the sake of peace. Non-Christians sometimes simply will not be reconciled or satisfied with anything less than a moral capitulation on our part. Paul cites Deuteronomy 32:35 to support his prohibition of revenge (v. 19). The best way to stifle our urge for revenge is to remember that a perfectly just God will one day right all wrongs. We can leave it to God to punish people who sin and resist him and persecute his people. In contrast to revenge, Paul urges us to feed and give drink to our enemy, for in doing so we "heap burning coals on his head" (v. 20). These words come from Proverbs 25:21–22, which Paul is quoting. We usually take them to mean that our kind actions will bring shame upon our enemy, perhaps causing him or her to repent and turn to Christ. This probably is the correct interpretation.[7] While the text is quite obscure, the Proverbs passage may allude to an ancient Egyptian practice whereby a penitent would carry a tray of burning coals on his or her head to symbolize repentance.[8]

17 Citizens of the World and Citizens of Heaven

Romans 13:1–14

Objectives

After reading this chapter, you should be able to

1. Explain what submitting to the governing authorities means.
2. Explain why Christians need to submit to governing authorities.
3. Explain how love for the neighbor fulfills the Old Testament law.
4. Appreciate the time in which Christians live and how that time should affect the way we live.

"In the world but not of the world" is a popular way of summarizing the Christian life. Though we live in this world, we are not to let the world "squeeze us into its mold" (to quote J. B. Phillips's paraphrase of Rom 12:2). The temptation that most of us face is to let the values of the world around us influence us too strongly. But the opposite temptation also exists: to think that not being "of the world" requires us to withdraw from or to ignore this world. While God calls us to live his heavenly values in the midst of the world, we must also recognize that God has not abandoned this world. He continues to work in it by his common grace. To turn our backs on everything associated with this world might be to turn our backs on some things that God intends to use for our good.

Government is one of those things. Paul knows that his teaching about "not being conformed to the world" in 12:2 might be taken by some Christians as a call to renounce all the institutions of this world. We have evidence from elsewhere in the New Testament that some early Christians took just such an attitude, condemning, for instance, marriage (see 1 Tm 4:3; cf. 1 Cor 7). So one of the reasons that Paul brings up the need for Christians to submit to governing authorities is to squelch this "antiworld" extremism. But he has at least two other reasons for introducing this topic here. First, Rome at about the time Paul writes is rife with antitax fervor. Paul may be afraid that the Christians will join in this movement, and so he reminds them of their obligations to government and of the need to pay their taxes (see v. 7). Second, Paul has just encouraged believers to avoid taking vengeance, leaving these matters in the hands of the Lord (12:19). Government, he now teaches, is one means that God is using to right wrongs and to punish evil (13:3–4). Christians therefore need to recognize government as one part of this world that they should uphold. But, after a short passage on love and the law, Paul reminds us again of the other side of the matter, the need to

Inscription of Romans 13:3 from Caesarea. (John McRay)

Dais in the Roman Senate, a symbol of Roman authority. (Ben Witherington III)

avoid the world's values and lifestyle (vv. 11–14).

Submitting to the Governing Authorities (13:1–7)

The point of this paragraph is clear enough: people are to "submit themselves" to the governing authorities (v. 1a, repeated in v. 5a). Paul provides two reasons why we should submit: God him-self ordains the authorities (v. 1b–2), and they have the right to punish people who do evil, or who do not submit (vv. 3–4). After repeating his basic command, Paul briefly touches on both these reasons again, in reverse (chiastic) order. We sub-mit "because of possible punishment" (v. 5b; cf. vv. 3–4) and "because of con-science" (v. 5c; cf. vv. 1b–2). Paul brings the teaching of the paragraph home with practical application: we must show our submission to government by paying our taxes (vv. 6–7).

Two words in verse 1 are critical for our understanding of this passage: "submit" and "authorities." "Authorities" trans-lates a word *(exousia)* that Paul often uses elsewhere to denote spiritual powers (see 1 Cor 15:24; Eph 1:21; 2:2; 3:10; 6:12; Col 1:16; 2:10, 15). Thus, a few interpreters—most notably theologian Karl Barth—thought that Paul here might be hinting at the spiritual beings that stand behind human rulers. We then should obey our earthly rulers, so this interpretation runs, only as long as they follow their spiritual counterparts in submitting to the ruler-ship of Christ.[1] Few interpreters today hold this view, and rightly so. While Paul can use the word *exousia* to refer to spir-itual beings, we have no evidence that he

The Structure of Romans 13:1–7

Submit to government! (v. 1a)	Submit to government! (v. 5a)
because:	because of:
God ordains it (vv. 1b–2)	fear of punishment (v. 5b)
government can punish you (vv. 3–4)	voice of conscience (v. 5b)
Therefore: Pay your taxes! (vv. 6–7)	

185

does so here. He interchanges that word with others in this context that clearly refer to human rulers (e.g., *archontes* in v. 3). The "authorities," then, are people who hold positions in human government—from the emperor or the president on down to the local bureaucrat.

What does it mean to "submit" to these authorities? As it is used in the New Testament, that word usually commands Christians to recognize that they stand in a certain hierarchy to others. Christian wives are called on to submit to their husbands (Eph 5:24; Col 3:18; Ti 2:5; cf. 1 Cor 14:35), Christian slaves to their masters (Ti 2:9; cf. Eph 6:5; Col 3:22), Christian prophets to other prophets (1 Cor 14:32), Christians in general to their spiritual leaders (1 Cor 16:16), and Christians in general to one another (Eph 5:21 [5:22–6:9 explains]). In each case, the believer is to recognize his or her need to "stand under" someone else. When applied to rulers, then (as here and in Ti 3:1), "submit" means to recognize that a hierarchy exists and that we stand under the rulers in that hierarchy. Normally, therefore, submission to the authorities will mean that we obey what they say. In all of Paul's hierarchical structures, however, the uppermost authority, though not always mentioned, is God. He stands at the top of all our hierarchies. What that means is that we must always submit to those over us in light of our ultimate submission to God. In certain cases, this might mean that we will disobey the authority immediately over us (a master, a husband, a ruler) in order to obey our ultimate authority. Paul, of course, does not spell this

Romans 13:4 and Capital Punishment

Debates over the legitimacy of capital punishment are nothing new. However, the debates have taken on new intensity in the wake of the use of DNA evidence in forensic police work. Several criminals condemned to die have been proved innocent through this type of evidence. Adding fuel to the fire of debate is the increasing recognition that the quality of legal defense plays a crucial role in whether a criminal is sentenced to death or not. People who can afford a good lawyer have a much better chance of avoiding execution than those who cannot. As a result of these factors, and others, people are less favorable toward capital punishment than in the past. And indeed, these issues should give us pause. They raise fundamental questions of fairness that must be addressed.

For Christians, the ultimate question must be, "Does the Bible sanction capital punishment?" This question is often answered from the Old Testament, where God himself institutes capital punishment in the nation of Israel. More important still is the principle that God announced to Noah: "Whoever sheds the blood of man, by man shall his blood be shed; for in the image of God has God made man" (Gn 9:6). Many Christians, however, wonder if the New Testament overturns this Old Testament principle. Thus, attention turns to Romans 13:4. In asserting the right of rulers to punish wrongdoers, Paul reminds us that the ruler "does not bear the sword for nothing." The sword might be an image of death by execution. If so, then Paul would implicitly be sanctioning the right of government to use capital punishment. However, we cannot be absolutely sure that this is what the imagery conveys. Paul simply might be referring to the "police powers" of the state, the right of the state to enforce law and order. Some ancient writers refer to police as "sword-bearers." The upshot is that Romans 13:4 probably cannot settle the matter one way or the other. I think it likely that it implies the right of rulers to execute criminals; but we cannot be sure.

out in this paragraph. His concern is with our submission, and he plainly expects that our submission will normally entail obedience. We are justified, however, in the light of the teaching of Scripture elsewhere (e.g., Acts 5:29; Revelation), to think that Paul would allow exceptions to his demand for obedience when the ruler insists that we do something contrary to the will of God.

Paul's first, and primary, reason for insisting that we submit to governing authorities is that God himself has appointed the authorities. God's role in raising up human rulers and casting them down again is taught throughout Scripture (e.g., Dn 4:17; cf. 4:25, 32; 5:21; 2 Sm 12:8; Jer 27:5–6; Prv 8:15–16; Is 41:2–4; 45:1–7). Paul allows no exceptions: "there is no authority except that which God has established." Our consciences, then, or our "consciousness of God," require us to submit to those whom God has appointed (v. 5). But there is another reason why we should submit. God has appointed rulers to carry out a definite purpose. They are to reward people who do good and punish people who do wrong (v. 3). God uses governing authorities as "agents of wrath" to visit his judgment on people who rebel against him and do evil. Christians therefore also should submit to rulers so that they avoid the punishment they would rightly deserve if they disobeyed. Again, we wonder as we read these verses about exceptions. Paul talks about rulers rewarding good and punishing evil. But suppose we find ourselves under rulers who reward evil and punish good. Suppose we find ourselves under a Hitler or a Stalin or an Idi Amin? Paul certainly was not so naive as to think such a situation would never occur. He knew his people's history, and he served a Lord who had been crucified unjustly by the governing authorities. So perhaps we can legitimately infer that Paul would allow us to disobey rulers when they fail to carry out their divine mandate to reward good and punish evil. Nevertheless, we must be very careful not to go too far down this road. Many interpretations of Romans 13:1–7 end up being explanations of what the text does not mean rather than what it does mean. Paul does not even mention exceptions. His concern is to get us to recognize the place that governing authorities rightly have under God as those placed over us. That should be the focus of our reading and application.

As we noted, Paul may conclude by calling on us to pay taxes (vv. 6–7) because Rome at the time of Paul's writing was wracked by antigovernment agitation over taxes (the Roman historian Tacitus mentions these disturbances [*Annals* 13]). But there might be another reason for Paul to bring up the subject of taxes. As we have seen in 12:9–21 particularly, Paul refers often in this context to the teaching of Jesus, and when Jesus taught about the disciple's responsibility to government, he did so in the context of a debate about taxes (Mt 22:15–22). In fact, some interpreters think that Paul might be alluding to Jesus' teaching directly in verse 7 when he requires us to give "respect" to whom it is due, for "respect" translates *phobos*, "fear," a word that often denotes the attitude we are to have toward God. Like Jesus, then, Paul might be calling on believers to "render to Caesar what is Caesar's" (e.g., taxes) and to render to God what is God's ("fear" and honor).[2] A direct allusion is not certain, resting, as it does, on a single word; dependence on the general teaching of Jesus is more likely.

Fulfilling the Law through Love (13:8–10)

Romans 13:1–7 is a bit of a detour in Paul's outline of the transformed Christian life. The passage is not unimportant or irrelevant to the overall topic,[3] but the general focus of 12:9–21 was Christian love, and 13:8–10 returns to this topic. The transition from verses 1–7 to verses 8–10 comes by means of the concept of "debt." In verse 7, Paul urges us to "give everyone what you owe him." Now, in verse

8, he repeats the idea, "Let no debt remain outstanding." But he then adds "except the continuing debt to love one another." Our obligation to love one another is a debt that can never be repaid. It always remains outstanding. We can never love enough. God will always be bringing new people into our lives whom we are called to love, and there are those people we have known for a long time whom we are called to love in new ways as they go through the ups and downs of life. But the bulk of this short paragraph is devoted to the reason we should love one another: loving one another fulfills the law. Whatever commandments of the law one might want to name, they all are "summed up" in the command to love the neighbor as ourselves (v. 9, quoting Lv 19:18). When we love the neighbor, we do no harm to him or her, and so love fulfills the law (v. 10).

But what, exactly, does Paul mean when he claims that loving others "fulfills" the law? The commandments that he cites in verse 9 reveal that he is thinking of—as he usually is when using the word "law" (nomos)—the law of Moses, the torah. Perhaps, then, he wants us to understand that we really have not obeyed the commandments of the Mosaic law until we add love to them. We can refrain from murdering someone, but our attitude toward that person might still be far from what God would want it to be. As Jesus reminded us, we must go beyond the outward act and deal with the inner attitude. We should not only refuse to murder people, but also cease being angry with them (Mt 5:21–22); indeed, we should love them (Mt 5:44; cf. Rom 12:14). So loving others might "fulfill" the law by "filling" it up to its ultimate meaning.[4] But there is another option, one that might do more justice to Paul's customary use of the language of fulfillment. In Paul's writings, and in the New Testament generally, this language usually refers to a new situation or teaching brought about by Jesus in the new age of redemption.

The "Day of the Lord" in the Old Testament and in Judaism

Some passages in which "day of the Lord" language appears will illustrate the conception:

The day of the Lord is near for all nations. As you have done, it will be done to you; your deeds will return upon your own head. Just as you drank on my holy hill, so all the nations will drink continually; they will drink and drink and be as if they had never been. But on Mount Zion will be deliverance; it will be holy, and the house of Jacob will possess its inheritance. (Ob 15–17)

"In that day," declares the Lord Almighty, "I will break the yoke off their necks and will tear off their bonds; no longer will foreigners enslave them. Instead, they will serve the Lord their God and David their king, whom I will raise up for them." (Jer 30:8–9)

Especially interesting is a passage from intertestamental Judaism that combines the two levels of meaning that we see in Romans 13:11–14:

The righteous ones shall be in the light of the sun and the elect ones in the light of eternal life which has no end. . . . The sun has shined upon the earth and darkness is over. There shall be a light that has no end. . . . For already darkness has been destroyed, light shall be permanent before the Lord of the Spirits, and the light of uprightness shall stand firm forever and ever before the Lord of the Spirits. (1 Enoch 58.2–6)

Thus, love's fulfillment of the law could be a matter of the love command standing in place of the other Mosaic commandments. Jesus himself singled out the love command as the essence of the law (along with, of course, love for God; cf. Mt 22:34–40 and parallels). Perhaps what Jesus intended is that true obedience to the love command would make unnecessary all the other commandments about our relationships with other people. If we truly love our neighbors, then murdering them, stealing from them, committing adultery with their spouses, and so on are unthinkable. Paul may intend a similar idea. Love is the essence of the Christian ethic. It is so important, so fundamental, that it can take the place of all the other commandments in the law about our relationships with other human beings.[5]

Living in Light of the Day (13:11–14)

The last paragraph of chapter 13 takes us back to the very beginning of this section, 12:1–2. Both these texts emphasize the nature of the time in which we live as a fundamental basis for our Christian obedience. These passages remind us that New Testament ethics is not simply a new moral code to be added to the list of other philosophies and religions. The ethical behavior that the New Testament requires is bound up inextricably with the New Testament teaching about the age of salvation that God has brought into being through Jesus Christ. In 12:1–2, Paul used the framework of old age/new age to make his point. Believers no longer should conform their behavior to the old age, which is passing away. They need to live out the values of the new age, to which they belong through Christ. Romans 13:11–14 uses the language of night and day to get a similar point across. But matters are complicated because Paul very skillfully uses the language of night and day at two different levels.

On one level, night and day refer simply to ordinary "nighttime" and "daytime." This application of the language is especially clear in verses 12b–13. (Note that the NIV distinction between "day" [v. 12a] and "daytime" [v. 13a] is an interpretation, as the Greek in both places is the same: *hēmera*, "day" [cf. the NRSV].) The ancient world, without electricity to keep cities lit at night, viewed darkness as the time of evil and corruption. Criminals could carry out their deeds under cover of night and escape detection. Decent people would fear to venture out after the sun went down. So it was natural for people to associate evil with the nighttime. Hence, Paul can call on us to put aside the "deeds of darkness" and to behave "decently, as in the daytime" (vv. 12b–13). Believers are to have nothing to do with those activities conducted in the dark—wild parties, excessive drinking, and sexual misbehavior. Instead of participating in activities such as those, we are to put on "the armor of light." Paul's introduction of a military metaphor, "armor," is striking. Perhaps he means, as Calvin suggests, that the believer is not only to be characterized by good deeds, the deeds done in daylight, but also to "carry on a warfare for the Lord."[6]

But "night" and "day" have another level of meaning. In the Old Testament,

Study Questions

1. How can we reconcile Paul's command that we submit to governing authorities with the teaching of Revelation that commends believers who disobey "the beast"?

2. How does love fulfill the law? What are the implications of this for the way believers are to view the Old Testament commandments?

3. How can Paul claim, "Our salvation is nearer now than when we first believed" (v. 11)? What does this say about salvation in the New Testament?

the prophets predict that God would fulfill his purposes for his people and bring redemption to the earth on "the day of the Lord." Jewish writers picked up this language, and it appears frequently in the New Testament as well, "Christianized" with references to Christ (e.g., 1 Cor 1:8; Phil 1:10; 2:16). When, therefore, Paul says that "the day is almost here" and that we are to live decently, as in "the day" (v. 13), surely we are to see allusion to this idea. Reflecting a typical New Testament perspective, Paul implies that that "day" is both present (v. 13) and future (v. 12). In his first coming, Christ inaugurated the "day of the Lord," but the culmination of that day, when our full salvation will be finalized (see v. 11), is still to come. What Paul wants us to do is to live in light of this period of time. We have new power to please God because we can draw from the power and blessings provided for us since that day of Christ has dawned. But at the same time, we long eagerly for the fulfillment of that day, when sin finally will be conquered and right will be established in all the earth.

18 A Plea for Unity in the Church

Romans 14:1–15:13

Outline

- Condemning Each Other Violates God's Prerogative (14:1–12)
- Limiting the Exercise of Liberty through Love (14:13–23)
- Receiving Each Other to the Glory of God (15:1–13)

Objectives

After reading this chapter, you should be able to

1. Explain the reason why Christians in the Roman church were condemning one another.
2. Identify the kinds of issues in our day that would correspond to the problem in the first-century Roman church.
3. Identify the theological bases of Paul's plea for reconciliation.
4. Relate the issue that Paul deals with in this section to the larger argument of the letter.

The New Testament repeatedly emphasizes the importance of unity in the church. God calls all believers to belong to one body, and that body is strong and has integrity in the eyes of the world to the degree that it functions in unison, with every member playing his or her necessary role (cf. 12:3–8). Yet often the Christian church as a whole, and Christian churches individually, are marked more by division and distrust than by unity and singleness of purpose. To be sure, division is sometimes necessary, for the New Testament also demands that Christians abide by apostolic teaching. When deviations from that teaching occur, the faithful need to respond and to criticize. And if faithful teaching cannot be restored, then Christians sometimes must make the sad decision to split from a church or denomination. Peace and unity are not the only virtues for the church; maintaining the truth is equally important. And there does come a time when unity might have to be sacrificed for the sake of truth.

But many, perhaps most, church divisions do not take place over serious doctrinal matters. Churches divide over what kind of instruments to use in worship, whether the pastor has the right kind of personality for the job, what color carpeting to put in the new sanctuary, and the like. Many of the quarrels and disunity that we see in the church are quite unjustified. Paul addresses this kind of situation in Romans 14:1–15:13. The Christians in Rome have divided into two groups. One of those groups, whom Paul calls the "weak" in faith (14:1, 2; 15:1), is criticizing the other group, accusing them of behavior that calls into question their status as Christians. The other group is responding in kind, accusing the weak of harboring silly prejudices that undermine their faith. Paul never explicitly labels this group, although 15:1—"we who are strong" —suggests that we can call them the "strong." Paul, of course, directs his teaching to this specific situation. But, as we will see in the comments that follow, this situation is analogous to many other situations that we confront in the church all the time. So what Paul writes about unity to the Roman Christians is both relevant and important for Christians today.

Because Paul repeats himself a bit in this section of the letter, and because we can understand his teaching in specific verses only by knowing something of the bigger issue, I begin by surveying the whole section for evidence of the specific issue that divided the Christians in Rome. I will then set this evidence against the background of the first-century world in an attempt to pin down the problem. Only then will we be in a position to interpret Paul's specific advice and to apply that advice accurately to our own day.

Paul mentions two, or perhaps three, specific issues over which the Roman Christians were quarreling. The biggest problem seems to have been whether Christians could eat anything they want or whether they should avoid eating meat (14:2–3, 14–15, 17, 20–21, 23). The weak apparently are those who refrain from eating any meat. The strong, on the other hand, think it quite all right to eat anything they want (see esp. 14:1–3). But Paul also refers explicitly to a second point of dispute: setting aside special days for religious purposes. Again, we can surmise that it was the weak who considered "one day more sacred than another," while the strong considered "every day alike" (14:5). There also might have been a third basis for division. In 14:21, Paul mentions drinking wine, along with eating meat, as the kind of behavior that Christians should avoid if they think that it might cause an-

Roman Colosseum as it appears today. (Ben Witherington III)

Sculpture of a Roman male offering a sacrifice. (Ben Witherington III)

the problem. A more attractive possibility is that the basic problem had to do with eating meat sacrificed to idols.[3] We find many parallels between Romans 14:1–15:13 and the passage in 1 Corinthians 8–10, where Paul deals with this problem. But this background, while it might explain the division over eating meat, does not explain why the Christians in Rome were also fighting over the observance of days and, possibly, the drinking of wine. We need to find a broader concern to explain all three of the specific points of conflict in Rome.

The best solution is to think that the weak were influenced by a Jewish tradition of asceticism based on the *torah*. The *torah*, the law of Moses, does not forbid eating meat or drinking wine. However, many Jews living in the midst of a pagan culture decided to avoid eating meat because they could not be sure that meat sold in the marketplace had been slaughtered and prepared in accordance with the requirements of Moses. For similar reasons, they would often refrain from drinking wine, for wine was associated with libations to the gods and was prepared in ways that might also violate Jewish kosher rules. The best biblical example of this tradition comes from the Book of Daniel. Immersed in the pagan culture of the Babylonian capital, Daniel "resolved not to defile himself with the royal food and wine" (Dn 1:8; cf. 10:3; and from Jewish intertestamental literature, Tobit 1:10–11; Judith 12:1–2, 19; Additions to Esther 14:17; *Joseph and Aseneth* 7.2). And, of course, Jews followed the law in observing the weekly Sabbath and the prescribed feasts.[4]

other brother or sister to fall. While not absolutely clear, it is likely that the weak refrained from drinking wine while the strong saw nothing wrong with it.

The crucial question is this: what was the underlying reason that led the weak to refrain from eating meat and drinking wine and to elevate some days over others in religious significance? Scholars have responded with a catalogue of answers to this question. Some think that the weak might have been legalists such as those Paul encountered in Galatia—people claiming that certain rules had to be followed if one were to be saved.[1] Others suggest that some kind of pagan religious influence might have been at work. We do know of a couple of pagan religions that taught asceticism—avoidance of the "pleasures" of food, drink, sex, and so on—and considered certain days "lucky" (a bit like the reverse of our "Friday the 13th" tradition).[2] Neither of these options seems likely. Surely Paul would have dealt more strictly with the weak if they really were trying to base salvation on following rules. And Paul uses several words and arguments that plainly point to a Jewish rather than pagan basis for

The scenario that best explains all the evidence of the text in its first-century context, then, would run something like this. Jewish Christians in Rome, convinced that the *torah* was still authoritative for Christians, claimed that a sincere Christian should avoid meat and wine and should observe the Sabbath and Jewish holy days. Only by following such practices could a Christian avoid ritual contamination and please God. These Jewish Christians, however, have ended up as a minority in the Roman church, and the now dominant Gentile majority thinks that such requirements are a ridiculous holdover from Judaism. Christians are no longer obliged to follow the *torah*, and the truly "liberated" Christian will understand that. Undoubtedly it was these Gentile Christians who labeled the other group in the church with the pejorative term "weak." They, for their part, prided themselves on being "strong." Paul makes clear his agreement with the "strong" (cf. 14:14; 15:1). He has taught in Romans itself that Christians are not "under the law" (6:14), and he himself did not always follow the practices of the Jewish law (see 1 Cor 9:19–23). Nevertheless, Paul's overriding concern in this passage is not with who is right and who is wrong. He is concerned about unity. He does not think that these particular issues are worth fighting over. Furthermore, he is particularly annoyed with the strong for their attitude of condescension toward the weak and the lack of love they are displaying toward them. So, although he rebukes the weak for their judgmentalism, he spends most of his time berating the strong for their selfish use (abuse) of their liberty in Christ. The bottom line for Paul in regard to those who pride themselves on being "strong" in their faith has never been expressed better than by Martin Luther: "A Christian man is a most free lord of all, subject to none. A Christian man is a most dutiful servant of all, subject to all."[5]

Condemning Each Other Violates God's Prerogative (14:1–12)

In this paragraph, Paul accomplishes two purposes. First, he gets the basic issue out on the table: the Christians in Rome are to stop judging each other (vv. 1–3). Second, he explains why they are to stop judging each other: they all are fellow slaves of Christ, to whom alone they an-

swer (vv. 4–9), and God alone has the right to judge his people (vv. 10–12). The shifts in the argument are marked by the second person singular address "you" (*sy* [Greek has separate words for the singular and plural of "you"]), that occurs at the beginning of verse 4 and verse 10.

A correct estimation of the problem that Paul is addressing must recognize the exact significance of the phrase "the one whose faith is weak." A more literal rendering would be "the one who is weak with respect to faith." Almost certainly this does not mean "a Christian who does not have much faith." In verse 2 Paul refers to the person whose "faith allows him to eat everything," as opposed to the one whose "faith is weak," who eats only vegetables. In other words, the issue is not who has the most faith. The issue is who thinks that his or her faith lets him or her do this or that. The "weak in faith" are not necessarily Christians who are more immature in their faith than the "strong"; they are Christians who do not recognize that the faith they have enables them to do certain things. The strong, on the other hand, think that their faith does give them the right to, for instance, eat meat and drink wine. An important, though not decisive, factor in where a Christian lands in these two groups is the way one was raised. Undoubtedly the weak in faith were mainly Jewish in background. They had been taught since birth that they must avoid certain practices in order to maintain their religious identity, especially as that identity was severely challenged by the overwhelmingly pagan environment in which they lived. It is no wonder that they found it difficult to discard some of their rituals when they became Christians. Nor, Paul implies, did they need to. He finds nothing wrong with the Jewish Christian who wants to continue to express his or her piety by following all the rules of the *torah* and of Jewish tradition. What he does object to is the tendency of the weak in faith to criticize other Christians for not following their practices. Christians no longer need to follow the ritual requirements of the law, Paul insists (see v. 14). Therefore, Jewish Christians must not condemn Gen-

Christians and the Sabbath

How should Christians observe the fourth commandment of the Decalogue? "Remember the Sabbath Day by keeping it holy" (Ex 20:8). Believers over the centuries have been uncertain about exactly what this commandment means in light of the coming of Christ. Some have insisted that the commandment means just what it says. As one of the Ten Commandments, a part of God's eternal moral law, the Sabbath command must be followed today just as it was in the days of Moses. So Christians should worship and rest on Saturday, the "seventh day" that God himself hallowed. A modern group espousing this view is the Seventh Day Adventists. Most Christians, however, have argued that the resurrection of Christ on a Sunday justifies moving the day of worship from the seventh day to the first day of the week. The New Testament itself hints that the early church did just this (e.g., 1 Cor 16:2; Rev 1:10). But what

about the requirement that God's people do no work on the Sabbath? Again, Christians have disagreed. Some have thought that the requirement still applies. Most have not, including most modern Christians. Probably most of us don't observe the Sabbath work prohibition, but more out of convenience than theological conviction.

Does Romans 14 have anything to contribute to the debate? I think it does. When Paul talks about disputes over "sacred days" (vv. 5–6) against a background of Jewish versus Gentile convictions, he almost certainly would include the Sabbath among those days. This is confirmed by his explicit inclusion of the Sabbath when dealing with a similar issue in Colossians (2:16). This means that Paul gives permission to Christians to observe or not observe the Sabbath as they see fit: "each one should be fully convinced in his own mind." Because Christians are not under the law (Rom 6:14),

Sabbath observance is no longer a requirement for God's people. As Hebrews suggests, the Sabbath command has found its fulfillment in Christ, so that all of us who have access to God through faith live in an eternal "Sabbath rest" (Heb 4:6–11).

Nevertheless, the Sabbath command suggests a principle that Christians can still learn from. One of the purposes of the Sabbath was to establish a rhythm of life in which the believer would take time off from the usual activities to worship God and to restore body and soul. There is much to be said for making such a rhythm a part of our lives. For instance, on Sundays I choose to avoid as much as possible any of my usual work. Not a word of this book was written on a Sunday! I find that a weekly break is vital to my own spiritual and physical well-being. But, as Paul makes clear in this text, we each need to make up our own mind on this matter.

---

adiaphora

tile Christians who ignore such requirements (v. 3). Neither, however, should the Gentile Christian scorn the Jewish Christian who wants to follow them (v. 3 again). Following the *torah* as a way of personal piety (not as a requirement of salvation) is in the category of what we call **adiaphora**—things neither prohibited nor required by the Christian faith.

Why is it wrong for weak and strong to be condemning each other? Because,

Paul reminds them, all Christians are fellow slaves (*oiketēs*, "household slave"). We all serve one master, one "Lord"— Jesus Christ (v. 4).[6] Whether we "stand" (are vindicated in the judgment) or "fall" (are condemned in the judgment) is up to Christ, not our fellow Christians. So what is important is that every believer behave with integrity. Each one should be convinced in his or her own mind (v. 5) and should do whatever he or she decides to do in honor of the Lord and in accordance with his will (v. 6). Everything that we do takes place before the Lord. There are no "neutral" areas of life; there is nothing we do or say or think that the Lord is unconcerned about. Death itself takes place in light of the Lord (vv. 7–8). Christ died and was raised precisely so that he might be the Lord of both "the dead and the living" (v. 9). All this means, to return to where Paul begins in this paragraph, that Christians should not condemn each other over the observance of sacred days and whether they eat meat or not (vv. 5–6).

Paul adds a second, closely related reason for his condemnation of the Roman Christians' infighting: God, and God alone, is the one who has the right to judge our conduct and determine whether it meets his standards or not. Therefore, the weak Christian should stop "judging" the strong Christian, and the strong Christian should stop "looking down on" the weak Christian (v. 10), for weak and strong alike will have to render an account of their behavior to God (vv. 10b, 12). Paul might mean that God will condemn believers for judging each other, but it is more likely that he reminds them again (cf. vv. 7–9) that God is the only one with whom we need to be concerned when it comes to eating meat and observing days. Paul's quotation of Isaiah 45:23 in verse 11 underscores the fact that all people will have to render an account to God in the end (cf. Phil 2:11).

Limiting the Exercise of Liberty through Love (14:13–23)

Paul begins his plea for unity in the church in Rome by calling on both the weak and the strong to discard their condemnatory attitudes. In verses 1–12, he focuses on the weak, but now he shifts gears. Verses 13–23 concentrate almost entirely on the strong. He rebukes the strong for having a selfish attitude in the way they use their liberty in Christ. Paul affirms the reality of that liberty (v. 14); no one, he implies, can take it away from us. But that liberty must be used in light of a more important consideration: love. The strong in Rome are ignoring the spiritual problems of their brothers and sisters as they flaunt their liberty before them. Their unconcern has the potential of doing real and lasting spiritual harm to their weaker brothers and sisters. Our liberty in Christ, a precious blessing, should be used instead to serve brothers and sisters. We should be focused not simply on what we *can* do, but on what we *should* do for the spiritual strengthening of other believers and the building up of the body of Christ. Paul issues this plea in verses 13–16 and verses 19–23; in between (vv. 17–18), he provides the theological rationale for that plea (see the sidebar "The Chiastic Structure of Romans 14:13–23").

Verse 13a seems to be addressed to both weak and strong, but it becomes clear as the passage unfolds that Paul really has the strong in view. They are the ones who pride themselves on having the insight to see that their faith allows them to eat meat, ignore holy days, and drink wine. And Paul has no quarrel with their basic theological view. He agrees: "no food is unclean in itself" (v. 14). Theologically, he is with the strong (see 15:1). His problem is with the way the strong are using their

The Chiastic Structure of Romans 14:13–23

A Warning about stumbling blocks (v. 13b)
  B Nothing is unclean (v. 14a)
    C Don't destroy one for whom Christ died (v. 15b)
      D *Theological rationale* (vv. 17–18)
    C' Don't destroy the work of God (v. 20a)
  B' All things are clean (v. 20b)
A' Don't do anything to cause a believer to stumble (v. 21)

The "Weaker Brother"

In Christian books and from Christian pulpits one sometimes hears Romans 14 applied something like this: believers should refrain from drinking alcohol out of deference to other Christians who might be inclined to overindulge and abuse alcohol. Those other Christians are the "weaker brothers" (or "sisters")—weak because they have a weakness for alcohol. The principle, of course, is valid enough. Christians should recognize the weaknesses of fellow Christians and do what they can to keep them from succumbing to those weaknesses. But we must point out that this idea of "weakness" is not what Paul is talking about in Romans 14. The "weak brother" in this chapter is the one who is "weak in faith." He believes that his faith does not allow him to do certain things. The weakness has nothing to do with an emotional or physical susceptibility. It is a theological weakness. Indeed, rather than referring to a Christian who is overly fond of alcohol, the "weak brother" is one who is convinced that drinking alcohol at all is wrong and condemns others for doing it.

theology. Right theology must be combined with insight into the needs of other believers, but the strong are ignoring the fact that there are other Christians who don't share their view. Other Christians cannot bring themselves to realize that their faith allows them to eat anything, and so for them, such food remains "unclean" (v. 14b). Although Paul does not use the word "conscience" in this context, that is the concern here (Paul does use that word as he deals with the similar problem in 1 Cor 8–10). That all food can be eaten by Christians is a truth that, theoretically, all Christians should know. Not all Christians, however, have been able to internalize this truth. The conscience of some Christians still tells them that eating certain foods is wrong, and Paul is worried that the activity of the strong in faith will create such pressure on the weak that they will cave in, go against their consciences, and eat meat. This is what Paul seems to mean by his language of "stumbling block" (v. 13b; cf. v. 20) and "dis-

tressing" the weak (v. 15a). The strong can cause spiritual harm to the weak by exercising their liberty to eat meat and drink wine in their presence. Since the strong are in a majority, the weak might be inclined simply to go along with the crowd and eat and drink as well. And by violating their consciences, the weak would be doing spiritual damage to themselves. Indeed, so serious might the situation become, Paul suggests, that the weak brother or sister might be "destroyed" (v. 15b; cf. v. 20). The language of "destroy," used in a spiritual sense, usually refers to eternal condemnation (see Rom 2:12; 1 Cor 1:18; 8:11; 15:18; 2 Cor 2:15; 4:3, 9; 2 Thes 2:10). Does this mean that Paul thinks that the behavior of the strong could lead a weak believer to lose his or her salvation? Some think so. But it might be that Paul simply warns about the ultimate destiny of those who keep violating their consciences, and perhaps he believes that the true believer always will be kept from that ultimate consequence.[7]

In addition to the practical issue that their behavior might lead to severe spiritual damage to other Christians, Paul adds three other reasons why the strong Christians should be careful about the way they exercise their liberty. First, they are not acting in love (v. 15a). As Paul has just reminded the Roman Christians (12:9–21; 13:8–10), love is the paramount Christian virtue. It must guide all Christian behavior. The strong indeed do have the liberty to eat meat and to drink wine. In the abstract, Paul would find nothing wrong with them doing so. But liberty is not as important as love. How and when a believer exercises liberty must be guided by love. And when a believer eats and drinks in a context that brings spiritual harm to another Christian, that believer clearly is not acting in love. A second reason that the strong need to refrain has to do with the liberty itself. That liberty is a "good" (v. 16), but if we abuse it and bring harm to other believers and dissension to the church, then it will begin to look like an evil thing. Third, believers should be willing to refrain from exercising their liberty because they should have a paramount concern for the well-being of the church. The kingdom of God, Paul reminds us, does not focus on "eating and drinking," but on "righteousness, peace and joy in the Holy Spirit" (v. 17). Our concern, therefore, should be to act in ways that enhance those virtues. We should be doing what leads to "peace" and to "mutual edification" (v. 19). Yet by insisting on eating and drinking whatever they want, the strong are disrupting the peace of the church. They "destroy the work of God for the sake of food" (the "work of God" probably refers to the church). What backward priorities!

Paul concludes with a final plea to the strong (vv. 22–23). Rather than trying to impose their views on the weak, they should be willing to keep them to themselves. What a shame if they had to blame themselves for harming believers and the church by doing what they approve of doing! And, for one last time, Paul reminds the strong how it is that they might be harming the weak (v. 23): if the weak go against what they believe, then they are sinning. It is not that their behavior in itself is wrong. Paul already has made clear that it is not. Their sin would arise from the fact that their actions would not be done out of faith, because anything not done out of faith, Paul claims, is sin. As we come to the end of this chapter, we must go back to where we began. The faith Paul refers to here probably is the same kind of faith he refers to in verses 1–2: faith that enables a Christian to do certain things. So verse 23 probably is not a general principle about sin and faith. In its context, it simply makes the point that weak believers sin if they act against what they believe they can and cannot do.

Paul's plea for unity takes a bit of a turn at 15:1, so we pause briefly to note the overall principle that Paul has established in chapter 14. That principle is clear: Christians must "agree to disagree" over matters that belong to the adiaphora. If a matter is not clearly prohibited in Scripture, or prohibited by virtue of clear theological reasoning, that matter should not lead believers to criticize each other or to break fellowship. Toleration, of course,

can be taken too far. Some theologians suggest that anybody who claims to be a Christian should have a right to his or her beliefs no matter what they are. The New Testament, however, sets clear boundaries, marking some matters as clear truths of the gospel. No Christian can deviate from these or tolerate those who hold different views on them. But toleration on the inessentials is what Paul calls for in this chapter. Many of the issues that divide Christians today fall into this category, and Paul would mourn over the divisions we have created over some of these matters.

Receiving Each Other to the Glory of God (15:1–13)

In verses 1–6, Paul issues a final, general plea to the strong. Then, in verses 7–13, he broadens his scope by calling on all the Christians in Rome to "accept one another." The theology that he uses to buttress that call in verses 8–13 casts an even wider net. His reminder of the way in which God has worked in salvation history to bring his salvation to both Jew and Gentile summarizes a key theme of the entire letter (e.g., 1:16, "everyone who believes, first for the Jew, then for the Gentile"; chs. 9–11).

Paul identifies with the strong and exhorts them to join with him in bearing with the "failings of the weak" (v. 1). The language of this verse is similar to Galatians 6:2, where Paul urges, "Carry each other's burdens, and in this way you will fulfill the law of Christ." Paul does not explicitly identify the law of Christ in Galatians 6, but certainly it includes, very prominently, the love command, which Paul has highlighted as the fulfillment of the law in Galatians 5:13–15. That command, from Leviticus 19:18, urges believers, "Love your neighbor as yourself." With this background in place, then, we can understand why Paul introduces the word "neighbor" in verse 2. By seeking the good of the weak and not just pleasing themselves by using their liberty in Christ in any way they wish, the strong will love their neighbors and so fulfill Christ's law. Christ did not simply issue the law of love; he also lived it. Christ, Paul reminds us in verse 3, did not "please himself." Rather, as the crucifixion story especially demonstrates, he bore the insults of those who had turned against God. Paul quotes Psalm 69:9 to make this point. This psalm features prominently as a source for language that the Gospel writers use to describe Christ's death (see Mt 27:34; Jn 2:17; 15:25; cf. Acts 1:20; Rom 11:9). So it is no surprise that Paul would turn to it here. But why this particular verse? Perhaps Paul is thinking of the insults that the weak are heaping on the strong for their failure to follow the strictures of the law. Rather than retaliating in kind, with criticism and mockery, the strong are to imitate Christ. They should refrain from insults and from any kind of mockery and content themselves with holding their own views and dealing gently with the weak.

Paul often teaches us in his letters by allowing us to overhear his prayers. In verses 5–6, he records a "wish prayer" for our benefit. Paul addresses God and asks for him to intervene in the lives of those to whom he writes. He thereby both seeks divine help for his readers so that they might be able to carry out his instructions and reminds his readers of the behavior they need to adopt. Paul calls on the "God who gives endurance and encouragement." Verse 4 (a parenthetical statement) reminds us that the Old Testament Scriptures were written so that we might have "endurance and encouragement." We need these qualities if we are to have the unity that is the heart of Paul's prayer here. We should be people who "think the same way" (*to auto phronein*; NIV: "spirit of unity"). Paul loves to use this word "think" (*phronein*) in these kinds of contexts (see esp. Phil 2:1–5; Rom 12:3–4). The word suggests a mind-set, a way of looking at life and steering our course accordingly. Paul does not require absolute uniformity of thinking, as if Christians need to be clones, never disagreeing about anything. Rather, it refers to a unity in spirit and attitude, an underlying sense of belonging to each other and loving each other that creates a loving context for the differences that inevitably exist among believers. It is when we exhibit this kind of united spirit that the church is able to praise God as he desires to be praised (v. 6). God is especially honored when his people unite, "with one heart and mouth," in their worship of him. Corporate worship should involve more than a group of isolated individuals who happen to come under the same roof at the same time of the week. It should be a union of like-minded people, all dedicated to God and to each other.

Romans 15:7 neatly summarizes all of 14:1–15:13: "receive one another, then, just as Christ accepted you." To "receive" another Christian means to recognize that person as a true brother or sister in Christ. It means to welcome other Christians into our worship services and give them a full place along with other worshipers. That reception should not be a grudging one (cf. 14:1); it should not come with a superior attitude, as if we are doing these brothers or sisters a favor by allowing them to worship with us. We may have differences over inessential points of theology or the way theology should be translated into practice, but these differences should not mitigate our wholehearted welcome. For the bottom line is that Christ himself has accepted us. Considering what we were in our sinful state, his acceptance of us is a matter of sheer grace. How can we withhold that grace from others when we ourselves have experienced it?

In verses 8–12, Paul grounds his appeal made in verse 7, and he does so by sounding very explicitly a note that runs as a constant theme throughout Romans: God has acted in salvation history to create a people composed of both Jews and Gentiles. Paul therefore implies quite clearly that the whole issue dividing the weak and the strong has to do with tensions between Jews and Gentiles. As we have seen, the specific problem seems to have been a sharp debate over whether Christians needed to observe the Mosaic law or not. The strong were not entirely made up of Gentiles, as Paul's standpoint makes clear (15:1), but most of them were probably Gentiles. And while there may have been some Gentiles who aligned themselves with the weak, we can conclude that most of the weak were Jewish. So Paul's reminder here of a key theological theme in the letter—the union of Jew and Gentile in Christ—provides perhaps the most important theological basis for his plea for unity.

The exact structure of verses 8–9a is debated. But the NIV reflects the better alternative:

> I tell you that Christ has become a servant of the Jews on behalf of God's truth,
> to confirm the promise made to the patriarchs
> so that the Gentiles may glorify God for his mercy.

Key Term

adiaphora

Christ's ministry to Jews leads, first of all, to the fulfillment of God's promise to the patriarchs. And by fulfilling that promise, Christ then also enables Gentiles to join with Jews in glorifying God. Throughout Romans, Paul has stressed that the gospel, as he puts it in 1:16, is "for the Jew first." The title "Christ" means "Messiah." Jesus was, first of all, the one whom God promised the Jews he would send to usher in the age of salvation. And so he has confirmed God's promise to Abraham, Isaac, and Jacob. As Paul points out in 9:4–5 and 11:28, God's continuing faithfulness to his promise means that the Jewish people still have a secure hope for God's mercy. However, in a theme equally important in Romans, Paul also has made clear that the fulfillment of God's promise given in the Old Testament spells blessing for the Gentiles as well. If the gospel is "first for the Jew," it is also "then for the Gentile" (1:16). As "all" have sinned, so "all" now have the opportunity to believe and receive God's forgiveness (3:22–24).

Paul has also shown that this extension of God's mercy to the Gentiles is in accordance with the Old Testament itself (see esp. ch. 4; 9:24–25; 10:19–20). Now he bolsters the point, citing a series of four Old Testament texts that speak of Gentiles joining with Jews in praising God as part of his people. Paul makes his case as comprehensively as he can, citing each of the three major sections of the Old Testament: the Law (Dt 32:43 in v. 10), the Prophets (Is 11:10 in v. 12), and the Writings (Ps 18:49 in v. 9b; Ps 117:1 in v. 11).

Paul concludes his plea for unity in the Roman church with another "prayer wish" (v. 13). The prayer touches on some of the major themes of the earlier exhortation. "The God of hope" reminds us of the opportunity Gentiles now have to

---

Study Questions

1. What underlying convictions led the weak in faith to adopt the practices that they did?

2. What kind of situations in the contemporary church might be similar to the situation that Paul addresses in 14:1–15:13? Be as specific as you can.

3. What implications does the teaching of these chapters hold for the ecumenical movement? Does Paul's argument support it or not? In what ways and with what limitations?

4. Explain how Paul's emphasis on the unity of Jew and Gentile in Christ (15:8–12) relates to his plea for unity.

5. Think a bit how the plea for unity, with its theological rationale, fits in with the general argument of the letter to the Romans.

"hope in him" (v. 12). When Paul prays that God might fill the Roman Christians with "joy and peace," undoubtedly he would have been referring back to 14:17: "For the kingdom of God is not a matter of eating and drinking, but of righteousness, peace and joy in the Holy Spirit."

By trusting in God, the Roman Christians will find that the Holy Spirit produces an overflow of hope. Jews and Gentiles alike can look ahead with eager anticipation to the time when together they can be set free from all remaining vestiges of sin and enjoy God's presence fully (cf. 8:19–25).

Part

7

Encountering the Letter's Conclusion

Romans 15:14–16:27

19 Additional Comments on the Concluding Material

Romans 15:14–16:27

Outline
- Paul, Apostle to the Gentiles (15:14–33)
- A Diverse Community (16:1–23)
- Glory to God! (16:25–27)

Objectives
After reading this chapter, you should be able to

1. Describe Paul's special sense of calling and apostolic ministry and relate them to the purpose of Romans.
2. Understand the purpose and significance of the greetings in Romans 16:1–16.
3. Appreciate the significance of Paul's references to women in Romans 16 for the ongoing debate about women in ministry.

apostle

Readers tend to lose concentration when they come to Romans 15:14. Here Paul starts talking about the specifics of the letter: why he has written, what his travel plans are, greetings to various individuals. All this does not seem very relevant to contemporary Christians. We have already dealt with much of this material in the two introductory chapters. We have seen that the specifics Paul gives in the concluding part of the letter are valuable for understanding the occasion and purpose of Romans. Our purpose here, then, is simply to touch on several passages and issues that we did not pay attention to in those earlier chapters. As we do so, I hope to show that the material in this part of Romans does have something to teach us.

Paul, Apostle to the Gentiles (15:14–33)

Paul's discussion of his ministry and travels falls into two temporal categories: his past ministry (vv. 14–22) and his future plans (vv. 23–33). In chapter 2, we surveyed these plans and estimated their significance for the occasion of the letter, but we did not look at what Paul says about his own ministry. Paul is concerned at least briefly to establish his credentials. He must have a good reason for addressing the Roman Christians as "boldly" as he does (to use his own word), and he makes clear that it is because of a special manifestation of God's grace that he can do so (v. 15). As Paul emphasizes in Galatians 1:1–7, his ministry is not the result of human appointment or self-advancement. God himself, through his Son, chose him to be an **apostle**—and to be a special apostle. God prepared and selected Paul to be the one through whom the gospel would be brought to the Gentiles. Much of Romans focuses on the way in which God has planned salvation history in such a way as to include Gentiles ultimately in the people of God. Paul is the perfect person to write about this because he was the one God used to accomplish much of

his purpose with the Gentiles. As Paul puts it in verse 16, he was given "the priestly duty of proclaiming the gospel of God, so that the Gentiles might become an offering acceptable to God, sanctified by the Holy Spirit." The priestly allusions in this verse are striking. Paul, of course, is not claiming to be a priest. He is simply using the language of the priesthood to make his point. He portrays himself as the one offering up the Gentiles as a sacrifice to God, and he suggests that he is fulfilling scriptural prophecies in this ministry. Verse 16 alludes to two Old Testament texts. The last phrase, "sanctified by the Holy Spirit," alludes to Ezekiel's prophecy that God would sanctify his name among the Gentiles in the last days (Ez 36:22–28).[1] And the reference to the Gentiles as a sacrifice recalls Isaiah 66:20: "And they will bring all your brothers, from all the nations, to my holy mountain in Jerusalem as an offering to the Lord."[2] Paul therefore sees his own ministry as a fulfillment of prophecies about the last days. Contributing to this emphasis on the unique significance of his own ministry is Paul's allusion to the "signs and wonders" that accompanied his ministry to the Gentiles (v. 19). This language is especially prominent in Old Testament descriptions of the exodus (e.g., Ex 7:3, 9; 11:9–10; Dt 4:34; Ps 78:43) and in the Book of Acts (e.g., 2:22, 43; 4:30; 5:12; 14:3; 15:12). Once again, the special place that Paul's ministry occupies in salvation history is accentuated.

As Paul writes to the Roman Christians, therefore, he writes from the consciousness of an authority that few others could claim. He is not simply an apostle, but *"the* apostle to the Gentiles." Despite the fact that he did not found the church in Rome or ever visit it (cf. vv. 20–22), Paul has every right to address the Roman Christians "quite boldly." And, of course, it is this same authority, under the inspiration of God, that gives Romans its special importance yet today.

In verses 19b–22, Paul briefly describes how his apostolic authority, exercised in the power of the Spirit, has enabled him to plant churches throughout the eastern

Mosaic map of Jerusalem, the earliest depiction of the city. (Ben Witherington III)

Mediterranean. But his gaze has now turned to the west. After delivering the collection to the saints in Jerusalem, Paul plans to initiate a new evangelistic enterprise in Spain. On his way to Spain, Paul intends to stop off in Rome to enlist the aid of the Roman Christians in this new enterprise (vv. 23–29). As we noted in chapter 2, Paul viewed the collection for the Jerusalem Christians as a significant step toward Christian unity. He therefore asks the Romans to pray that he, and his collection, might be received favorably in Jerusalem (vv. 30–33).

A Diverse Community (16:1–23)

Most of the matters that Paul touches on here are ones that Paul typically mentions at the end of his letters:

Commendation of a Christian fellow worker (16:1–2)
Greetings to Christians in Rome (16:3–15)
Exhortation to greet one another (16:16a)
Conveyance of greetings from other Christians (16:16b)

Warning about false teachers (16:17–19)
Eschatological promise and grace word (16:20)
Greetings from fellow workers (16:21–23)

But two of them are a bit unusual. First, Paul does not normally break into a tirade against false teachers in the midst of his closing remarks (vv. 17–19). We cannot be sure why he does so here. Perhaps he has a last-minute qualm about these teachers and wants to make sure that he gets in a word of warning before he closes. We cannot know who these teachers were or even what their agenda was, but Paul makes clear that they were typical of false teachers in creating divisions and distracting Christians from their true purpose. Second, while Paul often greets people in the conclusions of his letters, he never elsewhere comes even close to greeting as many people as he does here in Romans 16. What leads him to do so in this letter? He probably has two reasons. First, Paul has never been to Rome. He does not know all the Christians there, but only some of them—people he has met in the course of his ministry in the eastern Mediterranean. So he is able to single out those believers for special mention. And the reason why

207

Ruins of a temple in the Roman forum. (Ben Witherington III)

word "profitable" to the believer? I offer no definitive answer to that question. But one of the things that we learn indirectly from these verses is that the early Christian community was very diverse. In Paul's day, as in ours, people tended to gather with people who were like themselves. Greek men went with other Greek men to the gymnasium; Jews gathered at the synagogue, men together and women together. But the church, as far as we can tell from passages like this one, was quite a mixture of men and women from different ethnic backgrounds. Two aspects of this diversity are suggested in Romans 16.

First, the church in Rome seems to have been diverse ethnically and socially. We can surmise this from the many names that Paul includes in Romans 16. While not very interesting to the modern reader, these names are a gold mine for the social historian, because names in the ancient world were highly significant. People in our culture often choose names simply because they sound good or remind them of a movie star or athlete. But in Paul's culture, the names that people were given usually said something about their origin, profession, and/or social class. Peter Lampe has done a careful analysis of the names in Romans 16.[4] Several, of course, are Jewish names—Priscilla and Aquila (v. 3), Andronicus and Junia (v. 7), Herodion (v. 11a). But most are names that would have been given to Gentiles—for example, Hermes and Olympas, which refer to Greek mythology (vv. 14, 15). Furthermore, many of these Gentiles seem to have been "freedmen," a social class made up of people who had been released from slavery. And some were slaves still. To belong to the "household" of a certain person meant to be a slave of that person. Thus, those belonging to the households of Aristobulus (v. 10) and Narcissus (v. 11) were slaves. The names of Romans 16, then, imply a community made up mainly of Gentiles, and Gentiles from the lower strata of Greco-Roman society. Of course, these names are not necessarily representative of the entire church in Rome, nor can we assume that they are representative of the early church as a whole. Other

he has encountered so many is because the Roman emperor Claudius had expelled all the Jews, including Jewish-Christians, from Rome in A.D. 49 (see ch. 2 of this book). Second, Paul greets as many Christians as he can think of in Rome to establish common ground with the church. Writing to a church that he did not found and has never visited, he wants to make clear that a lot of the believers there already know and trust him.[3]

What are Christians who read Romans today supposed to learn from these seemingly irrelevant epistolary conventions and greetings? How is this part of God's

studies of the early church, however, have tended to confirm these findings.

Second, women were prominent in the Roman church, not just as attenders but as workers as well. Ten of the twenty-seven Christians whom Paul greets are women (more than one-third). Six of them (Phoebe [vv. 1–2], Priscilla [v. 3], Junias [v. 7], Tryphena [v. 12], Tryphosa [v. 12], and Persis [v. 12]) are specifically commended for their "labor in the Lord." The presence of these women fits in with what we know of the early church in general: it fostered an open atmosphere in which women participated alongside of men. This was unusual in the ancient world. Both Judaism and most of the Greco-Roman religions focused on men and often strictly segregated men and women. But what degree of prominence did the women in the ancient church hold? The answer to this question is important for the bearing it has on the ongoing and often volatile contemporary debate about the role of women in ministry. We can learn very little from most of the references to women in Romans 16; "working hard in the Lord" could take almost an infinite variety of specific forms.[5] Two passages,

however, are more specific and therefore have prompted considerable discussion.

In verses 1–2, Paul commends a Christian from Cenchrea, the seaport next to Corinth, who shortly will be traveling to Rome. He calls her a "servant of the church" (v. 1) and claims that she has been "a great help to many people, including me" (v. 2). The former designation does not necessarily prove very much: "servant" *(diakonos)* is a term used of all believers in the New Testament. It may have that sense here.[6] But the addition of the phrase "of the church" makes it more likely that *diakonos* here is an official title, designating Phoebe as a "deacon" (see the NIV marginal reading).[7] The "deacon" in the New Testament church is a bit of a shadowy figure; we simply don't have much information about what those who held this position did (see 1 Tm 3:8–12; Phil 1:1). Probably they were involved especially in the financial affairs of the community and were active in visiting the ill and administering the church's works of charity. The NIV translation "a great help" is a paraphrase of a single Greek word, *prostatis.* A few think that this word means "leader," but no matter how significant Phoebe may have been, it is quite unlikely that Paul would call her his leader. Rather, the word probably refers to the important ancient custom of patronage. People seeking to get ahead in the Greco-Roman world usually needed a sponsor—someone who could provide logistical and financial backing. Phoebe apparently was a wealthy woman who used her resources and clout to defend and sponsor Christian missionaries.[8]

The second debated text is verse 7, where Paul sends greetings to "Andronicus and Junias." "Junias" is a masculine name, but the Greek word here, *Iounian,* can be translated "Junia," a woman's name. The rarity of the former name and the commonness of the latter make it likely that "Junia" is the correct rendering.[9] Andronicus and Junia are probably a husband-and-wife team similar to Priscilla and Aquila (v. 3). What makes the debate about the name so important is that Paul goes on in verse 7 to call An-

A Fitting Conclusion: The Doxology and the Rest of Romans

Doxology (Rom 16:25–27)	Rest of Romans
who is able (power)	1:4, 16
establish you	1:11
my gospel	1:1, 9, 16; 2:16
revelation	1:17; cf. 3:21
prophetic writings	1:2; cf. 3:21
all nations (Gentiles)	1:5
believe and obey	1:5
only God	3:29–30
wise God	11:33–36

dronicus and Junia "apostles." Again, therefore, some claim that this verse provides New Testament evidence for women occupying the very highest and most authoritative positions in Christian ministry. However, it is quite unlikely that these two, never mentioned elsewhere in the New Testament, were "apostles" in the sense that Paul and Peter and John were apostles. The Greek word *apostolos* has a variety of meanings in the New Testament; the one that best fits this text is "commissioned missionary."[10]

Both Phoebe and Junia, therefore, stand as clear examples of the prominence that women had in the early Christian church and in its ministries. Neither, however, can prove that women in the early church held positions that put them in "authority over" men in the early community (cf. 1 Tm 2:12). The debate about whether it is appropriate today for women to hold such roles cannot be settled on the basis of these texts.[11]

Glory to God! (16:25–27)

Many scholars are convinced that Paul did not write these verses, that they were

---

Key Term

apostle

---

added to the end of Romans at some point after Paul wrote the letter.[12] However, the case against the authenticity of these verses is not compelling. The vast majority of manuscripts of Romans include these verses. They form an appropriate and natural conclusion to the letter.[13] Paul seems deliberately to have alluded to as many themes from the letter as possible in this brief doxology (see the sidebar "A Fitting Conclusion: The Doxology and the Rest of Romans"). Especially noteworthy are the reference to "my gospel" (v. 25) and the statement of a "two age" contrast between "mystery hidden for long ages past" and "now revealed and made known through the prophetic writings" (vv. 25–26). Salvation history provides the structure for the theology of Romans. Paul views Christ as the one who inaugurates the new and decisive age in the history of God's dealings with his people. Also characteristic is Paul's emphasis on the importance of this revelation for the Gentiles. Its purpose, Paul says, is "that all nations might believe and obey him" (v. 26). A literal translation of the Greek underlying that NIV paraphrase is "obedience of faith for all the nations." Thus, this phrase takes us directly back to the very beginning of the letter, where Paul says that his mission is to "call people from among all the Gentiles to the obedience of faith" (1:5 [a combination of NIV and my own translation]).

The deep theology and practical advice found in Romans have as their ultimate purpose the glory of God. It is when readers of Romans seek to understand that theology and to live out its consequences that God is glorified. May each of us reflect that doxology as we read and live out the message of this great book of the Bible.

Study Questions

1. On what basis could Paul claim the right to address the Roman Christians with authority?

2. What lessons might the modern church learn from the composition of the Roman Christian church?

3. What roles do Phoebe (vv. 1–2) and Junia (v. 7) play in the church?

4. Why does the doxology (vv. 25–27) make a fitting conclusion for the letter?

Notes

Chapter 1: Getting Oriented

1. K. Stendahl, "Paul and the Introspective Conscience of the West," *Harvard Theological Review* 56 (1963): 199–215.

2. E. P. Sanders, *Paul and Palestinian Judaism* (Philadelphia: Fortress, 1977).

3. Dunn has written about these matters in many places. Most accessible is his two-volume commentary on Romans (Word Biblical Commentary 38A, 38B [Dallas: Word, 1988]). One of his earliest writings on the matter was "The New Perspective on Paul," *Bulletin of the John Rylands Library* 65 (1983): 95–122.

4. Suetonius, *Life of Claudius* 25.2. The date has been disputed, but a solid case for A.D. 49 can be made. See, for example, E. M. Smallwood, *The Jews under Roman Rule*, Studies in Judaism in Late Antiquity 20 (Leiden: Brill, 1976).

5. For more detail, see D. J. Moo, *The Epistle to the Romans*, New International Commentary on the New Testament (Grand Rapids: Eerdmans, 1996), 211–17. Note also S. Westerholm, *Israel's Law and the Church's Faith* (Grand Rapids: Eerdmans, 1988), and M. A. Elliott, *The Survivors of Israel: A Reconsideration of the Theology of Pre-Christian Judaism* (Grand Rapids: Eerdmans, 2000). And see especially D. A. Carson, P. T. O'Brien, and M. A. Seifrid, eds., *Justification and Variegated Nomism*, vol. 1, *The Complexities of Second Temple Judaism* (Grand Rapids: Baker, 2001).

6. Augustine, *Confessions* 8.29.

Chapter 2: Paul and the Romans

1. *First Clement* 5.7: "He [Paul] taught righteousness to all the world, and when he had reached the limits of the West he gave his testimony before the rulers, and thus passed from the world."

2. See Acts 15:3; 20:38; 21:5; 1 Cor 16:6, 11; 2 Cor 1:16; Ti 3:13; 3 Jn 6.

Chapter 3: The Gospel of God

1. For further study, refer to D. J. Moo, *The Epistle to the Romans*, New International Commentary on the New Testament (Grand Rapids: Eerdmans, 1996), 70–76, 79–90; for other perspectives, see S. K. Williams, "The 'Righteousness of God' in Romans," *Journal of Biblical Literature* 99 (1980): 241–90; E. Käsemann, "The Righteousness of God in Romans," in *New Testament Questions of Today* (Philadelphia: Fortress, 1969), 168–82; J. D. G. Dunn, "The Justice of God: A Renewed Perspective on Justification," *Journal of Theological Studies* 43 (1992): 1–22.

2. A collection of essays that covers the field very well is K. Donfried, ed., *The Romans Debate*, rev. ed. (Peabody, Mass.: Hendrickson, 1991).

3. See J. Jervell, "The Letter to Jerusalem," in *The Romans Debate*, ed. Donfried, 53–64.

4. See in this regard the instructively titled book by A. J. M. Wedderburn, *The Reasons for Romans* (Edinburgh: Clark, 1991).

5. J. Denney, "St. Paul's Epistle to the Romans," in *The Expositor's Greek New Testament*, vol. 2, ed. W. R. Nicoll (1897; reprint, Grand Rapids: Eerdmans, 1970), 570.

6. A warning about imposing an "architectonic structure" on Romans has been sounded by J. C. Beker, *Paul the Apostle: The Triumph of God in Life and Thought* (Philadelphia: Fortress, 1980), 64–69.

Chapter 4: God's Wrath against Sinners

1. F. L. Godet, *Commentary on Romans* (1883; reprint, Grand Rapids: Kregel, 1977), 107.

2. See J. Boswell, *Christianity, Social Tolerance, and Homosexuality: Gay People in Europe from the Beginning of the Christian Era to the Fourteenth Century* (Chicago: University of Chicago Press, 1980), 111.

3. See, for example, *Testament of Naphtali* 3.4–5; Philo, *Change of Names* 211; *Special Laws* 4.79; *Decalogue* 142, 150; Josephus, *Against Apion* 2.273.

4. On the teaching of this text and of the New Testament generally about homosexuality, see R. Hays, *The Moral Vision of the New Testament* (San Francisco: HarperSanFrancisco, 1996), 379–406.

Chapter 5: Jews Are "without Excuse"

1. See F. L. Godet, *Commentary on Romans* (1883; reprint, Grand Rapids: Kregel, 1977), 119; C. E. B. Cranfield, *A Critical and Exegetical Commentary on the Epistle to the Romans*, 2 vols., International Critical Commentary (Edinburgh: Clark, 1975, 1979), 1.151–53.

2. For more details, see D. J. Moo, *The Epistle to the Romans*, New International Commentary on the New Testament (Grand Rapids: Eerdmans, 1996), 139–43; J. Murray, *The Epistle to the Romans*, 2 vols., New International Commentary on the New Testament (Grand Rapids: Eerdmans, 1959, 1965), 1.78–79.

3. See Cranfield, *Epistle to the Romans*, 1.155–56.

4. Failure to pay the "temple tax" was widely criticized (e.g., *Psalms of Solomon* 8.11–13; *Testament of Levi* 14.5).

5. See J. A. Fitzmyer, *Romans: A New Translation with Introduction and Commentary*, Anchor Bible 33 (Garden City, N.Y.: Doubleday, 1993), 318.

Chapter 6: The Universal Power of Sin

1. See L. E. Keck, "The Function of Rom 3,10–18: Observations and Suggestions," in *God's Christ and His People: Studies in Honour of Nils*

Alstrup Dahl, ed. J. Jervell and W. A. Meeks (Oslo: Universitetsforlaget, 1977), 141–57.

2. See J. D. G. Dunn, *Romans,* 2 vols., Word Biblical Commentary 38A, 38B (Dallas: Word, 1988), 1.158–60.

3. See D. J. Moo, "'Law,' 'Works of the Law,' and Legalism in Paul," *Westminster Theological Journal* 45 (1985): 90–96.

Chapter 7: God's Righteousness in Christ

1. Margin of the Luther Bible, on 3:23ff.

2. While details of interpretation differ, see, for this general approach, D. A. Campbell, *The Rhetoric of Righteousness in Romans 3:21–26,* Journal for the Study of the New Testament Supplements 65 (Sheffield: Sheffield Academic Press, 1992), 58–69; L. T. Johnson, "Romans 3:21–26 and the Faith of Jesus," *Catholic Biblical Quarterly* 44 (1982): 77–90.

3. See J. D. G. Dunn, "Once More, PISTIS CHRISTOU," in *Society of Biblical Literature 1991 Seminar Papers,* ed. E. H. Lovering (Atlanta: Scholars Press), 730–44.

4. See L. Morris, *The Apostolic Preaching of the Cross* (Grand Rapids: Eerdmans, 1965), 9–26.

5. See ibid., 136–56.

6. The most famous objector was C. H. Dodd; see Dodd's *The Bible and the Greeks* (London: Hodder & Stoughton, 1935), 82–95.

7. For this view, see A. J. Hultgren, *Paul's Gospel and Mission: The Outlook from His Letter to the Romans* (Philadelphia: Fortress, 1985), 47–72; D. J. Moo, *The Epistle to the Romans,* New International Commentary on the New Testament (Grand Rapids: Eerdmans, 1996), 231–37.

8. J. Denney, *The Death of Christ,* ed. R. V. G. Tasker (London: Tyndale, 1951), 98.

9. See J. D. G. Dunn, *Romans,* 2 vols., Word Biblical Commentary 38A, 38B (Dallas: Word, 1988), 1.185–86.

10. See C. E. B. Cranfield, *A Critical and Exegetical Commentary on the Epistle to the Romans,* 2 vols., International Critical Commentary (Edinburgh: Clark, 1975, 1979), 1.219–20.

Chapter 8: The Faith of Abraham

1. J. A. Fitzmyer, *Romans: A New Translation with Introduction and Commentary,* Anchor Bible 33 (Garden City, N.Y.: Doubleday, 1993), 385.

2. See, for example, Philo, *Special Laws* 4.187; see also C. E. B. Cranfield, *A Critical and Exegetical Commentary on the Epistle to the Romans,* 2 vols., International Critical Commentary (Edinburgh: Clark, 1975, 1979), 1.244–45.

Chapter 9: Rejoicing in Life and Hope

1. For this view, see J. Murray, *The Imputation of Adam's Sin* (Grand Rapids: Eerdmans, 1959). See also A. A. Hoekema, *Created in God's Image* (Grand Rapids: Eerdmans, 1986), 154–67.

2. See A. J. Hultgren, *Christ and His Benefits: Christology and Redemption in the New Testament* (Philadelphia: Fortress, 1987), 54–55.

Chapter 10: Freedom from the Power of Sin

1. Against, for instance, those who think that Paul might simply be using a metaphor (believers have been "immersed" in Christ) (so L. Morris, *The Epistle to the Romans,* Pillar New Testament Commentaries [Grand Rapids: Eerdmans, 1988], 246), and those who think that the reference might be to "baptism in the Spirit" (so D. M. Lloyd-Jones, *Romans: An Exposition of Chapter 6, The New Man* [Grand Rapids: Zondervan, 1973]).

2. See F. F. Bruce, *The Letter of Paul to the Romans,* Tyndale New Testament Commentaries (Grand Rapids: Eerdmans, 1985), 129.

3. See J. D. G. Dunn, *Baptism in the Holy Spirit* (London: SCM, 1970), 145, passim.

4. For this general interpretation, see G. R. Beasley-Murray, *Baptism in the New Testament* (Grand Rapids: Eerdmans, 1962), 133. This volume also provides the best overview of baptism in the New Testament.

5. See C. E. B. Cranfield, *A Critical and Exegetical Commentary on the Epistle to the Romans,* 2 vols., International Critical Commentary (Edinburgh: Clark, 1975, 1979), 1.308.

6. F. L. Godet, *Commentary on Romans* (1883; reprint, Grand Rapids: Kregel, 1977), 251.

7. See J. Murray, *The Epistle to the Romans,* 2 vols., New International Commentary on the New Testament (Grand Rapids: Eerdmans, 1959, 1965), 1.229.

8. D. M. Lloyd-Jones, *Romans: An Exposition of Chapter 6, The New Man* (Grand Rapids: Zondervan, 1972), 303–10.

Chapter 11: Freedom from the Law

1. See R. H. Gundry, "The Moral Frustration of Paul before His Conversion: Sexual Lust in Romans 7:7–25," in *Pauline Studies: Essays Presented to Professor F. F. Bruce on His Seventieth Birthday,* ed. D. A. Hagner and M. J. Harris (Grand Rapids: Eerdmans, 1980), 232–33.

2. See J. Murray, *The Epistle to the Romans,* 2 vols., New International Commentary on the New Testament (Grand Rapids: Eerdmans, 1959, 1965), 1.251.

3. See J. D. G. Dunn, *Romans,* 2 vols., Word Biblical Commentary 38A, 38B (Dallas: Word, 1988), 1.378–86.

4. See (combined with the first interpretation) D. J. Moo, *The Epistle to the Romans,* New International Commentary on the New Testament (Grand Rapids: Eerdmans, 1996), 423–31.

5. See, for example, Philo, *Decalogue* 142–143, 173; 4 Macc 2:6.

6. See, in detail, Moo, *Epistle to Romans,* 443–53.

7. See D. M. Lloyd-Jones, *Romans: An Exposition of Chapters 7:1–8:4, The Law: Its Functions and Limits* (Grand Rapids: Zondervan, 1974), 229–57.

8. See C. E. B. Cranfield, *A Critical and Exegetical Commentary on the Epistle to the Romans,* 2 vols., International Critical Commentary (Edinburgh: Clark, 1975, 1979),

1.344–47; Murray, *Epistle to the Romans,* 1.256–59; Dunn, *Romans,* 1.387–89, 1.403–12.

9. See Dunn, *Romans,* 1.395, and the broader treatment by K. Snodgrass, "Spheres of Influence: A Possible Solution for the Problem of Paul and the Law," *Journal for the Study of the New Testament* 32 (1988): 106–7.

Chapter 12: Life and Hope through the Spirit

1. Paul uses the Greek word for "condemnation," *katakrima,* only here and in Romans 5:16, 18—a lexical suggestion of the connection between the passages.

2. See K. Snodgrass, "Spheres of Influence: A Possible Solution for the Problem of Paul and the Law," *Journal for the Study of the New Testament* 32 (1988): 99; J. D. G. Dunn, *Romans,* 2 vols., Word Biblical Commentary 38A, 38B (Dallas: Word, 1988), 1.416–18.

3. "Sin offering," the NIV rendering, is probably justified, since the phrase Paul uses here, *peri hamartias,* frequently has this meaning in the Septuagint, the Greek translation of the Old Testament.

4. Note also that there is no word corresponding to the NIV's "your" in the text and that Paul refers to "life" (*zōē,* a noun), not "living" (the adjective presumed in NIV). Again, compare the NRSV.

5. So Augustine; cf. E. Käsemann, *Commentary on Romans* (Grand Rapids: Eerdmans, 1980), 232–33.

6. A few commentators have thought that the "one who subjected it" might be Adam (G. W. H. Lampe, "The New Testament Doctrine of *Ktisis,*" *Scottish Journal of Theology* 17 [1964]: 458) or even Satan (F. L. Godet, *Commentary on Romans* [1883; reprint, Grand Rapids: Kregel, 1977], 314–15).

7. Godet, *Commentary on Romans,* 320; Dunn, *Romans,* 1.476.

8. See G. Fee, *God's Empowering Presence: The Holy Spirit in the Letters of Paul* (Peabody, Mass.: Hendrickson, 1994), 588–90.

9. From Chrysostom's homilies on Romans.

Chapter 13: Israel and the Plan of God

1. See R. R. Ruether, *Faith and Fratricide: The Theological Roots of Anti-Semitism* (New York: Seabury, 1974).

2. See D. A. Hagner, "Paul's Quarrel with Judaism," in *Anti-Semitism and Early Christianity: Issues of Polemic and Faith,* ed. C. A. Evans and D. A. Hagner (Minneapolis: Fortress, 1993), 128–50.

3. This view can be traced back to the nineteenth century. Two prominent exponents in recent years have been K. Stendahl, "Paul among Jews and Gentiles," in *Paul among Jews and Gentiles and Other Essays* (Philadelphia: Fortress, 1976), and J. Gager, *The Origins of Anti-Semitism: Attitudes toward Judaism in Pagan and Christian Antiquity* (New York: Oxford University Press, 1983).

4. I emphasize that the problem is Israel's exclusion from salvation because a revisionist interpretation has received some support in recent years. According to this interpretation, Paul was not bewailing Israel's failure to be saved—Israel already is saved by virtue of the *torah* covenant—but Israel's failure to support the mission to the Gentiles. See L. Gaston, *Paul and the Torah* (Vancouver: University of British Columbia Press, 1987), 135–50; S. G. Hall III, *Christian Anti-Semitism and Paul's Theology* (Minneapolis: Fortress, 1993), 88–93, 113–27.

5. On this, see B. M. Metzger, "The Punctuation of Rm 9:5," in *Christ and Spirit in the New Testament: In Honour of Charles Francis Digby Moule,* ed. B. Lindars and S. Smalley (Cambridge: Cambridge University Press, 1973), 95–112; M. J. Harris, *Jesus as God: The New Testament Use of Theos in Reference to Jesus* (Grand Rapids: Baker, 1992), 144–72.

6. See R. N. Longenecker, *Galatians,* Word Biblical Commentary 41 (Dallas: Word, 1990), 297–99. For the opposite view, taking "Israel of God" to refer only to Jewish Christians, see

P. Richardson, *Israel in the Apostolic Church* (Cambridge: Cambridge University Press, 1969), 74–84.

7. See C. E. B. Cranfield, *A Critical and Exegetical Commentary on the Epistle to the Romans,* 2 vols., International Critical Commentary (Edinburgh: Clark, 1975, 1979), 2.480–81; J. A. Fitzmyer, *Romans: A New Translation with Introduction and Commentary,* Anchor Bible 33 (Garden City, N.Y.: Doubleday, 1993), 562–63; and, for a broader perspective on election, W. W. Klein, *The New Chosen People: A Corporate View of Election* (Grand Rapids: Zondervan, 1990).

8. See J. Piper, *The Justification of God: An Exegetical and Theological Study of Romans 9:1–23* (Grand Rapids: Baker, 1983), 45–54; T. Schreiner, *Romans,* Baker Exegetical Commentary on the New Testament (Grand Rapids: Baker, 1998), 497–503.

9. See Klein, *New Chosen People,* 166–67.

10. See G. K. Beale, "An Exegetical and Theological Consideration of the Hardening of Pharaoh's Heart in Exodus 4–14 and Romans 9," *Trinity Journal* 5 (1984): 129–54.

Chapter 14: Israel, the Gentiles, and the Righteousness of God

1. See J. Murray, *The Epistle to the Romans,* 2 vols., New International Commentary on the New Testament (Grand Rapids: Eerdmans, 1959, 1965), 2.43.

2. See D. P. Fuller, *Gospel and Law: Contrast or Continuum? The Hermeneutics of Dispensationalism and Covenant Theology* (Grand Rapids: Eerdmans, 1980), 71–79; C. E. B. Cranfield, *A Critical and Exegetical Commentary on the Epistle to the Romans,* 2 vols., International Critical Commentary (Edinburgh: Clark, 1975, 1979), 2.507–10.

3. See T. Schreiner, *Romans,* Baker Exegetical Commentary on the New Testament (Grand Rapids: Baker, 1998), 536–38; S. Westerholm, *Israel's Law and the Church's Faith* (Grand Rapids: Eerdmans, 1988), 127.

4. See J. D. G. Dunn, *Romans,* 2

vols., Word Biblical Commentary 38A, 38B (Dallas: Word, 1988), 2.587–88.

5. For argument and elaboration of this general interpretation of Romans 10:4, see D. J. Moo, *The Epistle to the Romans,* New International Commentary on the New Testament (Grand Rapids: Eerdmans, 1996), 638–41.

6. For this general approach, see esp. M. A. Seifrid, "Paul's Approach to the Old Testament in Romans 10:6–8," *Trinity Journal* 6 (1985): 35–37; Cranfield, *Epistle to the Romans,* 2.524–26.

Chapter 15: The Future of Israel

1. For this view, see J. Calvin, *Commentaries on the Epistle of Paul the Apostle to the Romans* (1540; reprint, Grand Rapids: Eerdmans, 1947), 410–11.

2. See J. Murray, *The Epistle to the Romans,* 2 vols., New International Commentary on the New Testament (Grand Rapids: Eerdmans, 1959, 1965), 2.79.

3. See C. E. B. Cranfield, *A Critical and Exegetical Commentary on the Epistle to the Romans,* 2 vols., International Critical Commentary (Edinburgh: Clark, 1975, 1979), 2.562–63; J. D. G. Dunn, *Romans,* 2 vols., Word Biblical Commentary 38A, 38B (Dallas: Word, 1988), 2.658.

4. See F. L. Godet, *Commentary on Romans* (1883; reprint, Grand Rapids: Kregel, 1977), 404; Murray, *Epistle to the Romans,* 2.82–84.

5. Murray, *Epistle to the Romans,* 2.92–93.

6. Cranfield, *Epistle to the Romans,* 2.573–74.

7. J. C. Beker, *Paul the Apostle: The Triumph of God in Life and Thought* (Philadelphia: Fortress, 1980), 333–35.

8. For a good criticism of bicovenantalism, or, as it is sometimes called, the *Sonderweg* ("special way") view, see R. Hvalvik, "A 'Sonderweg' for Israel: A Critical Examination of a Current Interpretation of Romans 11:25–27," *Journal for the Study of the New Testament* 38 (1990): 87–107.

9. One recent advocate is N. T.

Wright, *The Climax of the Covenant: Christ and the Law in Pauline Theology* (Edinburgh: Clark, 1991), 249–50.

10. See C. M. Horne, "The Meaning of the Phrase 'And Thus All Israel Will Be Saved,'" *Journal of the Evangelical Theological Society* 21 (1978): 331–34.

11. Some other significant texts are Nm 16:34; Jos 7:25; 1 Sm 7:5; 25:1; 1 Kgs 12:1; 2 Chr 12:1; Dn 9:11. Also frequently cited in this regard is the rabbinic text *Mishnah Sanhedrin* 10.1, which first affirms, "All Israelites have a share in the world to come," and then gives a list of exceptions.

Chapter 16: The Christian Mind-Set

1. See R. J. Karris, "Romans 14:1–15:13 and the Occasion of Romans," in *The Romans Debate,* ed. K. Donfried, rev. ed. (Peabody, Mass.: Hendrickson, 1991), 81–84.

2. See A. J. M. Wedderburn, *The Reasons for Romans* (Edinburgh: Clark, 1991), 78–81.

3. See C. K. Barrett, *A Commentary on the Epistle to the Romans,* Harper's New Testament Commentaries (New York: Harper & Row, 1957), 235.

4. See C. E. B. Cranfield, *A Critical and Exegetical Commentary on the Epistle to the Romans,* 2 vols., International Critical Commentary (Edinburgh: Clark, 1975, 1979), 2.613–16.

5. Several ancient writers use the human body to argue that the political state, although comprising many very different kinds of people, is a single entity. A few writers even call the state the "body" of the emperor.

6. F. L. Godet, *Commentary on Romans* (1883; reprint, Grand Rapids: Kregel, 1977), 435.

7. I should mention, however, that a few scholars think that Paul is suggesting that doing good to the enemy might increase his or her share in the judgment to come. They point out that in the Old Testament coals and fire are consistently images of judgment. See

J. Piper, *"Love Your Enemies": Jesus' Love Command in the Synoptic Gospels and in the Early Christian Paraenesis,* Society for New Testament Studies Monograph Series 38 (Cambridge: Cambridge University Press, 1979), 115–18.

8. See S. Morenz, "Feurige Kohlen auf dem Haupt," in *Religion und Geschichte des alten Ägypten* (Köln: Böhlau, 1975), 433–44.

Chapter 17: Citizens of the World and Citizens of Heaven

1. The best defense of this view is found in O. Cullmann, *The State in the New Testament* (New York: Harper & Row, 1956), 55–70; cf. K. Barth, *Church and State* (London: SCM, 1939), 23–36.

2. See C. E. B. Cranfield, *A Critical and Exegetical Commentary on the Epistle to the Romans,* 2 vols., International Critical Commentary (Edinburgh: Clark, 1975, 1979), 2.672.

3. A few interpreters go so far as to argue that 13:1–7 was not a part of Paul's original letter to the Romans (e.g., W. Munro, *Authority in Paul and Peter: The Identification of a Pastoral Stratum in the Pauline Corpus and 1 Peter,* Society for the Study of the New Testament Monograph Series 45 [Cambridge: Cambridge University Press, 1983], 56–67).

4. See T. Schreiner, *Romans,* Baker Exegetical Commentary on the New Testament (Grand Rapids: Baker, 1998), 692–95.

5. For this view, see S. Westerholm, *Israel's Law and the Church's Faith* (Grand Rapids: Eerdmans, 1988), 201–2.

6. J. Calvin, *Commentaries on the Epistle of Paul the Apostle to the Romans* (1540; reprint, Grand Rapids: Eerdmans, 1947), 489.

Chapter 18: A Plea for Unity in the Church

1. See C. K. Barrett, *A Commentary on the Epistle to the Romans,* Harper's New Testament Commentaries (New York: Harper & Row, 1957), 256–57.

2. See E. Käsemann, *Commentary*

on *Romans* (Grand Rapids: Eerdmans, 1980), 369.

3. A. Nygren, *Commentary on Romans* (Philadelphia: Fortress, 1949), 442.

4. This interpretation is supported by the wide majority of contemporary interpreters. See, for example, C. E. B. Cranfield, *A Critical and Exegetical Commentary on the Epistle to the Romans*, 2 vols., International Critical Commentary (Edinburgh: Clark, 1975, 1979), 2.694–97; J. D. G. Dunn, *Romans*, 2 vols., Word Biblical Commentary 38A, 38B (Dallas: Word, 1988), 2.799–802; D. J. Moo, *The Epistle to the Romans*, New International Commentary on the New Testament (Grand Rapids: Eerdmans, 1996), 826–33.

5. From *On the Freedom of a Christian Man*.

6. "Lord" could refer to God, but a good case can be made for thinking that the "Lord" here is Jesus Christ (see J. Murray, *The Epistle to the Romans*, 2 vols., New International Commentary on the New Testament [Grand Rapids: Eerdmans, 1959, 1965], 2.177).

7. It should also be noted in this regard that there is no word in the Greek corresponding to the NIV's "brother" in v. 15. Cf. the NRSV: "Do not let what you eat cause the ruin of one for whom Christ died."

Chapter 19: Additional Comments on the Concluding Material

1. See especially P. T. O'Brien, *Consumed by Passion: Paul and the Logic of the Gospel* (Homebush West, N.S.W., Australia: Lancer, 1993), 31, 50–51.

2. Note, however, that there is dispute about whether the "brothers" in Is 66:20 are Jews scattered outside Israel or Gentiles (as I am assuming). See Roger D. Aus, "Paul's Travel Plans to Spain and the 'Full Number of the Gentiles' of

Rom. XI.25," *Novum Testamentum* 21 (1979): 236–37.

3. P. Lampe, "The Roman Christians of Romans 16," in *The Romans Debate*, ed. K. Donfried, rev. ed. (Peabody, Mass.: Hendrickson, 1991), 218; J. A. D. Weima, *Neglected Endings: The Significance of the Pauline Letter Closings*, Journal for the Study of the New Testament Supplements 101 (Sheffield: JSOT Press, 1994), 226–28.

4. His major work is the monograph *Die stadtrömischen Christen in den ersten beiden Jahrhunderten: Untersuchungen zur Socialgeschichte*, 2nd ed. (Tübingen: Mohr, 1989). A summary of some of his main points is found in Lampe, "Roman Christians."

5. Some have made, however, exaggerated and, I think, unfounded claims on this point. E. S. Fiorenza, for instance, argues that these women were Paul's co-workers and therefore that most of them held ministries equal in authority to his ("Missionaries, Apostles, Coworkers: Romans 16 and the Reconstruction of Women's Early Christian History," *Word and World* 6 [1986]: 430).

6. See J. Murray, *The Epistle to the Romans*, 2 vols., New International Commentary on the New Testament (Grand Rapids: Eerdmans, 1959, 1965), 2.226.

7. So most commentators, among them F. L. Godet, *Commentary on Romans* (1883; reprint, Grand Rapids: Kregel, 1977), 488; C. E. B. Cranfield, *A Critical and Exegetical Commentary on the Epistle to the Romans*, 2 vols., International Critical Commentary (Edinburgh: Clark, 1975, 1979), 2.781.

8. See W. Sanday and A. C. Headlam, *A Critical and Exegetical Commentary on the Epistle to the Romans*, International Critical Commentary (Edinburgh: Clark, 1902), 417–18; J. D. G. Dunn,

Romans, 2 vols., Word Biblical Commentary 38A, 38B (Dallas: Word, 1988), 2.888–89; Cranfield, *Epistle to the Romans*, 2.782–83.

9. Indeed, some claim that "Junias," a contraction of the name "Junianus," is unknown. See Richard S. Cervin, "A Note Regarding the Name 'Junia(s)' in Romans 16.7," *New Testament Studies* 40 (1994): 464–70.

10. So most recent commentators, among them T. Schreiner, *Romans*, Baker Exegetical Commentary on the New Testament (Grand Rapids: Baker, 1998), 796; Cranfield, *Epistle to the Romans*, 2.789; Dunn, *Romans*, 2.894–95.

11. For further remarks on these texts and the general issue, see D. J. Moo, "What Does It Mean Not to Teach or Have Authority over Men (1 Timothy 2:11–15)?" in *Recovering Biblical Manhood and Womanhood*, ed. J. Piper and W. Grudem (Westchester, Ill.: Crossway, 1991), 179–93.

12. See E. Käsemann, *Commentary on Romans* (Grand Rapids: Eerdmans, 1980), 422, 427–28; J. A. Fitzmyer, *Romans: A New Translation with Introduction and Commentary*, Anchor Bible 33 (Garden City, N.Y.: Doubleday, 1993), 753; Cranfield, *Epistle to the Romans*, 2.808; Dunn, *Romans*, 2.912–13.

13. See L. Hurtado, "The Doxology at the End of Romans," in *New Testament Textual Criticism, Its Significance for Exegesis: Essays in Honor of Bruce M. Metzger*, ed. E. J. Epp and G. D. Fee (Oxford: Clarendon, 1981), 185–99; I. H. Marshall, "Romans 16:25–27—An Apt Conclusion," in *Romans and the People of God: Essays in Honor of Gordon D. Fee on the Occasion of His Sixty-fifth Birthday*, ed. S. K. Soderlund and N. T. Wright (Grand Rapids: Eerdmans, 1999), 170–84.

Glossary

adiaphora
Things neither prohibited nor required by the Christian faith.

apocalyptic
A movement among the Jews of the intertestamental period that emphasized God's vindication of his people at the end of history. Apocalyptic writers tended to divide history into two contrasting periods, the "old age" and the "new age."

apostle
Derived from the Greek *apostolos*, it can refer to those men specially selected by Christ to be the foundation of the church (e.g., Paul), but also can refer to messengers or commissioned missionaries.

Arminianism
A theological orientation derived from the seventeenth-century teacher Jacob Arminius. It highlights human involvement in the process of salvation, basing God's election on human believing and allowing for the possibility that Christians might lose their salvation.

atonement
The name given to the doctrine concerning what God did for us in Christ on the cross.

bicovenantalism
A sub-Christian view of salvation claiming that there are two covenants by which people can be saved: the torah covenant for Jews and the Christ covenant for Gentiles. *See "Sonderweg."*

Calvinism
A theological orientation derived from the teaching of the Reformer John Calvin. It stresses God's sovereignty in salvation, including the

ideas of unconditional election (God chooses who will believe) and eternal security (God infallibly preserves believers in their salvation to the end).

chiasm
The word is derived from the Greek letter *chi*, the shape of which looks like our letter *X*. It refers to a literary device in which items are arranged in an a-b-b'-a' pattern.

corporate solidarity
A way of thinking that pervades the Bible about the way human beings are linked together. The concept explains why Paul can view Adam and Christ as figures whose actions are at the same time actions of other people as well.

covenant
An agreement initiated by God through which he grants blessing to his people and demands response from them.

diatribe
A literary style featuring questions and answers, which Paul uses extensively in Romans.

election
The doctrine relating to the way God "calls" or "chooses" people to enter into relationship with him.

inclusio
A literary device in which an argument or section begins and ends with the same words or ideas.

justification
The judicial verdict of God declaring sinners innocent of their sin in God's eyes.

mercy seat
The traditional name for the place in the tabernacle of Israel where the blood of sacrifice on the Day of Atonement was sprinkled.

natural revelation
What God reveals about himself in the world itself. Distinguished from special revelation, God's specific communicative acts (the Bible, events in history such as the exodus, etc.). *See* "special revelation."

new age
Denotes the new era that began with the coming of Christ and the pouring out of the Holy Spirit. It is one segment of a salvation-historical scheme of approach.

new perspective
An approach to interpreting the apostle Paul's theology that has become popular in the last thirty years. It emphasizes Paul's concern with "people issues" (the relationship of Jews and Gentiles) and downplays traditional individual salvation concerns.

old age
Denotes the old era dominated by sin and death. While judged in Christ's coming, it continues to exert influence on believers.

patriarchs
The "fathers" of the nation of Israel, especially Abraham, Isaac, and Jacob. God's promises to them constitute the foundation for the people of God.

reconciliation
Bringing two parties together into a harmonious relationship. It is one metaphor for what Christ accomplished by bringing sinners and a wrathful God into relationship.

righteousness
An important theological term drawn from the Old Testament. It can refer to God's own "justice," to the upright behavior he expects of his people, and to his intervention

to put people back into a right relationship with himself.

salvation history
A phrase used to describe an approach to interpreting the gospel that emphasizes the way God has revealed himself in stages. *See* "old age," "new age."

Sonderweg
A German term, meaning "special way," often used to describe the way of salvation for Jews within the bicovenantal approach. *See* "bicovenantalism."

special revelation
God's revelation of himself and his purposes that comes to us in definite oral (e.g., prophecies) and written (the word of God) form. *See* "natural revelation."

torah
A transliteration of the Hebrew word for "law," used in this commentary to refer to the law given by God to Israel through Moses.

Select Annotated Bibliography

Barrett, C. K. *A Commentary on the Epistle to the Romans.* Harper's New Testament Commentaries. New York: Harper & Row, 1957. Brief but direct exposition by a noted British scholar.

Bruce, F. F. *The Letter of Paul to the Romans.* Tyndale New Testament Commentaries. Grand Rapids: Eerdmans, 1985. General exposition of Romans from the most famous evangelical Pauline scholar.

Calvin, J. *Commentaries on the Epistle of Paul the Apostle to the Romans.* 1540. Reprint, Grand Rapids: Eerdmans, 1947. Pithy, theologically insightful comments from one of the chief Reformers.

Cranfield, C. E. B. *A Critical and Exegetical Commentary on the Epistle to the Romans.* International Critical Commentary. 2 vols. Edinburgh: Clark, 1975, 1979. One of the most detailed commentaries in the modern era on the Greek text of Romans. Important for careful analysis of alternatives and marked by a Barthian theological stance.

Deidun, T. J. *New Covenant Morality in Paul.* Rome: Pontifical Biblical Institute, 1981. A stimulating study of the way Paul communicates the basic theology of his moral teaching.

Donfried, K., ed. *The Romans Debate.* Rev. ed. Peabody, Mass.: Hendrickson, 1991. Excellent collection of essays on issues pertaining to the nature and purpose of Romans.

Dunn, J. D. G. *Romans.* 2 vols. Word Biblical Commentary 38A, 38B. Dallas: Word, 1988. Especially strong on Jewish backgrounds, with constant interaction with other scholarly viewpoints. The best representative of the "new perspective" on Paul in Romans.

Fee, G. D. *God's Empowering Presence: The Holy Spirit in the Letters of Paul.* Peabody, Mass.: Hendrickson, 1994. Comprehensive and stimulating treatment of Paul's teaching on an important element of Pauline theology and of Romans.

Fitzmyer, J. A. *Romans: A New Translation with Introduction and Commentary.* Anchor Bible 33. New York: Doubleday, 1993. Extremely full bibliographies, sound and careful in interpretation. Roman Catholic in theology, but not aggressively so.

Godet, F. L. *Commentary on Romans.* 1883. Reprint, Grand Rapids: Kregel, 1977. A classic commentary on the Greek text from a great nineteenth-century expositor. Valuable for its generally Arminian approach to Paul.

Hays, R. B. *Echoes of Scripture in the Letters of Paul.* New Haven: Yale University Press, 1989. A groundbreaking study on the variety of ways in which Paul uses the Old Testament to make his points.

Käsemann, E. *Commentary on Romans.* Grand Rapids: Eerdmans, 1980. A translation of a classic German commentary, representing the post-Bultmannian perspective. Very technical, assuming considerable acquaintance with Greek and the history of interpretation.

Laato, T. *Paul and Judaism: An Anthropological Approach.* Atlanta: Scholars Press, 1995. An important response to many of the issues raised by the "new perspective" on Romans.

Lloyd-Jones, D. M. *Romans: An Exposition of Chapter 5, Assurance.* Grand Rapids, Zondervan, 1971. This volume and the three listed below it offer insightful, theologically oriented exposition from a great British evangelical preacher. Other volumes in this series by Lloyd-Jones (not listed here) treat other sections of Romans.

———. *Romans: An Exposition of Chapter 6, The New Man.* Grand Rapids: Zondervan, 1973.

———. *Romans: An Exposition of Chapters 7:1–8:4, The Law: Its Functions and Limits.* Grand Rapids: Zondervan, 1974.

———. *Romans: An Exposition of Chapters 8:5–17, The Sons of God.* Grand Rapids: Zondervan, 1975.

Moo, D. J. *The Epistle to the Romans.* New International Commentary on the New Testament. Grand Rapids: Eerdmans, 1996.

———. *Romans.* NIV Application Commentary. Grand Rapids: Zondervan, 2000.

Morris, L. *The Epistle to the Romans.* Pillar New Testament Commentaries. Grand Rapids: Eerdmans, 1988. Solid exposition from a broad evangelical viewpoint.

Munck, J. *Paul and the Salvation of Mankind.* London: SCM, 1959. A very significant study of the importance of salvation history in Paul's life and letters.

Murray, J. *The Epistle to the Romans.* 2 vols. New International Commentary on the New Testament. Grand Rapids: Eerdmans, 1959, 1965. Solid exposition of Romans from a generally Reformed perspective.

Nygren, A. *Commentary on Romans.* Philadelphia: Fortress, 1949. Less a commentary on Romans than a theological reflection on its key themes. Takes a Lutheran perspective.

Piper, J. *The Justification of God: An Exegetical and Theological Study of Romans 9:1–23.* Grand Rapids: Baker, 1983. A very careful exegetical-theological defense of a

Calvinist reading of Romans 9, along with important ideas about "righteousness" in Romans.

Ridderbos, H. N. *Paul: An Outline of His Theology*. Grand Rapids: Eerdmans, 1974. A very important, though rather technical, overview of Paul's theology from the "salvation-historical" perspective adopted in this commentary.

Sanday, W., and A. C. Headlam. *A Critical and Exegetical Commentary on the Epistle to the Romans*. International Critical Commentary. Edinburgh: Clark, 1902. Classic commentary with emphasis on exegetical and textual matters.

Schreiner, T. *Romans*. Baker Exegetical Commentary on the New Testament. Grand Rapids: Baker, 1998. A fine, balanced treatment combining exegesis with solid theological insight. An important response to the "new perspective" approach to Romans.

Stott, J. *Romans: God's Good News for the World*. Downers Grove, Ill.: InterVarsity, 1994. Excellent exposition with clear and valuable application.

Strickland, W. G., ed. *The Law, the Gospel, and the Modern Christian: Five Views* (Grand Rapids: Zondervan, 1993). A discussion of the New Testament teaching about the law of God from several theological perspectives.

Stuhlmacher, P. *Paul's Letter to the Romans*. Louisville: Westminster/John Knox, 1994. Translation of a brief exposition by a key German contemporary Pauline scholar.

Westerholm, S. *Israel's Law and the Church's Faith*. Grand Rapids: Eerdmans, 1988. A good, though dated, survey of recent developments among scholars in their interpretation of the law in Paul. An important response to the "new perspective" on Romans.

———. *Preface to the Study of Paul*. Grand Rapids: Eerdmans, 1997. An interesting attempt to apply the basic theological insights of Romans to contemporary postmodern thinking.

Scripture Index

Subject Index